NEW HANDBOOK OF
BASIC
WRITING
SKILLS

SECOND EDITION

NEW HANDBOOK OF
BASIC
WRITING
SKILLS

SECOND EDITION

Cora L. Robey
Tidewater Community College
Frederick Campus

Alice M. Hedrick   Ethelyn H. Morgan
Late of Tidewater Community College
Frederick Campus

EDITORIAL CONSULTANTS

Sarah E. Kreps   Helen M. Maloney
Tidewater Community College
Frederick Campus

HARCOURT BRACE JOVANOVICH, PUBLISHERS
San Diego   New York   Chicago   Atlanta   Washington, D.C.
London   Sydney   Toronto

(continued on inside back cover)

To the Instructor

The *Handbook of Basic Writing Skills* was originally written in response to a need for a reference and writing aid that could be readily understood by all students, regardless of their background in English. The *New Handbook of Basic Writing Skills*, Second Edition, is like the first edition in that it uses clear and simple language in its examples and explanations and contains an abundance of exercises. It offers assistance in all the areas covered by the traditional handbooks and gives special emphasis to the problems that trouble beginning writers—particularly verb endings, subject-verb agreement, noun plurals, fragments, run-together sentences, possessive endings, and sentence logic. It helps the student through each step from constructing a sentence to researching and organizing a full-length paper.

There are twenty-nine chapters in the *New Handbook of Basic Writing Skills*. You should be able to refer students to the appropriate section of the handbook for virtually any error found in a student paper. The first eight chapters cover such basic writing concerns as agreement, verbs, and fragments. The verb section (Chapter 7) is the largest in the book and contains many useful exercises. Chapters 9 through 11 cover other important elements of sentence structure. Chapters 12 through 19 cover spelling and punctuation, and focus on questions inexperienced writers are likely to ask about these matters. Chapters 20 through 23 represent a simple approach to the use of words. The dictionary chapter (20) should be helpful to students who need to build reading skills. Chapters 24 through 29 move from sentence improvement and variety through the paragraph (25), the full-length paper (26), and the research paper and manuscript form (27–28). The last chapter (29), a new one, is on business letter writing. These last few chapters offer practical suggestions on subjects like brainstorming, the selection and limitation of topics, organization of material, and editing. You might want to use these chapters for beginning the teaching of rhetoric.

The exercises in the *Handbook* are aimed particularly at areas in which students need practice. Not all exercises will be helpful to all students, of course, so you will probably want to use some as general class exercises and assign certain others—especially those in Chapters 1 through 8—to students with particular writing problems, on an individual basis. The examples used in the explanations and in the exercises are mainly student sentences; they are frequently interesting in themselves and are close to the style students use in their own writing.

Although the *New Handbook of Basic Writing Skills* has the strengths of the first edition, it is intended to be even more responsive to the needs of students. The Second Edition includes the following new features:

1. Standard grammatical terms are used where such terms will help clarify the writing process.

2. Extensive discussion of sequence of tenses and several verb charts are found in Chapter 7.

3. The exercises are greatly improved. There has been an attempt to emphasize the editing process in many of these exercises.

4. There is now a chapter (29) on business letter writing.

5. Chapter 25 on the paragraph has been expanded. It now describes several methods of organizing paragraphs using student models.

6. Chapter 26 on the full-length paper approaches organization in two ways. It helps the beginning writer brainstorm and plan a simple paper, and it shows the student how to organize a more complex paper, using a topic or sentence outline. There are now sample outlines for several kinds of papers.

7. There is a new research paper on a subject of general interest, the "Doonesbury" cartoons. This chapter (27) shows how to prepare the research paper using old MLA style footnotes and new MLA style so instructors may choose the type of documentation that they want their students to use. There are also many more kinds of sample entries provided.

8. The diction chapter (21) now includes a discussion of slang, clichés, and jargon.
9. There are now new or improved discussions of the following subjects:
   a. *this-these* confusion
   b. phrase and clause fragments
   c. comma splices
   d. *good* and *well*
   e. the *who-whom* confusion
   f. the passive and some uses of the subjunctive
   g. subject and object pronouns
   h. change of person
   i. spelling errors caused by vowel-*r* reversal
   j. spelling errors caused by miscounting syllables
   k. the parts of speech, including lists of pronouns and conjunctions
   l. unnecessary use of the semicolon

Throughout the book there are such labels as RIGHT and WRONG and WEAK and BETTER to identify example sentences. These labels are designed to help students recognize Standard American English. We are not commenting in any way on the acceptability of the language that students use in their own informal speech.

The *New Workbook of Basic Writing Skills,* Second Edition, can be used in conjunction with the *Handbook.* The *Workbook* follows the format of the *Handbook* and provides many additional exercises. An Instructor's Manual is also available and includes diagnostic tests and answers to all exercises in both the *Handbook* and *Workbook.*

I have worked on the *New Handbook of Basic Writing Skills* with a great deal of sadness because of the loss of my two co-authors and friends, Alice M. Hedrick and Ethelyn H. Morgan, who died just as we were beginning our work on the Second Edition. I have missed their talents, their enthusiasm, and their companionship more than I can say. I thank Bruce Busby of Ohio Dominican College, William Connelly of Middle Tennessee State University, Lorita Langdon of the Columbus Technical Institute, and Lorraine M. Murphy of the University of Dayton, who read and helped improve the manuscript. Special thanks go to the many people who helped me in the preparation of the manuscript for the Second Edition, especially Sarah

E. Kreps and Helen M. Maloney, who served as editorial consultants. I would also like to thank the staff at Harcourt Brace Jovanovich, particularly Margie Rogers and Marlane Agriesti, Judy Brown, Lynn Edwards, and Ann Smith, and my colleagues at Tidewater Community College, Frederick Campus, particularly W. P. Covington, Charles Earl, Walter Harris, Barbara Marr, Robert Marshall, Carolyn Melchor, Barbara Nudelman, and Betty J. Perkinson, who suggested specific improvements for this edition. Finally, I want to thank my family for their encouragement and assistance, especially my daughter Judith, who served as critic, typist, and proofreader during much of the editing process.

Cora Robey

To the Student

This handbook is designed to help you express your ideas correctly and clearly in writing. When you talk with your friends, you may use informal language or even leave out words and still be understood; but when you write for college classes or in your work, you need to be careful in your selection and use of words.

Since the words you use and the way you use them must be understood by both you and the person who reads what you have written, certain forms have been accepted as usual, or standard, ways to write what you want to write. In this book you will see examples with labels such as RIGHT and WRONG to help you recognize and use these standard forms.

Each section of the book covers a different area of writing skills. Your instructor will usually let you know, by chapter number, what chapters you need to refer to in order to correct errors in your papers. You do not have to start at the beginning of the book unless directed to do so. By doing the exercises in each chapter, you will have a chance to practice what you have learned.

If you are confused about how to organize your paper, which form of a word to use, or how to say clearly what you mean to say, you may want to look at a particular chapter for help while you are writing a paper. Chapters 1 through 23 help you construct sentences and choose correct words. Chapters 24 and 25 tell how to arrange sentences into paragraphs, and Chapters 26 through 29 help you plan a complete paper, do research, prepare the final version, and write acceptable business letters.

Learn to use this handbook both as a reference book while you are writing and to correct your finished work. Let it help you prevent errors as you fulfill your writing assignments.

Contents

MORE ABOUT SENTENCES

SPELLING AND PUNCTUATION

WORDS

MOVING TOWARD THE COMPLETE PAPER

THE COMPLETE PAPER

PART ONE
SENTENCE BASICS

CHAPTER ONE

Sentence Makeup

Learn some basic facts about sentences.

1a
What is a sentence?

You probably think about a sentence in one of three ways. Let us look at these ways one by one.

1a(1)
A sentence is a group of words beginning with a capital letter and ending with a period, a question mark, or an exclamation point.

The first way of viewing a sentence is the easiest to see. The most common type of sentence makes a statement. It begins with a capital letter and ends with a period.

> Some mothers never learn from experience.
> The Beatles changed the course of modern music.

Sometimes a sentence asks a question. It begins with a capital letter and ends with a question mark.

> Do mothers ever learn from experience?
> Did the Beatles change the course of modern music?

A sentence showing strong feeling or surprise begins with a capital letter and ends with an exclamation point.

> It's a miracle!
> Show me a 1964 Oldsmobile, and I'll show you a great car!

A command begins with a capital letter and ends with either a period or an exclamation point.

> Show me a 1964 Oldsmobile, please.
> Hold your horses!

EXERCISE 1

Test your ability to recognize sentences by adding a period, a question mark, or an exclamation point to mark the end of each sentence in the following paragraph.

> My friend Keith is a short, active fellow whose number one interest is dancing you can bet your bottom dollar that if there's a dance in town, Keith will be there as soon as he enters the D. J. will ask, "Is that you, Hollywood" Keith will grin from ear to ear do you know that he thinks if he isn't there, the dance can't go on the D. J. will then spin one of Keith's favorite records Keith will dance until his clothes are soaking wet, but nothing will keep him from dancing with every woman in the place he really knows how to have a ball show me someone like Keith, and I'll show you someone who can do it all

1a(2)

A sentence is made up of words that we call parts of speech.

Listed below are the most common parts of speech:

NOUN: the name of a person, place, thing, or idea

> <u>Mary</u> has a <u>bloodhound</u> guarding her <u>castle</u> in bad <u>weather</u>.
> The noisy <u>crowd</u> in the <u>park</u> demanded <u>justice</u>.

PRONOUN: a word that takes the place of a noun

> <u>I</u> want hand lotion because <u>it</u> is good for people <u>whose</u> hands are red.

VERB: a word that expresses action or state of being

ACTION VERBS	BEING VERBS
run, sit, stood, listened, repeats	is, are, was, were, will be, has been

The verb tells what the subject is doing.

> When Helen <u>worked</u>, she <u>was</u> always happy.

ADJECTIVE: a word that describes a noun or pronoun

> As a <u>happy</u> child, I enjoyed washing <u>dirty</u> dishes. <u>Crazy</u> me!

ADVERB: a word that describes a verb, adjective, or other adverb

> <u>Radiantly</u> beautiful Millicent dresses <u>elegantly</u>, but <u>not very conservatively</u>.

It tells how, when, or where.

> Al dances <u>divinely</u>, <u>often</u>, and <u>everywhere</u>

PREPOSITION: a word generally used to show how a noun or pronoun is related to another word in the sentence

COMMON PREPOSITIONS

about	as	during	on	under
above	at	for	out	up
across	before	from	outside	upon
after	behind	in	over	with
against	below	inside	since	without
along	between	into	though	
among	by	near	through	
around	down	of	to	

My brother lives <u>with</u> me <u>on</u> Hennepin Avenue <u>in</u> Minneapolis.

CONJUNCTION: a word used to connect words or parts of sentences

1. *Coordinating conjunctions* (*and, but, or, nor, for, so, yet*) join words, clauses, or other groups of words.

   You <u>or</u> I will visit Al now <u>and</u> then.

2. *Subordinating conjunctions* join clauses (groups of words containing subjects and verbs).

COMMON SUBORDINATING CONJUNCTIONS

after	because	since	when
although	before	unless	while
as	if	until	

I will see you <u>when</u> and <u>if</u> you arrive.

Jane rested <u>because</u> she was tired.

ARTICLE: a word (*a, an,* or *the*) coming before and usually limiting a noun

<u>A</u> beet and <u>an</u> apple are sitting on <u>the</u> table.

1a(3)
A sentence contains a subject and a verb.

Throughout this book we will be using these two words. The *subject* of the sentence is the person or thing you are writing about.

A *simple subject* is one word.

> Hubcaps are not essential parts of automobiles.

A subject may be two or more words, joined by *and, but, or,* or *nor.*

> Fathers and sons frequently don't get along.

A subject with some descriptive words in front of it or after it can be called a *complete subject.*

> My uncle Fred has eaten too much lunch.
> Part of my lunch is gone.

The *verb* tells what the subject is doing or what is happening to the subject.

A subject may have a one-word verb.

> Few domestic geese fly.

A subject may have a verb of more than one word.

> She should have waited at least an hour.

A subject may have more than one verb.

> Alice just sits and looks out the window.

There are usually many words other than a subject and a verb in a sentence, but the subject and verb are the only two words necessary to make a sentence.

> Frank cried.
> After many days of waiting and wondering, she finally left.

1a(4)

A sentence is made up of groups of words called clauses or phrases.

Clauses

A *clause* is a group of words with a subject and a verb. A clause is either main or dependent. A *main clause* is really a sentence; it can stand by itself.

> I am here.
> Sea water is very salty.

A *dependent clause* cannot stand by itself; it needs or depends on a main clause.

DEPENDENT CLAUSES		MAIN CLAUSES
If you need me,	←	I am here.
Although it looks good to drink,	←	sea water is very salty.

A *relative clause* is a dependent clause usually introduced by *who*, *which*, or *that*. It needs or depends on a main clause.

MAIN CLAUSES		DEPENDENT (RELATIVE) CLAUSES
John Glenn is an astronaut	←	*who* became a senator.
Sea water is a liquid	←	*that* is very salty.

Phrases

A *phrase* is a group of words that has no subject or verb. Three common phrases are the following:

1. *Prepositional phrase:* a group of words starting with a preposition and containing a noun or pronoun

   in the lake, at the last minute, about me

2. *Participial phrase:* a group of words containing a present or past participle, which is an adjective formed from a verb. Present participles end in *-ing*; past participles of regular verbs end in *-ed.*

> Brushing her beautiful hair, Gwendolen gazed at herself admiringly.
> Exhausted from studying, I left the campus for a rest.

3. *Infinitive phrase*: a group of words beginning with an infinitive, which is a verb form with no ending (-*s*, -*ed*, or other), usually introduced by *to*.

> I once had to interview a famous actress.

For more information on clauses and phrases, see **2a–e**.

1b

Recognize the subject and verb.

Before you can really understand and correct most writing problems, you must be able to identify the subject and verb of a sentence. In a very short sentence, this is no problem.

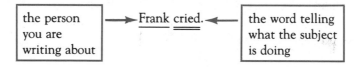

1b(1)

A sentence often begins with the subject and verb.

> Judgment is a necessity in surfing.
> I wanted a job working in a bank.
> We have enjoyed painting in our spare time.
> Stews are cooked slowly.

1b(2)

Words may come between the subject and its verb.

Although the subject and verb often appear first in the sentence, this is not the only possible word order, especially when a word like *one, all, each, everyone, any, some, many, none,* or *nobody* is the simple subject.

> One of my father's ties <u>fell</u> from the rack.
> <u>All</u> of the patients in the hospital <u>want</u> you to show a personal interest in them.
> <u>None</u> of the women <u>has</u> a different idea on the subject.
> After such a narrow escape, <u>he</u> never <u>went</u> there again.

When trying to locate the simple subject of a sentence, ask yourself *who* is doing something or *what* is happening. That *who* or *what* is the subject. Then look for the word that tells you what the subject is doing. That word is the verb.

> <u>One</u> of my father's ties <u>fell</u> from the rack.

What is being written about in this sentence is *one* of the ties—not all of them. The verb *fell* goes with the subject *one.* Do not let phrases beginning with *of* mislead you when they come between the simple subject and its verb.

> The <u>children</u> of today <u>will be</u> our salvation. [*Children,* not *today,* is the subject; *children* will be our salvation.]
> <u>Some</u> of the players <u>are doing</u> different things. [*Some,* not *players,* is the subject. *Some,* not *all,* of the players are doing different things.]

EXERCISE 2

In the following sentences, the simple subject is underlined once. Underline the verb twice.

■ **Example**   The <u>girl</u> of my dreams <u>is</u> Mimi.

1. The <u>cause</u> of all my troubles is lack of money.
2. Almost every <u>customer</u> in this restaurant asks the chef to cook bluefish.
3. The <u>rules</u> of that school seem very strict to me.

4. The eyes of everyone were on that one man.
5. A machine useful for cutting all types of wood and metal is called a lathe.

EXERCISE 3

In the following sentences, the verb is underlined twice. Underline the simple subject once.

■ **Example**   One of the students in this class registered last week.

1. The people involved in that project should feel a sense of accomplishment?
2. Many of the men on that ship surely miss home at this very minute.
3. Some of the most enthusiastic former supporters of that candidate voted for his opponent.
4. All of the money went to my sister.
5. One of the banks makes loans on automobiles.

1b(3)
The verb sometimes comes *before* the subject.

You usually expect the subject to come before its verb in a sentence, but that is not always the case. In a *there is (are)*, *here is (are)*, *where is (are)* sentence, the verb comes before the subject.

> There are mosquitoes all over the place.
> Here is the best reason for buying a new car.
> Where are my old friends?

There, *here*, and *where* are not subjects. The simple subjects of the sentences above are *mosquitoes*, *reason*, and *friends*. *There*, *here*, and *where* only introduce the subject.

   Be sure that when you use *there* to introduce the subject, you do not confuse it with *they* or *it*. *They* and *it* refer to definite persons or things, and unlike *there*, *they* or *it* can be the subject of a sentence.

They are late for dinner. [They (certain persons) are late for dinner.]
It is too early to visit your sister. [It (the time) is too early to visit your sister.]

Do not use *they* or *it* in place of *there* to introduce the subject of a sentence.

WRONG	Is they a place in Germany more dangerous than Berlin?
RIGHT	Is *there* a place in Germany more dangerous than Berlin?
WRONG	It is a very nice girl living on our block.
RIGHT	*There* is a very nice girl living on our block.
WRONG	It is only five of us at home now.
RIGHT	*There* are only five of us at home now.

EXERCISE 4

Copy the following sentences. As you do so, change *it* or *they* to *there* in any sentence where *it* or *they* is incorrectly used to introduce the subject. You may need to change *is* to *are* or *was* to *were* if you are talking about more than one person or thing.

■ Examples   They was a good reason for my mother's decision.
There was a good reason for my mother's decision.

It was many of us involved in that decision.
There were many of us involved in that decision.

1. It is usually several people waiting at that bus stop.
2. They were left by the side of the road.
3. In New York they were more jobs, but they were also more people applying for the jobs.
4. They are many differences between a truck and a car.
5. On that block they is a pool hall with a smoky ceiling.
6. It was five or six of us who signed up for the annual picnic.
7. It was time to go, and I still wasn't ready.

The verb may come before its subject in sentences other than those beginning with *there is (are)*, *here is (are)*, and *where is (are)*.

Next to his desk are four filing cabinets. [The subject is *cabinets*; the cabinets are near the desk.]

On the wall hang the racks that hold the cue sticks. [The subject is *racks*; the racks hang on the wall.]

1b(4)
In a command the subject is not written out in the sentence.

Since you are talking to someone when you command or request him or her to do something, the subject is *you* (understood).

SUBJECT	VERB
(You)	Leave my house immediately!
(You)	Please wear hiking boots if you are going into those woods.

EXERCISE 5

In the following sentences, the verbs are underlined twice. Underline the subjects once. If a subject is understood, write *you* next to the sentence.

■ **Example**   The man threw the frisbee over the woman's head.

1. All along the stairs were my brother's toys.
2. In the room there are three chairs, a sofa, a loveseat, and a cedar chest.
3. Please walk the dog on the other side of the street.
4. On top of the lockers sit piles of books.
5. Listen carefully to the news this evening.

1b(5)
A sentence must have at least one main clause.

A main clause has a subject and verb and can stand by itself. In addition to a main clause, a sentence may have one or more dependent clauses. When this happens, you need to recognize the subject and verb in the main clause. This subject and verb make the sentence complete.

Main clause (or sentence)

Herman waited for me.

A dependent clause needs a main clause before it completes its meaning. Both of the following are dependent clauses; each needs a main clause to produce a complete sentence.

Dependent clauses

1. Introduced by a subordinating conjunction (*because, when, although,* etc.)

   although he was very impatient
2. Usually beginning with *who, which,* or *that*

   who is very impatient

The following are complete sentences which include the dependent clauses given above. The subject and verb of the main clause are underlined.

Herman waited for me although he was very impatient.
Herman, who is very impatient, waited for me.

If you need help in deciding whether a sentence is complete, see **2b**.

EXERCISE 6

The following sentences have more than one subject and more than one verb. Underline the simple subject of the main clause once and its verb twice.

■ **Examples**   After the bell rang, the <u>students</u> <u style="text-decoration: underline double">wasted</u> no time in leaving the room.

An <u>announcer</u> who forgets his lines <u style="text-decoration: underline double">needs</u> to practice before his broadcasts.

1. Since the poll was taken close to the election, the results are surely reliable.
2. If this talk of a recession doesn't stop, interest rates will go higher than they are right now.
3. My brother, who is not the most courageous person in the world, decided not to ask that very attractive girl for a date.
4. The umbrella that you needed this afternoon seems to be hanging in your closet.
5. My research paper required more reliable sources before my instructor would accept it.

In locating the subject and verb, remember that

1. words may separate a subject from its verb—particularly a simple subject like *one, all, each, some,* and so on.
2. in a *there is (are), here is (are),* and *where is (are)* sentence, the verb comes before its subject.
3. in other sentences the verb sometimes comes before its subject.
4. in a command the subject (you) is understood.
5. a sentence may have more than one subject and verb, but it must have at least one subject and verb in a main clause.

EXERCISE 7

Copy these sentences, underlining the simple subjects of the complete sentences once and the main verbs that go with them twice. Do not underline the subject and verb of any dependent clause. When the subject is understood, write *you* next to the sentence.

■ **Examples**   When I finally met my roommate, <u>I</u> really <u style="text-decoration: underline double">got</u> a shock.

<u style="text-decoration: underline double">Go</u> home immediately. (You)

1. Gail bought a pair of sandals after she got her paycheck.

2. In 1865 he bought a small farm.

3. Of all the things that I like, my favorite pastime is fishing.

4. He stepped on the accelerator again and finally started his car.

5. Stop the car immediately!

6. According to the newspaper reports, none of the relatives or friends of Howard Hughes ever really knew him.

7. All across the hardening cement are the unmistakable pawprints of my curious cat, Tagi.

8. In case of an emergency, have several fuses in the house.

9. One of our airplanes has disappeared.

10. Mr. Vernon, who considered work in his garden more a labor of love than a weekly duty, grew some of the most marvelous vegetables that I have ever seen.

11. If the Jets don't win on Sunday, my sister will be in a bad mood all week.

12. For information on the essentials of automotive maintenance, people often sign up for some courses at a nearby community college.

13. Here in the newspaper, after the news, the comics, and all of the classified ads, is the notice of that great sale.

14. After all the kind words of encouragement and the frequently given, but not unwelcome, words of advice, I never dreamed of such an outcome.

1c
Write correct negative sentences.

1c(1)
The most common negative sentence uses one negative word, such as *no, not, never, nothing, nowhere,* or *hardly.*

In addition to telling the reader what is happening to the subject, a sentence can also tell what is not happening.

There are *no* drill bits in that drawer.
Midnight is *not* a good time to study.
You can *never* cheat an honest person.
I have *nothing* to do today.

Sometimes a contraction is used instead of the word *not*.

There are not any drill bits in that drawer.	OR There *aren't* any drill bits in that drawer.
Midnight is not a good time to study.	OR Midnight *isn't* a good time to study.
You cannot cheat an honest person.	OR You *can't* cheat an honest person.
I do not have anything to do today.	OR I *don't* have anything to do today.

Remember to use an apostrophe before the *t* in a contraction, since the *o* of *not* is omitted.

Note: *Ain't* is not a correct contraction for *am not, is not, are not, has not,* or *have not.*

WRONG   That ain't any way to run a railroad.
RIGHT   *That's* no way to run a railroad.

1c(2)
Use only one negative word, like *no, not, never, nothing,* or *nowhere,* to say that something is not true.

English is unlike most other languages in its negative sentences. In Spanish, for example, the more negative words you use, the more you deny that something is true.

No vi a *nadie* ni oí *nada* en *ninguna* parte.
I didn't see no one nor hear nothing nowhere.

An English reader would shriek in horror at that sentence. Remember not to use two negative words such as *no, no one, not, never, nothing, nowhere,* or *hardly* when you want to say that something is not so.

WRONG	I had never seen nobody as pretty as she.
RIGHT	I had *never* seen *anybody* as pretty as she.
WRONG	I did things for them no other person would never have done.
RIGHT	I did things for them *no* other person would *ever* have done.
WRONG	He is not hardly old enough to stay by himself.
RIGHT	He is *hardly* old enough to stay by himself.

To avoid using two negative words, you can usually do one of the following:

1. Eliminate one of the negative words.

WRONG	There are not hardly any peaches left.
RIGHT	There are *hardly* any peaches left.

2. Substitute *ever* for *never.*

WRONG	They're not never here.
RIGHT	They're not *ever* here.

3. Substitute *any* for *no* or *none.*

WRONG	I can't find him nowhere.
RIGHT	I can't find him *anywhere.*
WRONG	I don't see none on the shelf.
RIGHT	I don't see *any* on the shelf.

Note: The only time you do use two negative words to say that something is not true is when you use the pair *neither . . . nor.*

Neither my English teacher *nor* I can understand why I continue to make verb errors.

EXERCISE 8

Correct the following sentences by changing any incorrect negative words.

■ **Example**   I don't have no more money.
I don't have *any* more money.

1. I wouldn't trade my dog in for no one else's.
2. They knew we wouldn't like the idea of working in nobody's field.
3. It's not hardly early enough to call Sally.
4. I don't have no more coffee left.
5. Bowser ain't eaten nothing since the start of dog days.
6. I hate to tell you this, but you don't have no gas in that car.
7. Joey feels so bad he can't hardly hold his head up.
8. I don't never expect to do nothing with my education.
9. No wonder they didn't know how to act at her house; they've never been nowhere outside of New Jersey.
10. Didn't nobody figure out the ending to that story?
11. J.J. sits in the front of the store and won't let nobody enter.

1d
Use singular and plural nouns correctly.

Sentences make statements about *nouns* (persons and things). The words you use should show whether you are naming one person or thing or more than one.

1d(1)
Singular nouns do not add an ending. Words like *a, one, each,* and *every* describe singular nouns.

Do not add an *s* or another plural ending to a noun when it is used with a singular adjective. If you need help identifying adjectives, see Chapter 4.

WRONG	each members of the group
RIGHT	each *member* of the group
WRONG	a new records
RIGHT	a new *record*

1d(2)
Most plural nouns end in -s.

Words like *six, ninety, many, all, some, several,* and expressions like *a number, a few,* or *a group of* describe more than one person or thing. When these words are used, add an *-s* to the noun they describe, or use another plural form.

WRONG	five acre of wheat
RIGHT	five *acres* of wheat
WRONG	many young ballplayer
RIGHT	many young *ballplayers*
WRONG	all of the required adjustment
RIGHT	all of the required *adjustments*
WRONG	at least three time
RIGHT	at least three *times*
WRONG	a number of test
RIGHT	a number of *tests*
WRONG	I have a few ticket.
RIGHT	I have a few *tickets.*
WRONG	these kind of things
RIGHT	these *kinds* of things

Even when the number of persons or things is not mentioned in the sentence, do not carelessly forget the *-s* or other ending when you mean to name more than one person or thing.

WRONG	He invites guest to perform.
RIGHT	He invites *guests* to perform.

1d(3)
A few nouns use special plural forms.

Learn and use them when needed instead of a singular or another incorrect word. Some common plurals are *women, feet, teeth, people,* and *children.*

WRONG He is five foot tall.
RIGHT He is five *feet* tall.

Do not use a plural noun when you mean to use a singular one.

WRONG a women
RIGHT a *woman*

1d(4)
Some nouns have no plural forms.

Do not add an ending to these words. Some examples are abstract words like *happiness, violence, sincerity, laziness,* and the common words *fish, deer,* and *sheep.*

WRONG Think of the violences in the world!
RIGHT Think of the *violence* in the world!

1d(5)
This is a singular word; *these* is plural. Do not confuse them.

WRONG *these* type of driver
RIGHT *this* type of driver
     these types of drivers
WRONG *these* equipment
RIGHT *this* equipment
     these items of equipment

EXERCISE 9

This paragraph was written by a student who had trouble recognizing plural words. Proofread the paragraph, correcting any errors in the use of singular and plural nouns or in the use of *this* and *these*.

> One of America's biggest problem is the dumping of chemical wastes. These problem grows worse as time passes. In designated areas chemical waste is dumped and buried. It has recently been found, however, that these chemical do not go away. Many of them interact with one another and bubble and boil back to the surface, releasing toxic gases. Many seep down into underground water supplies. This is a very dangerous situations. Many community have felt the effects of these situations by experiencing birth defect and mutations in the new generations.

EXERCISE 10

Correct any incorrect singular or plural nouns.

1. Anesthesia is used in many hospital.
2. My father was always afraid that we would cut our hand.
3. His workshop has many tools and electric motor.
4. He eats at least six time a day.
5. I have two pair of tennis shoes.
6. At one time a phone call cost five cent.
7. I keep my bedroom slipper right beside my bed.
8. Buster has two bark—one for peoples and one for animals.
9. Lazy persons have never learned the value of work.
10. Handicapped student need a special area to take test.
11. I hope to finish this lessons before time to leave.
12. This is a time when my relatives get together to spread the latest gossips and to enjoy themselves.
13. In our neighborhood, people's lawn are well-kept.
14. Many people think I am bragging when I say positive thing about myself, but I'm really not.
15. Being shy can sometime be a blessing.

CHAPTER TWO

Incomplete Sentences

Be sure that your sentences are complete.

A complete sentence has a subject (the person or thing you are writing about) and a main verb (the word that describes what the subject is doing or what is happening to the subject). Remember that when you write a complete sentence, you are saying something about the subject and you finish saying it. When you write a fragment you do not complete your statement about the subject.

FRAGMENT	As a traveling salesman. [What are you saying about a traveling salesman?]
SENTENCE	He works as a traveling salesman.
FRAGMENT	And receives no fixed salary. [Who gets no fixed salary?]
SENTENCE	He works as a traveling salesman and receives no fixed salary.
FRAGMENT	Since he receives no fixed salary. [What happens since he receives no fixed salary?]
SENTENCE	Since he receives no fixed salary, it is hard for him to plan his expenses.

Usually a sentence can be completed in two ways:

1. You can rewrite the fragment completely.

   FRAGMENT   Fear that I would be unable to do the work.
   COMPLETE   I was afraid that I would be unable to do the work.

2. You can join the fragment to the complete sentence before or after it.

   FRAGMENT   Fear that I would be unable to do the work.
   COMPLETE   One of my biggest problems was fear of returning to school, fear that I would be unable to do the work.

It is often better to join a fragment to the sentence either before or after it. This is because a fragment is usually just a group of words that was left out of the sentence next to it. If you find a fragment in your paper, look to see if you really meant to join it to a sentence next to it.

2a
Correct a phrase fragment.

Remember that a group of words that does not have a subject and a verb is not a sentence; it is a *phrase fragment.* Whenever possible, join these words to the sentence next to them.

FRAGMENT	JOIN	COMPLETE
Without thinking about the danger.	People going downhill sometimes coast and ride their brakes. ← Without thinking about the danger.	People going downhill sometimes coast and ride their brakes without thinking about the danger.

2a(1)
Join a prepositional phrase fragment to the sentence next to it.

A prepositional phrase is a group of words starting with a preposition (*to, for, without,* and so on) and containing a noun or pronoun. Some of the common prepositions used in such a phrase are listed on page 6. When you try to separate a prepositional phrase like *for an hour* or *without it* from the rest of a sentence, you are writing a fragment.

FRAGMENT	JOIN	COMPLETE
For an hour	Bill did go to work on Friday. ← For an hour.	Bill did go to work on Friday for an hour.
Without it.	Linda came to get a particular book but left. ← Without it.	Linda came to get a particular book but left without it.

2a(2)
Join an *-ing* fragment to the sentence next to it.

FRAGMENT	JOIN	COMPLETE
Having no income of his own. [What happens because he has no income?]	Having no income of his own. ← George is always borrowing from his brother.	Having no income of his own, George is always borrowing from his brother.
Checking myself, proofreading, and correcting errors.	I have to write my paper very slowly. ← Checking myself, proofreading, and correcting errors.	I have to write my paper very slowly, checking myself, proofreading, and correcting errors.

EXERCISE 1

Write *F* to the left of any fragment listed below. Write *S* to the left of any sentence.

1. On the first day of spring.
2. Jeanette was trying to forget everything that had happened to her.
3. In August I plan to visit one of my childhood haunts.
4. Figuring his profits for the year, my boss wasn't very optimistic about employment prospects.
5. Without a word we departed.
6. Slamming the door behind him and hoping never to return.

7. Repeating the poem I had memorized, I entered the classroom.

8. The red carnation offering Paul a new beginning.

9. However, among Knute's many shattered dreams.

10. After being stationed in Germany for two and a half years.

EXERCISE 2

Complete all of the following sentences by joining the fragments to the sentences. Do not join any sentences that are already complete. Do not change or add any words to the sentences.

■ Example   For the entire week. I sat waiting for the telephone to ring.
             For the entire week, I sat waiting for the telephone to ring.

1. Don't waste time moving the person to a better place. Loosening the clothing or draining water from the lungs. Begin emergency treatment.

2. Mr. Evans locked the shop. After finishing all of his work for the day.

3. My mother never could get us all to supper. My brother was always practicing. In the gym.

4. Harry doesn't want to stay in that house. The windows are boarded up. Making the rooms seem like jail cells.

5. You can't go far in this town. Without friends. Anyone who has ever lived here can tell you that.

6. Let me give you an example. My friend Al is always riding his brakes. Causing himself to coast downhill.

7. My friend Lenore lives in Passaic. In a great place. With beautiful oaks and pine trees.

2b
Correct a clause fragment.

A group of words with a subject and verb is not always a sentence; sometimes it is a *clause fragment.*

2b(1)

Words like *because, when, after, before,* and *since* (subordinating conjunctions) often introduce dependent clauses. They help you recognize that something needs to be explained before the sentence is complete. For a list of these conjunctions, see page 6.

DEPENDENT CLAUSE FRAGMENT	Because gossip can get people into trouble. [What is true because gossip can get people into trouble?]
SENTENCE OR MAIN CLAUSE	Telling tales is bad because gossip can get people into trouble.
DEPENDENT CLAUSE FRAGMENT	As I was hanging out my wash. [What happened as I was hanging out my wash?]
SENTENCE OR MAIN CLAUSE	As I was hanging out my wash, I saw a beautiful puppy on my neighbor's steps.

2b(2)

Who, whose, whom, which, and *that* often signal relative (dependent) clauses.

When you use such clauses, make sure that your sentences are complete. A relative clause has a verb and a subject, but it needs a main clause to complete its meaning.

RELATIVE CLAUSE FRAGMENT	Which eats nasty houseflies.
COMPLETE SENTENCE	A Venus flytrap, which eats nasty houseflies, is a must for your screened porch.
RELATIVE CLAUSE FRAGMENT	A profession that makes me feel useful to others.
COMPLETE SENTENCE	Nursing is a wonderful profession, a profession that makes me feel useful to others.
RELATIVE CLAUSE FRAGMENT	Whose car wouldn't start yesterday.
COMPLETE SENTENCE	There is the man whose car wouldn't start yesterday

EXERCISE 3

Write *F* to the left of any fragment listed below. Write *S* to the left of any sentence.

1. If I see Jerry, I'll let you know.
2. Whereas in this present job I feel like a social security number.
3. Remember, if this is your first try, pick something that is simple to make.
4. This is the chair that I wrote to you about.
5. The letters, which the letter carrier delivered yesterday, are sitting on your desk.
6. While, on the other hand, I need pressure to force me to cope with my everyday problems.
7. Blizzards that leave our highways ice-covered and unusable for days.
8. Television shows that deal with the conservation of our natural resources.
9. If you know in advance the subject matter of the test and the time allowed to take the test.
10. If I am happy, everyone knows it.

EXERCISE 4

Turn all of the fragments into complete sentences. Write *S* to the left of any numbered item that is correct.

1. Although there are many jacks-of-all-trades who can produce quantity and not quality. We have a need for craftsmanship.
2. There are many steps. That lead up to the house.
3. If you didn't know better, you'd think she was a model.
4. There is always one person. Who must prove he is the best lover this side of the Mississippi.
5. As Helen walked through the swinging glass doors, she saw the display area.
6. When I picked up the telephone and the medical secretary gave me the decision of the board.

7. If you have to drive on rocks and mud. You need a heavy-duty tire.
8. Fishing is a sport. Which I really enjoy!
9. This is the best dinner that I have ever eaten.
10. The chair matches the wall. Which is dull pink.

2c
Correct a verb fragment.

A *verb fragment* has no subject. Most people write verb fragments when they are using the same subject with more than one verb.

> **WRONG** Most people hate to go to a dentist. And avoid going whenever possible.
>
> **RIGHT** Most people hate to go to a dentist and avoid going whenever possible.

One good way to correct a verb fragment is to join the fragment to the sentence that comes before it.

FRAGMENT	JOIN	COMPLETE
And in many cases share the bills. [Who shares the bills?]	Roommates share their food and time. ← And in many cases share the bills.	Roommates share their food and time and in many cases share the bills.

EXERCISE 5

In each of the following pairs of sentences, cross out the subject of the second sentence. Then combine each pair to make one sentence, using the same subject for both verbs, with the conjunctions *and, but,* or *or.* (Since the subject of both verbs is the same, you do not need a comma before the conjunction.)

■ Example   Linda heard the telephone ring. ~~She~~ knew it was not for her.
Linda heard the telephone ring but knew it was not for her.

1. We saw a diamondback rattlesnake. We decided to take it home.
2. My little sister raids the cookie jar every night. She is often sick the next morning.
3. I entered the house quietly. I hoped no one would hear me.
4. Helen counted sheep for an hour. She still couldn't get to sleep.
5. My cousin decided to pay us a visit. She forgot to let anyone know.
6. That movie is full of suspense. It has a very surprising ending.
7. Many cosmetics sell badly these days. They may not sell at all.
8. My brother is considerate in most ways. He makes my mother worry at times.

2d
Correct a noun fragment.

A *noun fragment* is a group of words containing a noun but no verb. Often you accidentally write a noun fragment when you are saying more than one thing about the subject. By mistake, you separate the noun fragment from the sentence itself.

> SENTENCE   There are three types of drivers I meet on the road.
> FRAGMENT   The fast driver, the slow driver, and the good driver.

You may rewrite the sentence, adding the information in the fragment.

> SENTENCE   The three types of drivers I meet on the road are the fast driver, the slow driver, and the good driver.

You may also use punctuation to join the fragment to the sentence. Try placing a comma or a colon (:) instead of a period after the sentence and joining the noun fragment to the sentence.

> SENTENCE   There are three types of drivers I meet on the road: the fast driver, the slow driver, and the good driver.

Here are some other noun fragments corrected by punctuation:

SENTENCE	He was from a military family.
FRAGMENT	The second son of a naval officer.
CORRECTION	He was from a military family, the second son of a naval officer.
SENTENCE	I have all I ever wanted.
FRAGMENT	Money, friends, and a nice apartment.
CORRECTION	I have all I ever wanted: money, friends, and a nice apartment.

If the noun fragment comes before the sentence, you may rewrite the sentence, adding the information in the fragment.

FRAGMENT	A phone call from his father.
SENTENCE	That was something Paul was dreading.
CORRECTION	A phone call from his father was something Paul was dreading.

You may instead use a comma or a dash and join the fragment to the sentence.

SENTENCE	A phone call from his father—that was something Paul was dreading.

(For more information on the dash and the colon, see pp. 235–37.)

EXERCISE 6

Correct all the fragments. Write *S* next to each sentence.

1. In every state there is an institution for lawbreakers. A reform school for teenagers and a jail for adults. Believe me.

2. There are three main types of fishing boats: rowboats, run-abouts, and cabin cruisers.

3. The coming of the Emotions and Earth, Wind and Fire to the Frank D. Lawrence Stadium. That was a big event. People waited in long lines for tickets.

4. There were no more happy times. No more baseball games. No more children laughing and playing.

5. The beautiful decorations that brought happiness to so many. They have been put away for the winter.

6. There are three kinds of sleepers who annoy me. The easy-to-wake sleeper, the hard-to-wake sleeper, and the sleeper who snores.

EXERCISE 7

In each of the following pairs of sentences, cross out the subject and verb of the second sentence. Then combine each pair to make one sentence, using the same subject and verb for both sentences. Add a dash (—), a colon (:), or *and* when you combine them.

■ **Example**   We could see many signs of a declining neighborhood. ~~They were~~ old wooden staircases, clotheslines in all the yards, and garbage all over the place.

We could see many signs of a declining neighborhood: old wooden staircases, clotheslines in all the yards, and garbage all over the place.

1. Our society puts the mentally ill in institutions. It puts the elderly in nursing homes.

2. Our town now has two fast-food restaurants. It has a drive-in movie theatre.

3. My children often tell me that they enjoy being at home. They say that my home is full of love and warmth.

4. The Welches' house has a well-equipped kitchen. It has a cozy family room.

5. My sister prefers a club where she can dance. She wants someplace that offers a lot of excitement.

2e
Correct an infinitive fragment.

An *infinitive* is a verb form with no ending (-s, -ed, or other), usually introduced by *to* (to laugh, to work). An infinitive is not a verb itself, but it usually appears with a verb.

            verb   infinitive
My uncle loves *to talk.*

An infinitive should not be left out of the sentence that comes before it.

   FRAGMENT   To solder a joint.
   SENTENCE   My mother showed me how to solder a joint.

EXERCISE 8

Correct all infinitive fragments.

1. It's always a good idea. To take along an extra diaper. You never know when you'll need it.
2. I can't help wondering. Did Sally ask you. To get the car keys from her mother?
3. Danny always manages. To get a speeding ticket on Saturday night.
4. It is important to know when to pass a hand and just as important. To know when to bluff.

EXERCISE 9

Correct all fragments. Write S next to each sentence that is complete.

1. Charles makes you smile. When you really don't feel like being bothered. How I admire him!
2. If you think Gloria is thin. You should see my Uncle Jim.
3. She dresses that way because she wants to clown around.
4. There aren't many people. Who like to watch that show.
5. By 1990. If people don't have a college degree, they won't be able to find jobs. That's why I'm going to college. Aren't you worried about your sister? Who didn't even finish high school?
6. There are many stores in the Suffolk Shopping Center. Which is found in the middle of town.

7. Hoping for the best but expecting the worst. Janet answered the telephone.

8. Frank has his own dance studio. And teaches all kinds of people. Who have never really learned to dance.

9. Jean was caught at her favorite vice. Sleeping in class.

10. Make sure you have the necessary tools. A crowbar and a jack.

CHAPTER THREE

Run-Together Sentences and Comma Splices

Separate your run-together sentences and comma splices

Read the following sentences aloud.

> I bought a used boat this past summer from a friend at work it needed
> several repairs
> Years have passed since I was last here now the windows are covered
> with boards.
> The score was eight to nine, the Mets were ahead.

As you read the sentences aloud, you probably found that you read each one as if it were two sentences. In the first two examples, the writers did not show that there were two complete thoughts or sentences and ran two sentences together. In the third example, the writer created a comma splice by using only a comma to join two complete thoughts. What should the writers have done? There are several ways to avoid running sentences together.

3a
Separate your sentences by using a period.

Notice that there are two complete sentences in each wrong example below. In the first sentence, *I* is the subject and *bought* is the verb; in the second sentence, *it* is the subject and *needed* is the verb. You can separate the sentences by placing a period after *work* and starting *it* with a capital letter; then the sentences will be correct.

WRONG	I bought a used boat this past summer from a friend at work it needed several repairs.
RIGHT	I bought a used boat this past summer from a friend at work. It needed several repairs.
WRONG	The room is lighted with large fluorescent lights some fixtures have both tubes missing.
RIGHT	The room is lighted with large fluorescent lights. Some fixtures have both tubes missing.

3b
Separate your sentences by using a semicolon.

Again, there are two complete sentences run together in the wrong example below. In the first sentence, the subject is *Years* and the verb is *have passed*. In the second sentence, the subject is *windows* and the verb is *are covered*. Since the thoughts in the sentences are closely related, the sentences can be separated with a semicolon instead of a period. Notice that the word following the semicolon does NOT begin with a capital letter.

WRONG	Years have passed since I was last here now the windows are covered with boards.
RIGHT	Years have passed since I was last here; now the windows are covered with boards.

EXERCISE 1

Each item below contains two complete thoughts. Show the separation clearly by adding, removing, or relocating periods, semicolons, commas, and capital letters where necessary. Write C next to any items that are separated correctly.

■ **Example**   Our neighbors have a beautiful yard every season of the year they enjoy taking care of the shrubs And flowers in hot weather and in cold.

1. Last year Diane received the school's drama award now she is saving her money for drama school; so that she can be an actress.

2. Most cars that drag race cannot pass inspection for street driving. They are too noisy.

3. Mr. Baker, my government teacher, plans to run for city council; in the next election, he thinks that his classes will learn about city government during the campaign.

4. The wind blowing across the campus was strong; it blew the papers from my hand.

5. Water pollution is a serious problem in many cities the water from the rivers and streams is dangerous to drink. Even after it has been treated.

6. Years have passed since I was here last now the doors and windows are covered with splintered boards; and the place has been sadly neglected.

7. After a day of hard work. I often fall asleep on the sofa sometimes my mother has to wake me to get me to go to bed.

8. My brother injured his leg when he was in the army he spent three months in the hospital; trying to regain the use of that leg.

9. After going back to school, I found that I had to change my lifestyle completely I had to get up much earlier. And stay up late working on assignments.

10. The carpet in the hall looks worn; after just a year of use the next time we should buy heavier carpeting.

3c
Separate your sentences by using a comma and a coordinating conjunction such as *and, but, or, nor, for, so,* or *yet.*

Sometimes you may not be sure what separating mark to use to separate your sentences, although you can tell that something is needed. Use a comma only when you also use a

$$
\text{coordinating conjunction}
\begin{Bmatrix}
and \\
but \\
or \\
nor \\
for \\
so \\
yet
\end{Bmatrix}
\text{after the comma.}
$$

A *coordinating conjunction* is a word that joins two equal elements: two words, two phrases, two clauses, or two sentences. You can use a coordinating conjunction like *and* or *but* to separate two main clauses or sentences.

WRONG	The score was eight to nine, the Mets were ahead.
RIGHT	The score was eight to nine, *and* the Mets were ahead.
WRONG	I want to go home, I have to stay at school.
RIGHT	I want to go home, *but* I have to stay at school.
WRONG	He had trouble driving, the visibility was poor.
RIGHT	He had trouble driving, *for* the visibility was poor.

Notice that all of these sentences are really two main clauses; each could stand by itself. If a comma is used between the two main clauses or sentences, a coordinating conjunction like *and* or *but* must also be used. When only a comma is used, the error is called a *comma splice.* (See **3e.**)

EXERCISE 2

Each of the following is the beginning of a sentence that contains one main clause and a coordinating conjunction (*and, but, or, nor, for, so,* or *yet*). Add another main clause to complete each sentence. Be sure your clause contains a subject and a verb.

■ Example   The prisoner arose and faced the jury, and *the whole courtroom awaited the verdict.*

1. The police had been watching my neighbor's house for an hour, and

   _____

2. I tried to warn my sister that her green shoes did not match her purple dress, but _____

3. When we get home, either there will still be water in the tea kettle you left on the hot burner, or _____

   _____

4. Many adults are going back to school to learn a trade, for _____

   _____

5. Try to get to bed early tonight, so _____

   _____

6. I know in my heart that you are right, yet _____

EXERCISE 3

Correct any of the following sentences that are run together or have comma splices, using periods, semicolons, or commas with coordinating conjunctions.

1. The piano in the old building needed tuning it sounded just like the wild west tin-pan piano in the movies.

2. John looked for his books for twenty minutes and was upset Bill found them under the desk that John had been using.

3. It is hard to believe that the garbage collectors could leave so much of our trash they are continually doing this.

4. When the light was green, I pressed the gas pedal then I had to brake because another driver was pulling in front of me.

5. Don't expect that you will never make a mistake, I don't.

6. Bus drivers need to stop students from disturbing others on the bus when people ride the bus every day, they expect to have a comfortable ride. Some students stand in the front of the bus this situation could lead to an accident.

7. I get up at seven o'clock first I turn on the radio to hear the weather forecast, then I go into the bathroom to take a shower.

8. Some people seem to attract misfortune, my friend Gwen is an example, when trouble comes, she never seems to move out of the way.

3d

Separate your sentences by making one of them a dependent clause.

Sometimes when you run two sentences together, you really should make one of them a dependent clause because you want to show a relationship between the two.

> **INCORRECT (run-together)**   The bus was late, Peter missed his train connection.

That run-together sentence can be corrected with a period, a semicolon, or a comma and a coordinating conjunction (*and, but,* and so on).

> **CORRECT BUT WEAK**   The bus was late, and Peter missed his train connection.

The relationship between the two complete thoughts would be clearer, however, if you put one of them in a dependent clause. Then the reader could easily see that one event led to the other.

CORRECT AND IMPROVED   Because his bus was late, Peter missed his train connection.

A dependent clause is introduced by a subordinating conjunction such as *because, since, before, after,* and *when.* When you are separating sentences by turning one into a dependent clause, use the subordinating conjunction that makes the relationship between the two sentences clear.

3d(1)

To make the time of an event clear, use *before, after, when,* and *while* to separate sentences.

BEFORE   Steve and Pete ran along the street and reached the building *before* the man saw them.

AFTER   He picked up the ball *after* it fell from the table.

WHEN   The car turned over *when* another car hit it.

3d(2)

To show the cause of something, use *because* and *since* to separate sentences.

BECAUSE   The rubber raft sank *because* it hit a sharp rock.

SINCE   I am finishing school *since* without an education I cannot reach my goal.

There are several other commonly used subordinating conjunctions. Some of these words are *although, as, if, unless, until,* and *where.* You can learn more about how these words are used by reading Chapter **24**.

Caution: If the dependent clause comes first in the sentence, use a comma after it. If it comes after the main clause, you do not need a comma.

After you get here, we will have lunch.
We will have lunch after you get here.

EXERCISE 4

Separate the sentences in the following paragraph, using any of the methods described in this chapter.

When I was a child and not so tall as a sewing machine, I watched my mother daily as she sewed as I grew older, I dreamed more and more about being a seamstress one day at the age of nine, I sat at the machine and pedaled it electric machines were not available for sewing in those days to hear the machine and to see it operate really fascinated me then I gathered pieces of scrap material, and my mother helped me cut out small things the first dress I made was for a doll in a few years I knew how to select material, cut it out by a pattern, and, in a few hours, produce a garment that was ready to wear now I sew my clothes instead of buying them being a seamstress is my favorite pastime, and I am delighted and proud that I learned to sew.

3e

Avoid the comma splice. Do not use a comma alone to separate your sentences.

Using only a comma between sentences is called *comma splice* or *comma fault*. When you signal a new thought, you need to do so in a definite way; a comma alone is not enough to give this signal.

WRONG   Mary left her new coat on the bus last week, she is now more careful about her possessions.

RIGHT	Mary left her new coat on the bus last week. She is now more careful about her possessions.
RIGHT	Mary left her new coat on the bus last week; she is now more careful about her possessions.
RIGHT	Mary left her new coat on the bus last week, so she is now more careful about her possessions.

EXERCISE 5

Correct all comma splices in the following paragraph, using any of the methods suggested in this chapter.

> If you are sick of your job, just plain tired of your boss, and annoyed by the menial work that you do, I would like to give you some suggestions on how to get yourself fired. The first step on the road to unemployment is the easiest—come in late, this move should gain you at least a reprimand from management, next you should ignore your work and gossip with your co-workers. If these steps don't work, insulting your boss should do the trick. You should now be walking the streets, but if you still find yourself at the same job, there is only one remaining step, take the coward's way out and just quit!

You have learned four ways to correct run-together sentences and comma splices. Read the example of a run-together sentence and study the ways to correct it. If one of the methods still gives you trouble, return to the section that explains it.

> Only a few leaves could be seen the earth was covered with a blanket of snow.

1. Separate the sentences by using a period.

   > Only a few leaves could be seen. The earth was covered with a blanket of snow.

2. Separate the sentences by using a semicolon.

   > Only a few leaves could be seen; the earth was covered with a blanket of snow.

3. Separate the sentences by using a comma and a coordinating conjunction such as *and, but, or, nor, for, so,* or *yet.*

> Only a few leaves could be seen, *for* the earth was covered with a blanket of snow.

4. Separate the sentences by using a dependent clause beginning with a subordinating conjunction such as *before, after, when, because,* or *since.*

> Only a few leaves could be seen *because* the earth was covered with a blanket of snow.

EXERCISE 6

Separate the sentences in the following paragraph, using any of the methods described in this chapter.

> Misleading commercials advertise everything from headache remedies to automobiles the advertisements for headache and cold remedies lead people to believe that the product will relieve their miseries in seconds most of these advertisements compare one product with another and make people believe the advertised product has a tremendous advantage over its competitors when in fact the advantage is only slight mouthwash, toothpaste, cologne, and perfume commercials hint that the only thing needed to meet and keep an attractive woman or man is to use the advertised product these advertisements are not true to life rarely will someone tell people that they have bad breath or an unappealing smell the appearance of famous movie stars and athletes in commercials can also mislead some people these famous people imply that it is easy to be handsome, beautiful, or athletic just by using the right product.

CHAPTER FOUR

Adjectives and Adverbs

Learn to recognize adjectives (words that describe persons and things) and adverbs (words that tell how, when, and where).

When you write a sentence, you are telling about someone doing something or about something happening. You might write:

The woman screamed.
OR
The clock fell.

As you know, not many sentences are so short. You will usually want to say something more about the woman or the clock. One of the ways you can do that is to use words that describe. You can say:

The *tall* woman screamed.
The *tall, mysterious* woman screamed.
One tall, mysterious, dark-haired woman screamed.

You can say:

The *large* clock fell.
The *large cuckoo* clock fell.
The *large, white, antique cuckoo* clock fell.

Adjectives

The words *one, tall, mysterious, dark-haired, large, white, antique,* and *cuckoo* describe persons and things and are called *adjectives.* Adjectives usually tell

> which one   (the *tall* woman)
> (the *antique* clock)
> how many or how much   (*one* woman)

The italicized words below all tell which one, how many, or how much about the things they describe.

> **WHICH ONE**   *first* mile
> *singing* bird
>
> **HOW MANY**   *four* movies
> *few* friends
>
> **HOW MUCH**   *great* success
> *little* food

Adjectives usually come before the nouns they describe.

> We have an *enthusiastic* teacher.

Adjectives can appear after forms of *to be* (*is, are, was, were,* and so on).

> Our teacher is *enthusiastic.*

Adverbs

In addition to describing people and things, you will want to use words that say something about how, when, and where something is happening. These words are called *adverbs.* You might write:

> **HOW**   The woman enters *suddenly.*
> **WHEN**   The woman enters *early.*
> **WHERE**   The woman enters *below.*

HOW	The clock fell *noisily*.
WHEN	The clock fell *yesterday*.
WHERE	The clock fell *there*.

Adverbs describe verbs, adjectives, or other adverbs. They usually tell how, when, and where about the words they describe.

HOW	It is *strangely* quiet.
	She works *really* hard.
	I will act *quickly*.
WHEN	We left *early*.
	I moved *soon*.
	You arrived *late*.
WHERE	They ran *far*.
	I lived *nearby*.
	I went *there*.

Notice that adverbs, which are words that tell how, when, and where, often end in -*ly* (sudden*ly*, occasional*ly*, sharp*ly*, rude*ly*, happi*ly*).

EXERCISE 1

In the following sentences, underline all of the adjectives.

1. If you work very hard, you can finish two papers in class.
2. The frightened child cried for her mother.
3. Liz has black hair.
4. Suddenly there was a dark cloud in the sky.
5. Tom quickly refused John's kind offer.
6. If you should sneeze in the quiet library, do it as unobtrusively as possible.
7. Her youngest and laziest daughter has a job that pays well.
8. The singing birds disturbed us.
9. An egg-shaped ball is used to play football.
10. That poor dog has no juicy bones to chew.

EXERCISE 2

In the following sentences, underline all of the adverbs.

1. The frightened cat moved very cautiously.
2. Suddenly, the rain began.
3. The sleepy students entered the room slowly.
4. My older brother has always done his job well.
5. The crackling fire soon cheered us up.

4a

Learn participles used as adjectives.

4a(1)

Use participles ending in -ed and -ing correctly.

Adjectives ending in -ed or -ing come from regular verbs. They are participles used as adjectives, so they use the participle endings. The regular past participle ending is -ed.

-ed FORM USED AS A VERB	-ed FORM USED AS AN ADJECTIVE
The gun is not *loaded.*	Don't carry a *loaded* gun.

The present participle ending is -ing.

-ing FORM USED AS A VERB	-ing FORM USED AS AN ADJECTIVE
The girls are *working* hard.	They are *working* girls.

Here are some participles used as adjectives.

> *Mimeographed* copies are available. [copies that have been mimeographed]
> This is an *aged* cheese. [a cheese that has been aged]
> Don't open any *closed* doors. [doors that have been closed]
> My *sewing* box is on the desk. [a box used in sewing]
> We have no more *washing* powder. [powder used for washing]
> She saw a *purring* cat. [a cat who was purring]

Do not omit the *-d* or *-ed* participle ending.

WRONG	a love one
RIGHT	a love*d* one
WRONG	a load gun
RIGHT	a load*ed* gun
WRONG	a toss salad and a bake potato
RIGHT	a tossed salad and a baked potato

Do not omit the *-ing* participle ending.

WRONG	a change opinion
RIGHT	a chang*ing* opinion
WRONG	a gather storm
RIGHT	a gather*ing* storm
WRONG	a work girl
RIGHT	a work*ing* girl

When words like *love, load, toss, bake, change, gather* and *work* are used as adjectives, remember to add *-ed* or *-ing* to them.

EXERCISE 3

Copy the examples below. Then make a participle from each of the following verbs, and use it in a sentence: *help, admire, work, shout,* and *finish.*

■ Examples   *burn*
    The *burned* child dreads the fire.
    wish
    I need a *wishing* well to make my front yard complete.

EXERCISE 4

In the following sentences, underline the correct word in parentheses.

1. Health spas are popular with middle- (age, aged) men and women.
2. Who is the (injure, injured) party in this case?
3. My niece is a (comfort, comforted) to me.

4. Everyone had to bring a (cover, covered) dish to the picnic.

5. Low (cook, cooking) temperature softens the tissues and makes meat tender.

6. People are afraid of Mr. Schneider's (terrified, terrifying) temper.

7. A successful football team needs a good (pass, passing) attack.

8. You have to be on your guard when buying a (use, used) car.

9. Parents who show (concern, concerned) will worry when their children stay out late.

10. (Fish, Fishing) tackle should be available at any store in that area.

11. No Thanksgiving dinner is complete at my house without (stew, stewed) tomatoes and (candy, candied) yams.

4a(2)

Learn irregular past participles used as adjectives.

Not all verbs are regular. Some are irregular; that is, their past and past participle forms do not always end in *-ed.* Irregular verbs have special past participle forms. When these forms are used as adjectives, they, of course, are irregular too.

> My coat was *torn.*   I have a *torn* coat.
> My fingers were *frozen.*   I had *frozen* fingers.

These are some common past participles used as adjectives.

> a *beaten* egg   a *homegrown* vegetable
> a *broken* glass   the best *laid* plans
> a *chosen* few   the *spoken* word
> a well-*done* hamburger   a well-*written* letter
> the *stolen* camera   a *worn* garment

If you are not sure whether an adjective form is regular or irregular, look up the present form of the verb it comes from in the dictionary. The past participle (adjective) form comes after the past form of an irregular verb.

> Example   shake (shāk), *vb.,* shook,
>   shaken (shakən), shaking

In this example, the past participle (adjective) form, *shaken*, follows the past form, *shook*.

4b

Use adverbs, not adjectives, to tell how, when, and where something happens.

Adverbs describe just as adjectives do, but adverbs do not describe nouns and pronouns. They describe verbs, adjectives, and other adverbs. They also tell how, when, or where something happens.

ADJECTIVE	ADVERB
The clock is *slow*.	The clock chimed *slowly*.
[*slow* describes the noun, *clock*.]	[*Slowly* describes the verb *chimed*; it tells *how* the clock chimed.]

Remember to use adverbs, not adjectives, when you are describing verbs, adjectives, or other adverbs.

WRONG	The accident happened quick.
RIGHT	The accident happened *quickly*.
	[*Quickly* is an adverb that describes the verb *happened*.]
WRONG	He is breathing normal.
RIGHT	He is breathing *normally*.
	[*Normally* is an adverb that describes the verb *breathing*.]
WRONG	My sister doesn't sing very good.
RIGHT	My sister doesn't sing very *well*.
	[*Well* is an adverb that describes the verb *sing*.]

Many adverbs end in *-ly*. When adjectives already end in *-l*, the adverbs formed from them end in *-ly*.

usual   usual*ly*

Caution: Do not forget that adverbs describe adjectives as well as verbs and adverbs. Words describing adjectives like *good*, *easy*, and *young* should have *-ly* or other appropriate adverb endings.

WRONG   I feel *real* good today.
RIGHT   I feel *really* good today.

EXERCISE 5

Correct any errors in the use of adjectives and adverbs in the following sentences. Write a C next to any sentence in which there is no error.

1. My employer told me to finish the job as quick as I could and to stop for the day.
2. Almost anyone works bad when he is in a terrible big hurry.
3. I can finish this ice cream easily before it melts.
4. Jimmy Connors played badly at Wimbledon, but he still won the tournament.
5. If you drive too slow, you may not be safe on the roads.
6. This week's lesson is a real hard one.
7. Talk soft because my sister is not sleeping very sound.
8. It is a real problem getting a good job if you write badly.
9. In order to clean windows properly, you will need paper towels, window cleaner, rags, and some windows.
10. My nephew Bryant does things different from everyone else.

EXERCISE 6

Underline the correct word in parentheses in the following sentences.

1. David is a (real, really) good friend of mine.
2. The furniture in my room fits my personality (perfect, perfectly).
3. Renee wears glasses, and she is (constant, constantly) pulling them off and putting them on again.
4. The game started (slow, slowly), but after the first quarter, the Cowboys made a touchdown.
5. You will need a large pot for your geranium (immediate, immediately).

6. After I wash my hair, I rinse the shampoo out (careful, carefully).

7. I recently visited my hometown and found it changed (considerable, considerably).

4c
Use adjectives and adverbs correctly after linking verbs like *look, feel, seem, appear, taste,* and *sound.*

Often these verbs mean the same as *is, are, was, were,* or some other form of *to be.* When they do, they are called *linking verbs* because they link adjectives with the words they describe.

> Strawberry shortcake *tastes* delicious [Strawberry shortcake *is* delicious.]
> I *feel* restless. [I *am* restless.]

Whenever you use a verb like *look, feel, seem,* or *taste* as a linking verb, use an adjective with it. When you are just telling how something is done, use an adverb.

LINKING VERB *Use an Adjective*	NOT A LINKING VERB *Use an Adverb*
The teacher looked angry. [looked = was]	The teacher looked angrily at me. [looked does not = was]
She felt cautious about making a decision. [felt = was]	She felt cautiously under the bed, not knowing what she would find. [felt does not = was]

Remember that you almost always want to say that someone feels *bad,* not *badly.* A person who feels badly is probably looking for something in the dark.

EXERCISE 7

In the following sentences, underline the correct word in parentheses.

1. Your decision seems (hasty, hastily) to me.
2. She ate (hasty, hastily), not certain when the doorbell would ring.
3. With all you ate, I'm not surprised you feel (bad, badly).

4. Your decision appeared (sudden, suddenly) to me.
5. My sister appeared (sudden, suddenly) in the doorway.
6. Rock music always sounds (noisy, noisily) to me.
7. I'm afraid that that flounder doesn't smell very (fresh, freshly).

4d
Use adjectives and adverbs correctly when comparing two or more persons or things.

Use a comparative form of adjectives and adverbs when comparing two; use a superlative form when comparing more than two.

4d(1)
Short adjectives and some adverbs add an -er ending when they compare two persons or things (comparative form).

> Today is *hotter* than yesterday.
> Herb is *lazier* than Jim.
> Ed snores *louder* than Joe does.
> Lisa talks *longer* than Julie does.

4d(2)
The word *more* comes before longer adjectives and most adverbs that compare two persons or things (comparative form).

> Ted is *more* interesting than Lee.
> I talk *more* freely when Sue is not around.

4d(3)
Short adjectives and some adverbs add an -est ending when they compare more than two persons or things (superlative form).

> This is the hot*test* room in the house.
> Herb is the lazi*est* person I know.

Ed snores loud*est* of all.
Lisa talks the long*est* of any of the speakers.

4d(4)

The word *most* comes before longer adjectives and most adverbs that compare more than two persons or things (superlative form).

Ted is the *most* interesting person I know.
I talk *most* freely when no one else is listening.

Do not use *more* or *most* before a descriptive word that ends in -*er* or -*est*.

WRONG	more prettier
RIGHT	*prettier*
WRONG	most loveliest
RIGHT	*loveliest*

If *more* or *most* comes before a descriptive word, do not put -*er* or -*est* at the end of that word.

WRONG	more likelier
RIGHT	*more likely*
WRONG	most wonderfulest
RIGHT	*most wonderful*

4d(5)

Learn the special comparative and superlative forms of *good* and *well* and *bad* and *badly*.

Words that describe or compare persons and things

Janice is a *good* daughter.
Janice is a *better* daughter than Sarah. (comparative)
Janice is the *best* daughter anyone could have. (superlative)

I have a *bad* hangover.
I have a *worse* hangover than Earl. (comparative)
I have the *worst* hangover I have ever had. (superlative)

Words that describe or compare verbs

Janice obeys *well.*
Janice obeys *better* than Sarah. (comparative)
Janice obeys *best* of all. (superlative)

I drive *badly* when I am tired.
I drive *worse* when I am tired than when I am rested. (comparative)
I drive *worst* of all when I drink. (superlative)

4d(6)
Summary of Comparisons—Adjectives and Adverbs

BASIC FORM	COMPARATIVE FORM *For Two Items*	SUPERLATIVE FORM *For More Than Two*
small	smaller	smallest
fast	faster	fastest
beautiful	more beautiful	most beautiful
rapidly	more rapidly	most rapidly
good, well	better	best
bad, badly	worse	worst
much, many	more	most

EXERCISE 8

Correct the incorrect adjectives and adverbs in the following sentences by using the right form to compare the persons or things. Write C next to any sentences that are correct.

1. The ten-speed is one of the most fastest bikes.
2. A house is more safer than a trailer.
3. Mosquitoes are becoming a bigger problem than ever.
4. One of the loveliest places to visit in the fall is the mountains.
5. Friday is the most greatest day of the week.

6. My father hit me the hardest I had ever been hit.

7. My pastor spoke more longer this Sunday than he did last Sunday.

8. I think my hands are stronger than my little brother's.

9. We jumped off the porch and ran the most fastest we had ever run in our lives.

10. Bill is the most funniest person I know.

EXERCISE 9

Underline the correct adjectives or adverbs in parentheses.

1. My father cooks (better, more better) than my mother does.

2. The lectures we get at orientation are (worse, worst) than you can imagine.

3. My girlfriend is the (best, bestest) listener I know.

4. At boot camp we were treated (worse, worser) than animals.

5. Irene drives (better, best) than Frank does.

4e
Learn the special uses of *good* and *well*.

Good is always used as an adjective.

> *Bleak House* is a *good* book.
> Joe is *good* to me.
> Al looks *good* in brown.

Well can be used as an adjective or an adverb. It is an adjective when it describes someone's health or appearance; it is an adverb when it describes how something is done.

> A completely *well* person would not have spent the day in bed. [adjective—describes someone's health]
> The children usually play *well* together. [adverb—describes the way the children played]

EXERCISE 10

Underline the correct descriptive word in parentheses.

1. That stew smells (good, well).
2. Homemade ice cream always tastes (good, well).
3. That red hat looks (good, well) with your purple skirt.
4. My father was sick, but today he feels as (good, well) as he ever did.
5. Some athletes do (good, well) at every sport they try.

EXERCISE 11

Correct any incorrect adjectives or adverbs in the following sentences. Write C next to each sentence that is correct.

1. All my brothers have jobs that pay good.
2. When you're doing bad in high school, you're called to the counseling office.
3. It is now time for Hank to think serious about his life.
4. When I was inducted into the army, I thought it was the worse thing that could have happened to me.
5. Amy seems to have a more bigger writing problem than ever.
6. An F pencil lead is the softer of all the leads.
7. Drafting paper will not tear easily.
8. When you get married, it is for better or worst.
9. My aunt is a middle-age woman who loves to eat.
10. The expressway traffic situation is looking well today.
11. Turn left at the next flash red light.
12. Who was the most admire of all presidents?
13. That was a well-wore dress that your aunt was wearing.
14. I am feeling badly about losing your pen.
15. Music helps me release all of my build-up tension.

CHAPTER FIVE

Subjects, Possessive Words, and Objects

Learn to recognize when nouns and pronouns are subjects, possessive words, and objects.

The following table shows the different forms of nouns and pronouns. It shows subjects, possessive words, and objects.

	SUBJECTS	POSSESSIVE WORDS	OBJECTS
NOUNS:	John	John's	John
	nation	nation's	nation
PRONOUNS:	I	my, mine	me
	you	your, yours	you
	he	his	him
	she	her, hers	her
	it	its	it
	we	our, ours	us
	they	their, theirs	them
	who	whose	whom

Pronouns (I, you, they, and so on) replace words that name someone or something (nouns).

John is usually late. [*He* could replace *John.*]
He is usually late.

The *nation* is in economic trouble. [*It* could replace *nation.*]
It is in economic trouble.

Both nouns and pronouns have special forms. Nouns like *John* and *nation* change only to show possession, but pronouns like *I*, *he*, and *who* have special object forms as well (*me*, *him*, and *whom*).

> *John* is happy. (subject)
> I saw *John's* book. (possessive)
> I saw *John*. (object)
>
> *He* is happy. (subject)
> I saw *his* smile. (possessive)
> I saw *him*. (object)

Subjects

I, you, he, she, it, we, they, and *who* are used as subjects of sentences or dependent clauses. They tell who the subject is.

> *I* waited for hours.
> *They* listened carefully.
> This is the man *who* called you.

Possessives

My, mine, your, yours, his, her, hers, its, our, ours, their, theirs, and *whose* show possession. These words cannot be used as subjects. Instead they tell who or what owns a particular thing. If you wanted to say, "I own a house, and it is large," you would probably say:

> *My* house is large.

If you wanted to say that the roof belonging to the house was large, you would say:

> *Its* roof is large.

Objects

Me, you, him, her, it, us, them, and *whom* are used as objects. Pronouns (like nouns) can be objects of verbs or objects of prepositions. They are objects of verbs when they receive the action of these verbs.

Harry saw *them* (the children) across the street.

Pronouns are objects of prepositions when they appear after these prepositions in phrases.

I lent some money to *her* (the woman).

Sometimes the preposition *to* is omitted, but *her* is still the object; it is called the *indirect object*.

I lent *her* some money.

Nouns (*children, woman*) look the same whether they are subjects or objects. The pronouns *I, he, she, we, they,* and *who* change when they become objects.

I	→	me
he	→	him
she	→	her
we	→	us
they	→	them
who	→	whom

We avoided the spiders,
    but
the spiders also avoided *us*.

5a

Use *I, he, she, we, they,* and *who* only as subjects (persons or things being talked about); use *me, him, her, us, them* and *whom* as objects.

Do not confuse
$$\left\{ \begin{array}{l} \text{I with } me \\ he \text{ with } him \\ she \text{ with } her \\ we \text{ with } us \\ they \text{ with } them \end{array} \right\}$$
when your sentence has two subjects.

WRONG	Me and Althea always come home late.
RIGHT	Althea and *I* always come home late.
WRONG	Him and me lost a bet.
RIGHT	*He* and *I* lost a bet.
WRONG	Her and Joe are really close.
RIGHT	*She* and Joe are really close.

When a sentence has a double subject, there is a simple test that you can use to see whether you have used the right word. Try using each subject by itself as the subject of the sentence. In the sentence

Me and Althea always come home late.

you would not say

Me always come home late.

because *I*, not *me*, is the subject of the sentence. Therefore, if it is correct to say

I always come home late.

it is also correct to say

Althea and *I* always come home late.

Notice *Althea* and *I* is correct, not *I* and *Althea*; writers should always put themselves last.

5a(1)
Use *me* instead of *I* as an object. *I* can only be used as a subject.

In sentences like

Sally gave the tickets to Jim and *me*.
                    OR
Mrs. Hodges invited Joan and *me* to the party.

remember that *me* is used as an object even though it does not directly follow the verb.

> **WRONG** She called to Ed and I to come in.
> **RIGHT** She called to Ed and *me* to come in.

5a(2)
Do not use *us* instead of *we* as the subject of a sentence.

> **WRONG** Us girls go bowling every Friday.
> **RIGHT** *We* girls go bowling every Friday.

Since *we* is the subject of the sentence, if you want to show that you are one of the girls, you have to say, "We [girls] go bowling."

5a(3)
Them cannot be used to describe nouns.

If you want to say that certain persons or things are in a particular place, use the words *these* or *those* to express that idea.

> **WRONG** Them books are on the table.
> **RIGHT** *Those* books are on the table.

5a(4)
Whom, not *who,* should be used when you need an object.

> **WRONG** This is the man to who I gave the tickets.
> **RIGHT** This is the man to *whom* I gave the tickets.

EXERCISE 1

Underline all pronouns in the following expressions. Write *S* above all subject pronouns; write *O* above all object pronouns.

1. he and I
2. we brothers
3. who among you

4. Nancy and me
5. many of us
6. she or Sarah
7. the man whom I saw
8. a picture of Helen and me

EXERCISE 2

In the following sentences, underline the correct word in parentheses.

1. That gift brought happiness to my husband and (I, me).
2. I told him that (we, us) ex-Marines would have to stick together.
3. When I was in the Army, (my friends and I, me and my friends) saved enough money to start a business.
4. Everyone left except (my brother and me, my brother and I).
5. To (who, whom) were you referring in your letter?
6. (He and I, Him and me) went downstairs to see what was going on.
7. My mother took (Janet and I, Janet and me) out to dinner.
8. I just told you that (those, them) glasses have already been washed.
9. (She and Lou, Her and Lou) were already in line when we got to the theater.
10. The people (who, whom) are called good drivers fall into three categories.

5b
Show possession clearly by using the correct forms.

5b(1)
Be sure that you change *you to your, it to its, and who to whose* **to show possession.**

> **WRONG** In an emergency you know who you friends are.
> **RIGHT** In an emergency you know who *your* friends are.

WRONG	Every nation has it secrets.
RIGHT	Every nation has *its* secrets.

5b(2)
Remember the two common ways that a pronoun can show possession.

THESE PRONOUNS COME BEFORE THE NOUN	THESE PRONOUNS SUBSTITUTE FOR A PRONOUN AND A NOUN
This is *my* cover.	This cover is *mine*. (my cover)
This is *your* cover.	This cover is *yours*. (your cover)
This is *his* cover.	This cover is *his*. (his cover)
This is *her* cover.	This cover is *hers*. (her cover)
This is *our* cover.	This cover is *ours*. (our cover)
This is *their* cover.	This cover is *theirs*. (their cover)

5b(3)
A pronoun does not use an apostrophe to show possession.
***Yours, his, hers, its, ours,* and *theirs* do not have an apostrophe (') before the *s. Mine* does not have an apostrophe (') or an *s*.**

WRONG	mine's, mines, your's, hi's, her's, it's, our's, their's
RIGHT	mine, yours, his, hers, its, ours, theirs
WRONG	That's mine's.
RIGHT	That's *mine*.
WRONG	I'm not using that pan because it's lid is missing.
RIGHT	I'm not using that pan because *its* lid is missing.

Remember that a pronoun with an apostrophe always means a contraction, not possession.

CONTRACTION	POSSESSION
You're here	Use your head.
They're wrong.	Those are their raincoats.

For more information on contractions, see 15d, p. 220.

5b(4)

Be sure to add an apostrophe (') and s to a noun to show possession.

> the book belonging to John → John's book
> the playground for the children → the children's playground
> the health of a person → a person's health

Do not carelessly omit the ending that shows ownership.

> **WRONG**   John book
> **RIGHT**   John's book
>
> **WRONG**   Children playground
> **RIGHT**   Children's playground

5b(5)

When a word ending in -ing is used as a noun, use a possessive pronoun to describe it.

> **WRONG**   I don't like you sleeping until noon.
> **RIGHT**   I don't like *your* sleeping until noon.

Sleeping is a thing (an activity); therefore, it is a noun. The possessive pronoun *your* rather than the object pronoun *you* should then be used to describe *sleeping*. The writer does not object to *you*; he just objects to *your sleeping*.

5b(6)

Do not confuse a word that shows possession with a word that merely ends in s.

Be sure that you have a reason for putting an apostrophe before an s. Do not put an apostrophe before an s used to indicate the plural of a word or to mark the present form of a verb.

WRONG	Sue is alway's in the way.
RIGHT	Sue is *always* in the way.
WRONG	Joe work's on Saturday's. [*Works* is the present form of *work; Saturdays* is the plural form of *Saturday.* Apostrophes are not needed.]
RIGHT	Joe works on Saturdays.

EXERCISE 3

Underline the word groups that are correctly written.

1. you raincoat; your raincoat
2. This is mines. This is mine. This is mine's.
3. its story; it story; it's story
4. they house; their house
5. What's mine is yours. What's mine's is your's. What's mine is your's.
6. That bar is theirs. That bar is their's.
7. Is it ours or his? Is it our's or hi's? Is it ours or hi's?

EXERCISE 4

Correct all errors in words showing possession. Write C next to each sentence that is correct.

1. I think that patience and understanding are your greatest strengths.
2. Tom is a dear friend of mine's.
3. Some baggers don't care how they handle you groceries.
4. I didn't like the idea of their going away to school.
5. Several coaches want him to attend they school.
6. My TV set has definitely reached the end of its useful life.
7. Get you equipment ready.
8. They are only giving their opinion.
9. I remember hi's saying he would never let a smaller man beat him.
10. Every marriage has it ups and downs.

EXERCISE 5

Copy the following sentences, using an apostrophe and *s* when needed to show possession. Remove the apostrophe when it is not needed.

1. All the women are waiting for the fishermen return.
2. Some people homes are large enough to have laundry room's.
3. The employer's always wanted more than a high-school diploma.
4. Getting into someone business can cause a lot of trouble.
5. He was always right by his father side.
6. To the right of the jewelry counter is the children department.
7. Dan Rather news coverage is very interesting.
8. The walls in Larry room were filled with hubcaps.
9. My sister name is Barbara.
10. Al likes to drive large cars like Cadillac's.

EXERCISE 6

Put a check mark next to any of the following word groups that show possession correctly. Rewrite any of the word groups that do not show ownership correctly.

1. from Joe point of view
2. in today world
3. the student name
4. a citizen's property
5. today's time's

5c

Myself, yourself, himself, herself, itself, ourselves, yourselves, and *themselves* are never used alone.

Use these words with subjects and objects to give them emphasis.

I walked by *myself.*

Charles thinks for *himself*.
We *ourselves* want to get the job finished.
The lesson *itself* is not difficult.

Do not use objects (*me, him, them*) for this purpose.

WRONG	I bought me a milkshake.
RIGHT	I bought *myself* a milkshake.
WRONG	My brother found him a good wife.
RIGHT	My brother found *himself* a good wife.

5c(1)
Myself, yourself, himself, herself, itself, ourselves, yourselves, or *themselves* cannot be the subject of a sentence.

WRONG	Myself and some friends moved all the furniture.
RIGHT	Some friends and I moved all the furniture.

5c(2)
Be sure to spell *himself, itself, ourselves,* and *themselves* correctly.

himself	NOT	hisself
itself	NOT	its self
ourselves	NOT	ourself
themselves	NOT	theirself
		theirselves
		themself

EXERCISE 7

In the following sentences, underline the correct word or words in parentheses.

1. Most of the time he is by (hisself, himself).

2. (My wife and myself, My wife and I) didn't want our daughter to move into an apartment.

3. We wanted to finish painting the barn by (ourself, ourselves).

4. Jenny and Lynn picked all those strawberries by (theirselves, themselves).

5. I know that mirror didn't get broken all by (its self, itself).

EXERCISE 8

Correct the incorrect sentences by changing the italicized words to the correct forms. Write C next to each sentence that is correct.

1. *Myself and three other people* were participating in the talent show.

2. Pope John Paul was injured by a would-be *assassin* bullet.

3. Did he mean to keep that letter a secret from *you and I?*

4. Around the corner *he and George* were waiting for us.

5. Are these children *their's* or *her's?*

6. *Her and I* were planning to go to the dance until you called.

7. *We kids* ought not to get in trouble right before Christmas.

8. That red motorcycle is *mine's;* the other one is *his.*

9. Remember that a sales tax takes money out of *you* pocket.

10. I call what he has on *his* face a *rat* nest, but he thinks it's a beard.

11. I found all of *those* stones in *them* beans I just washed.

12. I thought no one would ever break *Babe Ruth* home-run record.

13. In cold weather most people bundle *themself* up in warm clothing.

14. Every summer some good friends and *myself* go surfing.

15. I need to think about getting *me* a good job.

CHAPTER SIX
Agreement

> *Make a subject agree with its verb; make singular and plural words agree with the words they refer to.*

6a
Make each subject agree with its verb.

Many of your papers will be written in the present tense. A verb in the present tense has an -*s* ending or no ending. It is important to be sure that every present tense verb you use agrees with its subject.

In the following lists you can see that most subjects agree with present-tense verbs that have no ending; only *he, she,* and *it*—or nouns that can be replaced by *he, she,* and *it*—agree with verbs that end in -*s*.

I _____	we _____	I __sit__	we __sit__
you _____	you _____	you __sit__	you __sit__
he __s__	they _____	he __sits__	they __sit__
she __s__		she __sits__	
it __s__		it __sits__	

6a(1)

In the present tense, singular *(he, she, it)* subjects agree with verbs that end in *-s,* and plural *(they)* subjects agree with verbs that do *not* end in *-s.*

The present tense tells what is happening now or what happens on a regular basis or as a matter of habit. When you use the present, make sure to add *-s* to the verb with a singular *(he, she, it)* subject.

SOME SUBJECTS AND VERBS THAT AGREE

(he subject)	Bob often *writes* letters to his friends.
	[*Bob* could be replaced by *He.*]
(she subject)	Lisa *smiles* and *looks* happy when she *sees* you.
	[*Lisa* could be replaced by *She.*]
(it subject)	A party sometimes *lasts* all night.
	[*A party* could be replaced by *It.*]
(they subject)	The neighbors always *finish* dinner before we do.
	[*The neighbors* could be replaced by *They.*]
(they subject)	The weird noises outside *keep* us awake.
	[*The weird noises outside* could be replaced by *They.*]

Caution: Words sometimes come between a singular subject and the verb that goes with it. When this happens, be very careful to make the verb end in *-s* to agree with its subject.

WRONG	One of my best friends sing off key.
RIGHT	One of my best friends *sings* off key. [*One* is the subject of the sentence, not *friends.* Since *one* is singular, *sings* should end in *s* to agree with it.]

a. The following singular *(he, she, it)* subjects agree with verbs that end in *-s:*

one	*One* of the children *plays* quietly by himself.
everyone	*Everyone tries* to get her attention.
someone	*Someone waits* for Jane after class every day.
something	*Something falls* in the attic every night.
everything	*Everything happens* to me.
each	*Each* of the police officers *guards* one section of the mall.

kind	This *kind* of jewelry *costs* a lot.
either	*Either* drink *tastes* good to me.
neither	*Neither* of the students *works* very hard.

b. The following plural *(they)* subjects agree with verbs that do not end in -s:

lots	*Lots* of my friends *attend* this school.
kinds	Many *kinds* of clothes *cost* a lot.
both	*Both* of the boys *study* four hours a day.
many	*Many* of us *worry* about the future.
several	*Several* members of the club always *come* late to the meetings.

c. *All, some,* and *none* can be singular or plural, depending on meaning.

SINGULAR SUBJECT	PLURAL SUBJECT
Verb Ends in -s	*Verb Does Not End in -s*
All candy *tastes* delicious.	All jellybeans *taste* delicious.
Some of the mail *seems* to be lost.	Some of the husbands *seem* to be male chauvinists.
None (not one) of the students *is* prepared.	None (not any) of the students *are* prepared.

d. Units of money are considered singular subjects; they agree with verbs that end in -s.

Five dollars *seems* to be all the money I have.

EXERCISE 1

In the following sentences, underline the verb in parentheses that agrees with its subject.

1. Vernon (talks, talk) from the time he (start, starts) cutting your hair until the time he is finished.
2. Sometimes she (dresses, dress) that way to clown around.
3. Every time he has some extra money, he always (spend, spends) it.
4. Those children (makes, make) you smile when you really don't feel like it.
5. Most people (finish, finishes) eating before my cousin Rhonda.

EXERCISE 2

In the following sentences, underline the verb in parentheses that agrees with its subject.

1. One of my cousins (play, plays) the piano beautifully.
2. The mall has several kinds of stores that (stays, stay) open late.
3. Some of my friends (spends, spend) their evenings in that bar.
4. Everything (bother, bothers) me today.
5. All of my new friends (seem, seems) to look up to me.

EXERCISE 3

Correct the incorrect italicized verbs in the following sentences so that they agree with their subjects. Write C next to each sentence that is correct.

1. The hallway *look* like a racetrack.
2. She always *want* me to invest my money in her company.
3. Bill usually *sing* in the chorus.
4. Ten cents *buys* very little these days.
5. Becky always *look* her best.
6. Slow drivers *causes* many accidents.
7. Sammy told me about the parts of the movie that *scares* everybody.
8. Everyone *enjoys* a good laugh.
9. He *drive* a 1982 Buick.
10. Not one of the students *seem* to realize that the bell has rung.

6a(2)

In the present tense, *I, we,* and *you* subjects agree with verbs that do not end in *-s*.

SOME SUBJECTS AND VERBS THAT AGREE

I *like* to visit him.
You always *finish* first.

I *work* every day from 8:00 to 4:30.
We *understand* your problem.
You *treat* John unfairly.

EXERCISE 4

Circle the verbs that can be used with the following subjects. There may be more than one.

■ **Example**   I passes, thinks, (listen), (work)

1. We races, drinks, shout, dance
2. I sings, play, twirls, strut
3. Each of us swim, row, fishes, float
4. Not one of the snakes bite, hiss, strikes, rattles
5. Several newcomers in the area talk, smile, greets, waves
6. You cry, fights, scratch, sleep
7. I scream, laugh, hears, works
8. You collapse, jog, blinks, touch
9. Rusty, a member of the club for years, swims, ask, chairs, seek
10. We snores, delivers, act, sounds

EXERCISE 5

Correct the incorrect verbs in the following sentences so that the subjects and verbs agree. Write C next to each sentence that is correct.

1. I tries to avoid gossiping about others.
2. You always thinks of others.
3. You eats too much junk food.
4. I read the directions carefully.
5. You never seem to care about other people.
6. I wishes you would come.
7. We dances to the music.
8. Bill and I never see each other.

6a(3)
Learn the forms of the verb *to be* that agree with their subjects.

The present tense of *to be* has three verb forms: *am, is,* and *are. Am* agrees with *I; is* ends in *-s* to agree with *he, she,* and *it* subjects; and *are* agrees with all other subjects.

SINGULAR	PLURAL
I am	we are
you are	you are
he, she, it is	they are

To be is the only verb that has two past forms that need to agree with their subjects: *was* and *were. Was* agrees with *I, he, she,* and *it; were* agrees with all other subjects.

SINGULAR	PLURAL
I was	we were
you were	you were
he, she, it was	they were

Caution: In *here is (are), there is (are),* and *where is (are)* sentences, the subject comes after the verb. Be sure to look after the verb for its subject in such sentences, and make the verb agree with its subject.

> Here is the key you have been looking for. [*Is* agrees with the singular subject *key.*]
> There are definitely mice in this attic. [*Are* agrees with the plural subject *mice.*]
> Where were those shoes when you found them? [*Were* agrees with the plural subject *shoes.*]

EXERCISE 6

In the following sentences, underline the correct verb form in parentheses.

1. Empty beer cans and wine bottles (was, were) all over the yard.
2. I (am, is) taking a make-up test on Wednesday.
3. There (is, are) only a few days of vacation left.
4. Scrubbing floors (is, are) easy.
5. I never suspected that you (was, were) the one who called.
6. There (was, were) about fifteen men in my section.
7. On that shelf there (is, are) several of my favorite knickknacks.
8. There (is, are) about twenty-five seats in our classroom.
9. Where (is, are) the mountains you said would be covered with snow?
10. Here (is, are) the books and tapes the language lab supplies to help you.

6a(4)

Singular subjects *(he, she,* and *it)* agree with the verb form *has;* all other subjects agree with the verb form *have.*

SUBJECT	VERB
I	have
you	have
he, she, it	has
we	have
you	have
they	have

EXERCISE 7

In the following sentences, underline the correct verb form in parentheses.

1. My high school (has, have) its first game of the season this weekend.
2. The boat (have, has) a tall mast with sails flying.
3. You (has, have) to jog every morning to keep your weight under control.
4. My uncle (have, has) things well-organized.
5. Tina and Carol (has, have) to be in bed by 9 P.M.

6a(5)

Singular subjects *(he, she,* and *it)* agree with the verb forms *does* and *goes;* all other subjects agree with the verb forms *do* and *go.*

SUBJECT	VERB	SUBJECT	VERB
I	do	I	go
you	do	you	go
he, she, it	does	he, she, it	goes
we	do	we	go
you	do	you	go
they	do	they	go

EXERCISE 8

In the following sentences, underline the correct verb form in parentheses.

1. My best friend (do, does) better in math than I (do, does).

2. It looks as though they (go, goes) to all of the school activities.

3. Many young parents today (does, do) seem too busy to take care of their babies.

4. Ann will see that everything (go, goes) well.

5. It just (go, goes) to show you that a daughter (do, does) not always do what you would have done in her place.

6a(6)

Learn the subjects that agree with the contracted forms of the verb + *not.*

I subjects agree with the verbs *don't, wasn't, haven't.*
He, she, it subjects agree with the verbs *isn't, doesn't, wasn't, hasn't.*
We, you, they subjects agree with the verbs *aren't, don't, weren't, haven't.*

SOME SUBJECTS AND VERBS THAT AGREE

     (*I* subject)   I *don't* understand you.
     (*he* subject)   Dennis *doesn't* like Janis.

(*she* subject)	Rhonda *hasn't* heard the news.
(*it* subject)	My car *doesn't* start on cold days.
(*we* subject)	We *weren't* going to tell him.
(*they* subject)	Joe and Richard *weren't* always friends.
(*they* subject)	His teeth *aren't* straight.

Spell these verbs correctly. The apostrophe goes between the *n* and the *t* because the *o* has been left out.

isn't	NOT	is'nt
aren't	NOT	are'nt
wasn't	NOT	was'nt
weren't	NOT	were'nt
doesn't	NOT	does'nt
don't	NOT	do'nt
hasn't	NOT	has'nt
haven't	NOT	have'nt

EXERCISE 9

Correct the incorrect italicized verbs in the following sentences so that they agree with their subjects. Write C next to each sentence that is correct.

1. Larry *don't* ever catch any fish.
2. Lucy *wasn't* very friendly yesterday.
3. David and Josephine *aren't* going together anymore.
4. This book *haven't* a very good ending.
5. You *wasn't* very fair in your decision.
6. I *wasn't* very happy about getting that teacher.
7. People *isn't* likely to watch that show.

EXERCISE 10

Proofread the following paragraph. Your instructor may ask you to copy it. The student who wrote the paragraph at times forgot to use an -s ending where it was needed and sometimes used an -s where it was not really needed. Circle any errors in agreement, and write your corrections above them.

> Some of my friends says that I treat my dog Nancy like a person instead of a dog. I enjoys my dog for the way she act and for the things she do. When Nancy want water, something makes her stands in front of the refrigerator and bark for ice to be put in it. She don't like lukewarm water from the sink. Nothing can make her eat her food from a dog's bowl. She insist on one of our china dishes. She also want to sleep in a regular bed just as we does. She have a special pillow that she drag around the house all the time. Nancy love to chew ice and eat candy. She adore ice cream. I treat Nancy like a person because she do act more like a person than a dog.

6b
Make pronouns agree with the words they refer to.

You wouldn't expect to read a sentence like

> Joe reads Joe's book.
>> OR
> The children took the children's places in the classroom.

To keep from using the same word over and over, sometimes you may want to use another word to refer to that word. When you do this, it is important that the two words agree.

6b(1)
Use singular pronouns *he, she, it, its, his, him, her,* or *hers* to agree with a singular noun or pronoun.

Use $\begin{Bmatrix} he \\ him \\ his \end{Bmatrix}$ to agree with *Sam.*

> Sam hides *his* beer cans when *his* father comes into the room.

Use $\begin{Bmatrix} \text{she} \\ \text{her} \\ \text{hers} \end{Bmatrix}$ to agree with *mother*.

Mother said *she* would see *her* lawyer on Thursday.

Use $\begin{Bmatrix} \text{it} \\ \text{its} \end{Bmatrix}$ to agree with *beer*.

I poured the beer slowly, but *it* still has a head on *it*.

Note: When a subject could be either male or female, many writers like to make the subject plural and to use a plural pronoun to refer to it.
Instead of: A visitor should check his packages at the door.
It is better to say: Visitors should check *their* packages at the door.

6b(2)

Use plural pronouns *they, them, their,* or *theirs* to agree with a plural noun or pronoun.

Use $\begin{Bmatrix} \text{they} \\ \text{them} \\ \text{their} \\ \text{theirs} \end{Bmatrix}$ to agree with $\begin{Bmatrix} \text{students} \\ \text{desks} \\ \text{children} \end{Bmatrix}$.

Students shouldn't write on *their* desks or leave *their* gum stuck to *them*.
If Joe cleans his room, my *children* may clean *theirs*.

SOME NOUNS AND PRONOUNS THAT AGREE

A boy who prepares carefully for class will probably pass *his* exams.
Since a school desk is used by so many students, *it* always loses *its* shine.

6b(3)
Use singular pronouns to agree with special singular words.

The following are singular pronouns:

he	she	it
his	her	its
him	hers	

Use one of these pronouns to agree with one of the following singular words:

anyone	someone	no one	everyone	kind	each
anything	something	nothing	everything	type	either
anybody	somebody	nobody	everybody	sort	neither

SINGULAR WORDS THAT AGREE

Neither of the men left *his* name with the secretary.
What else can *someone* ask of *his* mother?
It is the *kind* of class I like best.

EXERCISE 11

In the following sentences, underline the word or words in parentheses that agree with the italicized noun or pronoun.

1. *Each* of my friends gave me (her, their) phone number.
2. *One* of the books had lost (its, their) cover.
3. Bill dropped *something.* Will you pick (it, them) up?
4. (He is, They are) the *kind* of teacher I like.
5. *Everyone* brought (his, their) own beer.
6. (It is, They are) the *types* of exercises all the students do.
7. I babysit so often that when *someone* comes to visit me, (they get, he gets) the impression that I am running a nursery.
8. When the time comes for a football game, *everyone* is excited because each thinks that (his, their) team is going to win.

6b(4)

Use a singular pronoun to agree with two or more singular subjects joined by *or* or *nor*. Use a plural pronoun to agree with two or more plural subjects joined by *or* or *nor*.

SOME NOUNS AND PRONOUNS THAT AGREE

Either Bill or Bob left *his* own work unfinished.
Neither the daughters nor the sons ever clean *their* own rooms.

When one of the subjects is singular and the other is plural, the pronoun agrees with the nearer subject.

Neither the teacher nor the *students* remembered *their* books.
Abandoned cats or even a stray *dog* has *its* problems finding enough food.

EXERCISE 12

In the following sentences, underline the word in parentheses that agrees with the italicized words.

1. *Neither Barbara nor Pam* finished (her, their) paper in class.
2. Did *your truck or your trailer* fail (their, its) inspection?
3. *Neither the fathers nor the children* lost (their, his) temper.
4. *Either the rain or the wind* had (its, their) effect on the garden.
5. Will *Bill or Ed* take (their, his) vacation in August?

EXERCISE 13

Copy the following paragraph, changing any words necessary to make all subjects and verbs agree and to make all pronouns agree with the words they refer to.

The detective will always be a favorite character on American television because people enjoys seeing how police protection work.

The TV detective always seem to know the solution to the crime without really thinking the case over. They are a superhuman mastermind, as well as an expert in self-defense, a good citizen, and a hero to all the kids. The TV detective is also so good-looking that all the women wants to kiss them. The real detective, though, are not like this. They has to think over dangerous situations because it could endanger their loved ones.

CHAPTER SEVEN
Verbs

Learn to recognize the correct forms of verbs.

In a sentence, a verb is a word that tells what the subject is doing or what is happening to the subject. You can usually use verbs correctly if you know how verb forms are spelled and if you understand their purpose in a sentence.

A verb can stand by itself *(love, loves, loved)*, or it can appear with another verb—often called a *helping verb*.

COMMON HELPING VERBS

has	is	do	can	will	must	shall
have	are	does	could	would	might	should
had	was					
	were					

VERB BY ITSELF

I *love* money.
He *loves* money.
We *loved* money.

VERB WITH HELPING VERB

Money *is loved* by many.
I *have loved* money.

I *could love* money.
They *do love* money.
We *will love* money.

A verb can be helped by one helping verb or by more than one
helping verb.

I *have* loved money.
I *could have* loved money.

A verb that is sometimes used as a helping verb can also appear by
itself as the main verb of a sentence.

I *have* money.

Most verbs have no more than four basic forms or principal parts.
If you know the principal parts of a verb, you can express any number
of ideas. Here are the four principal parts of the regular verb *learn*
and the irregular verb *give*.

	PRESENT	PAST	PAST PARTICIPLE	PRESENT PARTICIPLE
Regular:	learn(s)	learned	learned	learning
Irregular:	give(s)	gave	given	giving

Here are the main ways these principal parts are used.

Present: learn(s), give(s)

1. Used to form the present tense; *-s* is added to present tense verbs that
   agree with *he, she, it* subjects
   I learn; he learns; we give; it gives

Note: The tense of a verb shows then the action takes place. More information on verb tenses appears in Section **7g.**

2. Used after *will* to form the future
   I will learn; he will give

3. Used after helping verbs *can, could, will, would, should, must, might, ought,* and with *do* and *did*

> I can learn; we did give

Past: learned, gave

Used by itself to show past action

> She learned; you gave

Past participle: learned, given

1. Used after a form of the helping verb *have*

> he has learned; we have learned; we had given

2. Used after a form of the helping verb *be*

> it is learned; they will be learned; I was given

Present participle: learning, giving

Used after a form of *be* to show continuing action

> I am learning; they were giving

The use of the present tense is covered in Chapter **6** (agreement). The uses of other verb tenses are dealt with in this chapter. Pages **125–26** have a chart listing the tenses of regular and irregular verbs. The principal parts of irregular verbs are listed on page **106.**

7a
Learn the past tense of verbs.

Each verb except *be* has only one past form.

I
you
he
she   } *gave*
it
we
they

Be has two past forms: *was* and *were;* for more information, see
6a(4).

The past just says that something happened, and it says it using
one verb. No helping verbs are used. The italicized verbs in the
following sentences all tell about something that happened in the
past.

> I *sang* in the choir.
> You *lost* your way in the woods.
> We *laughed* on the way home.
> She *danced* all night long.
> It *was* under the sofa.
> They *were* in the bathtub.

7a(1)
Past forms ending in *-ed*

All verbs have a one-word form that expresses the past. It usually
ends in *-ed.* Only a *-d* is added when the verb already ends in *-e*
(*add* + *ed* → *added; change* + *-d* → *changed*). Sometimes the ending
is not clearly heard in speech, but it always appears in writing.

> **WRONG**   I notice that there were some buses full of people.
> **RIGHT**   I *noticed* that there were some buses full of people.
>
> **WRONG**   I watch the news last night.
> **RIGHT**   I *watched* the news last night.

Be sure to add *-d* or *-ed* to express the past of *use* and *happen.* If you
do not do this, it will sound as if you are talking about something
happening in the present.

> **PRESENT**   I use my commuter tickets. [I use them every day.]
> **PAST**   I *used* my commuter tickets. [I used them all.]
>
> **PRESENT**   I happen to be against that plan. [I am against it now.]
> **PAST**   I *happened* to be against that plan. [I was against it.]

EXERCISE 1

If any of the following sentences show that something happened in the past, make the italicized verb past by adding *-d* or *-ed*. If you cannot tell whether the past or present is intended, do not change the verb.

1. Everybody *finish* eating an hour ago.
2. The last time Sid *play* cards was a year ago.
3. The bus *approach* as I saw my father's car.
4. I *realize* that you are right.
5. I *like* this class.
6. We *use* to have money.
7. We all *decide* to go fishing last Saturday.
8. I *open* the door, and there she was!
9. People with allergies often *use* a special soap.
10. We *happen* to be wrong in this case.

7a(2)
Irregular past forms (listed on p. 106)

PAST FORMS HAVING THE SOUND *an*

began	sang
drank	sank
ran	shrank
rang	sprang

Some common verbs end in *-an* or have *an* (as in *and*) as the main sound when they express the past. These verbs are the past forms of *begin, drink, run, ring, sing, sink, shrink,* and *spring.* They appear without a helping verb.

> Eve *ran* home.
> We *began* to sort the mail.
> Phil *drank* all the beer.

We *sang* silly songs.
The leaky boat *sank*.

Do not confuse a past form with the past participial form that must be used with a helping verb.

WRONG	I have ran.
RIGHT	I *ran*.
	I *have run*.
WRONG	I have began.
RIGHT	I *began*.
	I *have begun*.
WRONG	We had drank water.
RIGHT	We *drank* water.
	We *had drunk* water.

EXERCISE 2

When the past is expressed *without* a helping verb, change the italicized verb to *ran, began, drank, sang,* or *shrank*.

1. When we heard that noise, we *run* all the way home.
2. I *begun* to worry about my clothing.
3. I can see that your dress *shrunk* in the wash.
4. Walter had *drunk* a lot before he came.
5. That song was *sung* at the band concert on Saturday.

Blew, drew, flew, grew, *and* knew

Blew, drew, flew, grew, and *knew* are the past forms of *blow, draw, fly, grow,* and *know*. Notice the contrast between the present and the past.

PRESENT	Today I blow bubbles.
PAST	Yesterday I *blew* bubbles.
PRESENT	Today I draw a picture.
PAST	Yesterday I *drew* a picture.

PRESENT	Today I fly planes.
PAST	Yesterday I *flew* planes.
PRESENT	Today I grow gardenias.
PAST	Yesterday I *grew* gardenias.
PRESENT	Today I know everything.
PAST	Yesterday I *knew* everything.

Do not make the mistake of thinking that *blow, draw, fly, grow,* and *know* are regular verbs that add *-d* or *-ed* to form the past.

| WRONG | blowed, drawed, flied, growed, knowed |
| RIGHT | *blew, drew, flew, grew, knew* |

EXERCISE 3

Write two sentences using each of the following beginnings: I blew, He drew, We flew, It grew, They knew.

Swore, tore, *and* wore

Swore, tore, and *wore* are the past forms of *swear, tear,* and *wear.* They cannot be used with helping verbs.

WRONG	I have tore my dress
RIGHT	I *tore* my dress.
WRONG	He has wore out that lawnmower.
RIGHT	He *wore* out that lawnmower.

EXERCISE 4

Write two sentences using each of the following beginnings: He swore, She tore, They wore.

Came *and* became

Be sure that you know the past forms (*came* and *became*) of the verbs *to come* and *to become.*

PRESENT	They come to our house. [They come every year.]
PAST	They *came* to our house. [They came last week.]
PRESENT	I become jealous easily. [I become jealous often.]
PAST	I *became* jealous when I saw them. [I became jealous that one time.]

Do not use *came* or *became* with a helping verb.

| WRONG | He has often came to our house. |
| RIGHT | He often *came* to our house. |

EXERCISE 5

Write two sentences using each of the following beginnings: They came, It became.

Did, saw, *and other unusual forms*

The following lists show some very common verbs that have unusual past forms.

PRESENT	PAST
go	went
do	did
eat	ate
fall	fell
forget	forgot
give	gave
see	saw
shake	shook
take	took

Remember not to use the past with helping verbs.

WRONG	They have did their English lesson.
RIGHT	They *did* their English lesson.
WRONG	He has already went home.
RIGHT	He already *went* home.

Do not use the incorrect forms *done, seen,* or *seed* as past forms.

WRONG	I done all that you asked.
RIGHT	I *did* all that you asked.
WRONG	I seen the motorcycle in the rear-view mirror.
RIGHT	I *saw* the motorcycle in the rear-view mirror.

EXERCISE 6

Write two sentences using each of the following beginnings: We did, It went, They fell, I forgot, You forgave, I gave, They shook, It took, She saw, He ate.

PAST FORMS HAVING THE SOUND o

arose	rose
broke	shone
chose	spoke
drove	stole
froze	wrote
rode	

These are the past forms of *arise, break, choose, drive, freeze, ride, rise, shine, speak, steal,* and *write.* When you say these words, you hear the sound *o* as in *hole.* All these forms end in a silent *-e.* Do not use a helping verb with any of them.

WRONG	A dispute has arose.
RIGHT	A dispute *arose.*
WRONG	The glass has broke.
RIGHT	The glass *broke.*
WRONG	He has chose a partner.
RIGHT	He *chose* a partner.
WRONG	I have spoke to him about it.
RIGHT	I *spoke* to him about it.
WRONG	You have never wrote to her.
RIGHT	You never *wrote* to her.

EXERCISE 7

Write two sentences using each of the following past forms: *arose, broke, chose, drove, froze, rode, spoke, stole, wrote.*

EXERCISE 8

If the italicized verbs in each of the following sentences express the past correctly, write C next to the sentence. If the past is not used, change the form of the verb to the past.

1. I had friends who *had went* into the Navy.
2. Al often *has rode* up and down the street to catch a glimpse of a pretty girl.
3. Sara *done* a lot for me when I *lived* in the dorm.
4. Many problems *have came* to the surface.
5. There was so much wind my house almost *blowed* away.
6. Leo *has swore* to tell the truth, the whole truth, and nothing but the truth.
7. The men who held me up *took* all my money.
8. I *knowed* it was wrong when I *saw* it.
9. Jo *has wore* my dress three times, and I haven't even had it on.
10. Edna *has gave* that dog all the bones she could find in the house.
11. They *have* all *chose* to stay in the same group.
12. Phil *became* angry when Ed *told* him the news.
13. They *have drove* that way for years.
14. He *flied* his plane into a mountain.
15. We *seen* him coming.
16. George and Steve *run* all the way home.
17. Eileen and I *had ate* too much that time.

Burst, caught, dug, led, *and* passed

The irregular past forms of *burst, catch, dig, lead,* and *pass* are often used incorrectly.

WRONG	The balloon bursted when it hit the window.
RIGHT	The balloon *burst* when it hit the window.
WRONG	I catched the flu.
RIGHT	I *caught* the flu.
WRONG	I digged a hole.
RIGHT	I *dug* a hole.
WRONG	I lead the list yesterday.
RIGHT	I *led* the list yesterday.
WRONG	I past (OR pasted) the chicken.
RIGHT	I *passed* the chicken.

EXERCISE 9

Write a sentence using each of the following past forms: *burst, caught, dug, led,* and *passed.*

Review **7a** carefully. Then do Exercises 10, 11, and 12.

EXERCISE 10

Write the past form of the verb given in parentheses in the space provided in each sentence.

(do)   1. We all _____ our homework.
(see)   2. I _____ the dog.
(burst)   3. Harvey _____ the bubble.
(take)   4. She _____ a letter.
(run)   5. They _____ down the hill.
(steal)   6. Milly and I _____ some money.
(draw)   7. Joan and Peggy _____ some pictures.
(break)   8. Marty _____ a bottle.
(know)   9. I _____ the answer.
(catch) 10. You _____ a cold.

EXERCISE 11

Rewrite the following sentences so that each verb is in the past. Follow the pattern given in the examples and begin each of your sentences with *They.*

■ **Examples**   It was seen as a big problem.
They *saw it as a big problem.*

Sugar was used to make a cake.
They *used sugar to make a cake.*

1. Plenty of examples were given.

   They _____.

2. The escapees were seen in this area.

   They _____.

3. The actor was chosen for the part.

   They _____.

4. The mayor was welcomed.

   They _____.

5. The work was soon done.

   They _____.

6. All the facts were known.

   They _____.

7. The boy's kite was torn.

   They _____.

8. The mirror was accidentally broken.

   They _____.

9. The hamburgers were soon eaten.

   They _____.

10. All the bad memories were forgotten.

    They _____.

11. The letter was written too late.

    They _____.

12. My good advice was not taken.

    They _____.

13. The ice cream was frozen.

    They _____.

14. Many gifts were given.

    They ——————————————————————————— .

15. Only one fish was caught.

    They ——————————————————————————— .

EXERCISE 12

If the italicized verb in each of the following sentences expresses the past correctly, write C next to the sentence. If the past is not used, change the form of the verb to the past.

1. I *notice* many buses full of people.
2. I *watched* the news that night.
3. My neighbor's dog *digged* a big hole in my yard.
4. They *ask* us what was going on.
5. After an hour *pasted,* I went to look for him.

7b

Learn to use regular and irregular past participles with helping verbs.

Four of the verbs used with helping verbs (such as *has, have, had, is, was, will be,* and *has been*) are the past participles *loved, given, done,* and *run.* The past participle *loved* is regular. It looks just like the past and is constructed by adding -d to the present form (*love* + -d → *loved*). The others (*given, done,* and *run*) are not regular, and you must learn them separately. Here are some of the different ideas you can express by using past participles with helping verbs:

> I have loved (given, gone, run)
> he has loved (given, gone, run)
> I will have loved (given, gone, run)
> I would have loved (given, gone, run)
> I can have loved (given, gone, run)

I could have loved (given, gone, run)
it is loved (given, gone, run)
it was loved (given, gone, run)
they will be loved (given, gone, run)
they have been loved (given, gone, run)

Cautions: 1. Remember that the past participle does not mean that the verb expresses past time.

> Everyone *is loved* by someone.
> Romeo *will be loved* by Juliet by the end of Act I.

2. Remember that a verb may be separated from its helping verb by other words in the sentence. Do not let this situation make you forget to use the correct verb form.

WRONG	I have never love you.
RIGHT	I *have* never *loved* you.
WRONG	Was her favorite doll gave to her sister?
RIGHT	*Was* her favorite doll *given* to her sister?

7b(1)
Regular past participles (ending in -ed)

Regular past participles end in -ed. They are often used with helping verbs like *has, have, had, is, are, was, were,* and *has been.* Some regular past participles are *loved, danced, watched, waited,* and *listened.* Remember that you do not always hear the -d ending clearly in speech, but it always appears in writing.

WRONG	Our group was single out for criticism.
RIGHT	Our group *was singled* out for criticism.
WRONG	The air is then push out of the carburetor.
RIGHT	The air *is* then *pushed* out of the carburetor.

Be especially careful to add -d or -ed to *use, happen,* and *suppose* when these words are used with helping verbs.

WRONG	He is use to hard times.
RIGHT	He *is used* to hard times.

WRONG	We are suppose to be there.
RIGHT	We *are supposed* to be there.
WRONG	It has happen many times.
RIGHT	It *has happened* many times.

EXERCISE 13

In the following sentences, underline the correct form of the verb in parentheses.

1. Was your brother (suppose, supposed) to work at the Mt. Olive pickle factory?
2. At an R-rated movie a child should be (accompany, accompanied) by an adult.
3. Many people have (call, called) about the party I am giving next week.
4. Mr. Sellers is the carpenter who has just (install, installed) my garage door.
5. Have you ever, even by accident, (finish, finished) your homework before midnight?

EXERCISE 14

Edit the following paragraph for errors in the use of *-ed* endings. Circle each error, and write your correction in the space above it.

My favorite hours have been pass working in my flower beds.

Each plant has always seem special to me. When I have problems of

one sort or another, my flowers become imaginary friends, and I have

often talk to my flowers, confiding in them all the secrets of my life.

In the past, when I have been upset, my flowers have always seemed

understanding and have always nodded to show their agreement with

all my decisions. My flowers are much cheaper than a psychiatrist.

7b(2)

Irregular past participles (listed on p. 106)

PAST PARTICIPLES HAVING THE SOUND *un*

begun	sung
drunk	sunk
run	shrunk
rung	sprung

These past participles are used with helping verbs such as *has, have, had, is,* and *was.* When you pronounce them, you hear that *un* (as in *under*) is their main sound. Do not confuse these words with the past verbs, which are not used with helping verbs.

> WRONG   I have just began.
> RIGHT   I *have* just *begun.*
>
> WRONG   They are ran by electricity.
> RIGHT   They *are run* by electricity.
>
> WRONG   He didn't know you had drank all his beer.
> RIGHT   He didn't know you *had drunk* all his beer.

You should not hear an *un* sound when you use *bring* with a helping verb. *Brought* is the form of *bring* used with helping verbs; there is no word *brung.*

> WRONG   She has brung her lunch.
> RIGHT   She *has brought* her lunch.

EXERCISE 15

Write at least ten sentences using the past participles *run, begun, sung, sprung,* and *shrunk* with the helping verbs *is, was, has,* and *had.*

EXERCISE 16

In the following sentences, underline the correct form of the verb in parentheses.

1. Heats are (ran, run) until there is only one racer left.
2. Your troubles with that child have just (begun, began).
3. I couldn't believe that my mother had (shrank, shrunk) my sweatshirt again.
4. I hope that the McDonalds have (brought, brung) salt.
5. That surprise was (sprung, sprang) on Tim last week.

PAST PARTICIPLES ENDING IN -n OR -en

Many past participles used with the helping verbs *have, had, is, are, was,* and *were* end in -n or -en. Some common examples are

arisen	forgiven	spoken
beaten	forgotten	stolen
broken	frozen	sworn
chosen	given	taken
driven	hidden	torn
eaten	seen	worn
fallen	shaken	written

Do not confuse these past participles with the past forms, which are not used with helping verbs.

WRONG   He had swore to be true.
RIGHT   He *had sworn* to be true.
WRONG   He was beat by ²⁄₁₀ of a second.
RIGHT   He *was beaten* by ²⁄₁₀ of a second.

EXERCISE 17

Respond to the following commands by writing a sentence using *have* and the past participle of the underlined verb in each command.
■ **Example**   Please beat the eggs.

I have already beaten the eggs.

1. Write me a letter.

   I have _____ .
2. Eat all of your lunch.

   I have _____ .

3. Take as much time as you need.

I have _____ .

4. <u>Forget</u> what you just saw.

I have _____ .

5. <u>Give</u> me your promise.

I have _____ .

6. <u>Speak</u> to Mr. Johnson about your sister's problem.

I have _____ .

7. <u>See</u> your teacher today.

I have _____ .

8. <u>Tear</u> the coupon out of the newspaper.

I have _____ .

EXERCISE 18

Change the italicized verb in each of the following sentences so that it will go with its helping verb. If any sentence is correct, write C next to the sentence.

1. Amy likes to be *seed* in the best places.

2. The police officer has *swore* out a warrant for his arrest.

3. That merchandise is sure to be *stolen*.

4. A student from my high school was *chose* to represent Dayton in the debating finals.

5. I think Ali was definitely *beat* in a fair fight.

6. All first offenders were *given* a warning.

7. Come home; all is *forgave*.

8. Larry has often *spoke* to me about her.

9. It would have *took* even longer if I hadn't called home.

10. My father has to be *driven* to work every morning because our car is still in the shop.

PAST PARTICIPLES ENDING IN -wn

blown	grown
drawn	known
flown	shown

These past participles, all of which end in -wn, are used with the helping verbs *has, have, had, is, are.* Do not make the mistake of thinking these are regular past participles that end in -d or -ed.

WRONG	The wind has blowed us about.
RIGHT	The wind *has blown* us about.
WRONG	You have drawed an accurate picture.
RIGHT	You *have drawn* an accurate picture.
WRONG	She is really growed up.
RIGHT	She *is* really *grown* up.
WRONG	We have knowed this for over a year.
RIGHT	We *have known* this for over a year.

EXERCISE 19

Using each of the six participles ending in -wn that you have just learned, write a sentence beginning "My sister has" and a question beginning "Have you."

■ **Examples**   My sister has *flown to Chicago.*
Have you ever *flown to Honolulu?*

Gone, done, come, *and* become

Four of the verbs you use often are *go, do, come,* and *become.* When they are used with helping verbs,

go changes to (have) *gone*
do changes to (have) *done*
come and *become* do not change: (have) *come*
(have) *become*

It is important not to confuse *gone, done, come,* and *become* with the past forms, which are not used with a helping verb.

WRONG	Many of my friends had went into the Army.
RIGHT	Many of my friends *had gone* into the Army.
WRONG	I have did everything I know how to do.
RIGHT	I *have done* everything I know how to do.
WRONG	This had all came to pass.
RIGHT	This *had* all *come* to pass.
WRONG	In just one more year we will have became rich.
RIGHT	In just one more year we *will have become* rich.

EXERCISE 20

Write a sentence using the past participle of *go, do, come,* and *become* with the helping verbs *will have* and another sentence with the helping verbs *could have*.

■ **Examples**   In one year I *will have become* a millionaire.
He *could have become* another Humphrey Bogart.

Burst, caught, dug, found, *and* passed

Burst, caught, dug, found, and *passed* are some irregular past participles used with helping verbs like *has, have, was, were.* If you do not know them well, you will have to study them. They are often used incorrectly.

WRONG	It has bursted.
RIGHT	It *has burst.*
WRONG	He has been catched.
RIGHT	He *has been caught.*
WRONG	We have digged.
RIGHT	We *have dug.*
WRONG	He was founded.
RIGHT	He *was found.*
WRONG	The day has past (OR pasted).
RIGHT	The day *has passed.*

EXERCISE 21

Using the beginning "It will be" or "We have been," write a sentence using each of the following verbs: *caught, dug, found, passed.*

Review **7b** carefully. Then do Exercises 22, 23, and 24.

EXERCISE 22

In the following sentences, add *-d* or *-ed* to the italicized verb only when needed. Correct any incorrect italicized forms. If any sentence is correct, write C next to it.

1. Joe Riddick has *retire* from the shipyard.
2. I have *learned* many things in my new job.
3. That would not have *happen* if you had been on time.
4. All of the fishing tackle can be *founded* on the table.
5. None of us was really *suppose* to be there.
6. After an hour had *past*, I went to look for Jack.
7. Clay refused the order and was *fined*.
8. We were *showed* the microfilm section.
9. Only fresh whole eggs are *used* in making an orange dream cake.
10. We have all *knowed* girls like Ava.

EXERCISE 23

In the following sentences, underline the correct form of the verb in parentheses.

1. Bob should have (gave, given) the car more gas.
2. Many problems have (came, come) to the surface.
3. I know I could have (become, became) a long-distance runner.
4. Buck's job was to look for mines that had not (gone, went) off.
5. I sometimes think the government is (ran, run) by idiots!

6. Have they (did, done) everything possible to find my records?

7. My sister has (worn, wore) every dress I own.

8. In spite of all my letters of inquiry, that company has never (wrote, written) me.

9. Fried chicken is often (ate, eaten) with the fingers.

10. That ship was (sank, sunk) in the Atlantic about twenty-five years ago.

EXERCISE 24

In the following paragraph, blanks appear where verbs have been omitted. Supply your own verbs to complete the paragraph.

My car has (1) _____ a unique appearance. When my car was just (2) _____, it must have (3) _____ one of the finest cars on the road. Now, twelve years later, it has (4) _____ an eyesore. It has (5) _____ rust spots from one end to the other. The vinyl roof is badly (6) _____, and many dents can be (7) _____ on the fenders. The paint job looks as though the painter had (8) _____ drinking. When it rains, you can take a shower while you ride down the road. The only good thing that can be (9) _____ about my car is that it is reliable. In fact, I have (10) _____ myself that, ugly or not, my car will have a home with me for many years to come.

IRREGULAR VERBS

Present	Simple Past	Past Participle	Present Participle
arise	arose	arisen	arising
beat	beat	beaten	beating
become	became	become	becoming
begin	began	begun	beginning
blow	blew	blown	blowing
break	broke	broken	breaking
bring	brought	brought	bringing
build	built	built	building
burst	burst	burst	bursting
buy	bought	bought	buying
can	could	been able	being able

IRREGULAR VERBS (*continued*)

Present	Simple Past	Past Participle	Present Participle
catch	caught	caught	catching
choose	chose	chosen	choosing
come	came	come	coming
cut	cut	cut	cutting
deal	dealt	dealt	dealing
dig	dug	dug	digging
dive	dove (dived)	dived	diving
do	did	done	doing
drag	dragged	dragged	dragging
draw	drew	drawn	drawing
drink	drank	drunk	drinking
drive	drove	driven	driving
eat	ate	eaten	eating
fall	fell	fallen	falling
feed	fed	fed	feeding
feel	felt	felt	feeling
fight	fought	fought	fighting
find	found	found	finding
fly	flew	flown	flying
forget	forgot	forgotten	forgetting
forgive	forgave	forgiven	forgiving
freeze	froze	frozen	freezing
get	got	got	getting
give	gave	given	giving
go	went	gone	going
grow	grew	grown	growing
have	had	had	having
hear	heard	heard	hearing
hide	hid	hidden	hiding
hit	hit	hit	hitting
hold	held	held	holding
hurt	hurt	hurt	hurting
keep	kept	kept	keeping
know	knew	known	knowing
lay	laid	laid	laying
lead	led	led	leading
leave	left	left	leaving
let	let	let	letting
lie	lay	lain	lying
lose	lost	lost	losing
make	made	made	making

IRREGULAR VERBS (continued)

Present	Simple Past	Past Participle	Present Participle
meet	met	met	meeting
pay	paid	paid	paying
put	put	put	putting
quit	quit	quit	quitting
read	read	read	reading
ride	rode	ridden	riding
ring	rang	rung	ringing
rise	rose	risen	rising
run	ran	run	running
say	said	said	saying
see	saw	seen	seeing
seek	sought	sought	seeking
sell	sold	sold	selling
send	sent	sent	sending
set	set	set	setting
shake	shook	shaken	shaking
shine	shone	shone	shining
show	showed	shown	showing
shut	shut	shut	shutting
sing	sang	sung	singing
shrink	shrank	shrunk	shrinking
sink	sank	sunk	sinking
sit	sat	sat	sitting
sleep	slept	slept	sleeping
speak	spoke	spoken	speaking
spend	spent	spent	spending
spring	sprang	sprung	springing
stand	stood	stood	standing
steal	stole	stolen	stealing
swim	swam	swum	swimming
take	took	taken	taking
teach	taught	taught	teaching
tear	tore	torn	tearing
tell	told	told	telling
think	thought	thought	thinking
throw	threw	thrown	throwing
understand	understood	understood	understanding
wake	woke (waked)	woken (waked)	waking
wear	wore	worn	wearing
win	won	won	winning
write	wrote	written	writing

7c
Use the present participle (*-ing*) ending that tells the reader that something is continuing.

In addition to saying that something is happening now,

> He *bothers* me.
> He *is bothered* by a fly.

or that something happened in the past,

> He *bothered* me.
> He *has bothered* me.
> He *was bothered* by a fly.

or that something will happen,

> That fly *will bother* him.
> He *will* not *want* to be bothered.

verbs also distinguish between something that happens all at once and something that happens over time. Verbs that end in *-ing* (*bothering, saying, doing, wanting, loving*) tell the reader that something is, was, or will be going on or continuing. They appear with helping verbs like *am, is, are, was, were,* and *will be*. These verb combinations are called *progressive forms* and are listed and described in **7g**.

ALL AT ONCE	I worked at the Credit Union. [I worked there at one time.]
CONTINUING	I *am working* at the Credit Union. [I am still working there.]
CONTINUING	I *was working* when you saw me. [I was working over a period of time.]
ALL AT ONCE	I will work late tonight. [I will work at one particular time.]
CONTINUING	I *will be working* tomorrow. [I will be working for awhile.]

Cautions: 1. Remember that the present participle does not necessarily mean present action.

When you came in, I *was saying* something to her.

2. Not all words ending in *-ing* are verbs. They may come from verbs, but unless they are used with helpers, present participles are not verbs. (See **7h(1).**)

PRESENT PARTICIPLE USED AS A VERB	PRESENT PARTICIPLE NOT USED AS A VERB
Betsy was *calling my name.*	*Calling my name,* Betsy chased me down the street.

Even though present participles like *calling* are not always used as verbs, they express continuing action as verbs do. Do not forget to add *-ing* to a word that expresses continuing action even though it does not appear with a helping verb.

WRONG	Carl had a sign on his door say "Do not enter."
RIGHT	Carl had a sign on his door *saying* "Do not enter."
WRONG	He made a sharp U-turn, bring the ambulance to a complete stop.
RIGHT	He made a sharp U-turn, *bringing* the ambulance to a complete stop.

For more information about these *-ing* words that look like verbs, see **7h(1)**.

EXERCISE 25

Copy the first sentence of each of the following pairs of sentences. Then complete the second sentence, beginning the part you write with an *-ing* word.

■ Example   Sam wrote a good composition, *following the suggestions of his teacher.*

Ida wrote a funny letter, *telling her sister all the news.*

1. I find out many things by *listening to my sister talk.*

   I learn a lot by _____.

2. The students are still *playing cards in the lounge.*

   My father is always _____.

3. I worked the dough on the counter, always *rolling it from the center toward the sides.*

   Sue finished the chores assigned, always _____.

4. My solution is *adding another room and calling this room the lounge.*

   My suggestion is _____.

5. My buddies and I were late as usual, *giving excuses you wouldn't believe.*

   My daughter forgot my birthday as usual, _____.

7d

Learn to use the verb *be* correctly.

Be is the most useful verb in English. A form of *be* can appear either by itself or with other verbs.

These are the basic forms of *be*:

INFINITIVE	PRESENT	PAST	PAST PARTICIPLE	PRESENT PARTICIPLE
be	am, is, are	was, were	been	being

The present tense of *be* tells what is happening.

I *am*
You *are*
He *is*
She *is* ⎬ very silly.
It *is*
We *are*
They *are*

The past tense of *be* tells what happened.

$$
\left.\begin{array}{l}
\text{I } \textit{was} \\
\text{You } \textit{were} \\
\text{He } \textit{was} \\
\text{She } \textit{was} \\
\text{It } \textit{was} \\
\text{We } \textit{were} \\
\text{They } \textit{were}
\end{array}\right\} \text{very silly.}
$$

A form of *be* can be used as a helping verb to help the verb say something about the subject.

It can express present time.

The library *is* located in this building.

It can express past time.

My father *was* waiting for hours.

Sometimes a form of *be* appears with other helping verbs to tell what the subject is doing.

I *have been* studying for an hour.
Edith *is* being teased.
You *will be* waiting.

7d(1)
Is and *are* are used more than any other forms of the verb *be*.

Be sure to use the verbs *is* and *are* or their contractions ('s) and ('re) to complete the meaning of a sentence.

> **WRONG** My roommate snores sometimes, but otherwise he great.
> **RIGHT** My roommate snores sometimes, but otherwise he *is* great.

WRONG	It not often that teenagers are on time.
RIGHT	It *is* not often that teenagers are on time.
WRONG	What happening?
RIGHT	What*'s* happening?
WRONG	They gone!
RIGHT	They*'re* gone!

Do not use *be* in place of *is* or *are* to complete the meaning of a sentence.

WRONG	He be waiting here.
RIGHT	He *is* waiting here.
WRONG	These children be very happy.
RIGHT	These children *are* very happy.

7d(2)
Being and *been* are used with helping verbs.

He *is being* hassled.
We *have been* worried.

Be sure to remember that a helping verb is needed to complete the meaning of such sentences.

WRONG	He being stubborn.
RIGHT	He *is* being stubborn.
WRONG	We been here a long time.
RIGHT	We *have* been here a long time.

7d(3)
Forms of *be* such as *is, are, was, were,* and *will be* + a past participle express an idea called *the passive.*

The passive suggests that something is happening to someone or something. Use the passive for a particular reason. Usually you want to tell what a person or thing is doing, and you use the active form of the verb (in this case, *set*).

> We *set* the table.

Sometimes, however, you want to emphasize the action being done, or you may not know who is performing the action. You then may use a passive verb form.

> The table *was set*.

It is not a good idea to use the passive except when you do not know who is performing the action or when you want to emphasize the action itself. If you overuse the passive, you will probably produce wordy or awkward sentences.

> PASSIVE   A mistake *has been made* by Harry. (wordy)
> ACTIVE   Harry *has made* a mistake. (better)

Caution: Do not shift from the active to the passive within a sentence. Such a shift merely confuses the reader.

> *Confusing:*   The building inspector *examined* the work carefully, but no violations *were found.*
> *Better:*   The building inspector *examined* the work carefully, but he *found* no violations.

EXERCISE 26

In each of the following sentences, the passive form of the verb is underlined. Rewrite each sentence, making the emphasis active instead of passive.

■ Examples   A good time <u>was had</u> by everyone.
            Everyone had a good time.

1. The Christmas presents <u>are opened</u> by the children.
2. The books <u>were checked out</u> by the students.
3. Current issues of magazines <u>were displayed</u> by the librarian.

4. A thorough knowledge of the subject <u>is required</u> by that teacher.

5. Joe <u>is liked</u> by many people.

7d(4)
Were can signal the subjunctive.

Were is usually the past form of the verb *be* that is used with a plural subject (they *were*). Sometimes, however, you will want to use it to express a wish or suggest a situation that might be true (but is not). This way of using *were* is called the *subjunctive*.

> I wish I *were* president. (I am not.)
> He acts as though he *were* president. (He is not.)

When *were* is used as a subjunctive, it does *not* agree with *he, she,* or *it* subjects (I wish he *were*). A subjunctive expression uses *were* no matter what the subject is.

EXERCISE 27

Insert *is* or *are* when needed to complete the meaning of the sentence. Write C next to any sentence that is correct.

1. If it not her head that hurts, it is her back.
2. This is a description of my brother.
3. Marty very slim and handsome.
4. The noise of the pool hall is still ringing in my ears.
5. They supposed to be here by 5:30.

EXERCISE 28

Write two sentences using *being* and two sentences using *been* with helping verbs.

EXERCISE 29

In the following sentences, underline the correct verb forms in parentheses.

1. They (being, are being) foolish about those children.
2. The child cried often, but otherwise he (been, has been) great.
3. If those girls (be, are) any later, they won't find any barbecue left.
4. I know Judy (been, has been) waiting a long time.
5. The whole time it (is, be) so noisy, you can't hear yourself talk.
6. If it (wasn't, weren't) for you, I would be in California now.
7. If there (was, were) no such thing as love, where would we be now?
8. You are being (call, called) to the telephone.
9. I wish I (was, were) a millionaire.
10. I knew that his decision (was, were) the right one.

7e
Change the form of a verb only when necessary.

You may find that you are occasionally confused about how to spell a verb form. You cannot always depend on what you hear because the verb ending does not always have a distinct sound. You remember that a verb has a special ending when used with a helping verb like *has, have, had, is, are, was,* and *were:*

NO HELPING VERB	They *dance.*
HELPING VERB	They *have danced.* (past participle ending)
NO HELPING VERB	We *sing.*
HELPING VERB	We *are singing.* (present participle ending)

But *has, have, is, was,* and other forms of *have* and *be* are not the only helping verbs. Verbs like *do, did, can, could, will,* and *would* are also helping verbs, but they are used with present forms, not with participles. These present forms have no endings.

7e(1)

Learn how to spell the verb forms that are used directly after the helping verbs *will, would, do, did, can, could, should, may,* and *might* and their negative forms (*won't, wouldn't,* and so on).

These helping verbs (unlike *has, have, is, are,* and so on) do not change the spelling of the verbs they help. They are used with the present form—the form with no ending.

WRONG	You did needed to study.
RIGHT	You *did need* to study.
WRONG	They would reacted badly.
RIGHT	They *would react* badly.
WRONG	He will tries to jump over the fence.
RIGHT	He *will try* to jump over the fence.
WRONG	A roofer can used both sides at once.
RIGHT	A roofer *can use* both sides at once.
WRONG	Alice won't wanted to be too early.
RIGHT	Alice *won't want* to be too early.

7e(2)

When there are two helpers (*will be, could have, can be,* and so on), the one directly before the verb controls the spelling of the verb.

will be visited [*Be* controls the spelling of *visited.*]
could have gone [*Have* controls the spelling of *gone.*]

The helping verbs *be* and *have* change the spelling of the verbs that follow them.

WRONG	In time, I would have react better.
RIGHT	In time, I *would have reacted* better. [*Have* comes before the verb, so you must add *-ed* to *react.*]

WRONG	Meanwhile, I can be use the book.
RIGHT	Meanwhile, I *can be using* the book. [*Be* comes before the verb, so you must add *-ing* to *use*.]

7e(3)

Use *have* (not *had*) after other helping verbs, such as *will, would, should, could, can, may,* and *might.*

WRONG	They might had encountered some problems while looking for a job.
RIGHT	They might *have* encountered some problems while looking for a job.
WRONG	I should had given up my old habits.
RIGHT	I should *have* given up my old habits.

EXERCISE 30

Correct any errors in the italicized verbs in the following sentences. Do not change any verb forms that are already correct.

1. When she did *arrived*, everyone was ready to go.
2. If children are forced to do what does not *interests* them, they will put forth little effort.
3. If I had known Lisa was going to be at the dance, I might *had* gone somewhere else.
4. I can still *heard* Daddy going up the creaking steps.
5. The car won't *rolled* down the hill.
6. Jimmy does *wants* some rock candy.
7. My mother-in-law did *come* early, as usual.
8. I could only *see* and *believed* in him.
9. Julie figured they needed help, but she didn't *figured* they would *refuse* it.
10. If you get overtired, you can *began* to lose your patience with others.

7f

Use the correct forms of *lay* and *lie* and *set* and *sit.*

The verbs *lay* and *lie* and *set* and *sit* have been bothering students for a long time. Here are the guidelines you need to remember to use these verbs correctly.

7f(1)

Be sure to use the correct forms of *lay* and *lie.*

Lay means "place" or "put something down."

WHEN WRITING ABOUT	USE	EXAMPLES
the present:	lay	They *lay* canvas over it each night.
with a helping verb:	laying	She *is laying* it on the counter.
the past:	laid	He *laid* the book on the table.
with a helping verb:	laying	They *were laying* the bricks too far apart.
	laid	We *have laid* boards over the muddy spots.

Lie means "rest" or "be in a horizontal position."

WHEN WRITING ABOUT	USE	EXAMPLES
the present:	lie	They *lie* on the grass every afternoon.
with a helping verb:	lying	The pen *is lying* on the desk.
the past:	lay	He *lay* there for an hour.
with a helping verb:	lying	The muddy dog *was lying* on our new chair.
	lain	It *has lain* there for an hour.

Present

Lay (or *laying*) in the present means "place" or "put." It needs an object (the person or thing receiving the action). When you lay something or someone down, you are doing something to that person or thing. In the following sentences, *lay, laying,* and *lays* take objects.

> We *lay* the packages down on the table. (packages = the object)
> They *are laying* aside their prejudices. (prejudices = the object)
> She *lays* the sleeping baby on his bed. (baby = the object)

Lie (or *lying*) in the present means "stretch out and rest." When you lie down, you are not doing anything to another person or thing.

The verbs *lie, lying,* and *lies* have no object in the following sentences; in other words, there is nothing receiving the action.

> We often *lie* on the beach for hours.
> The alligators *are lying* in the sun.
> She *lies* in bed too long every morning.

Past

Laid (or *laying*) in the past means "placed" or "put." When you laid something or someone down, you did something to that thing or person (the object).

> We *laid* our brushes down. (brushes = the object)
> They *laid* their sleeping children on the mattress. (children = the object)
> The workers *were laying* brick. (brick = the object)

Lay (or *lying*) in the past means "stretched out." When you lay down last night, you were not doing anything to anyone else; you were just resting.

The verbs *lay* and *lying* have no object in the following sentences:

> Yesterday we *lay* on our backs in the calm water.
> A jellyfish *was lying* near the shore.

Laid *and* lain *with helping verbs*

Laid with a helping verb means "put down." It takes an object.

> I *have laid* my work aside. (work = the object)

Lain with a helping verb means "stretched out." It does not take an object.

> The dog *has lain* under the rosebush for a long time. [This form is not often used. Most writers prefer to write: "The dog *has been lying* under the rosebush."]

EXERCISE 31

In the following sentences, underline the correct form of *lay* and *lie* in parentheses.

1. A bank employee who was (laying, lying) in the corner got a look at both the robbers.
2. He ordered me to (lay, lie) face down on the floor.
3. Engine parts are (laying, lying) in huge piles in the garage.
4. Henry was (laying, lying) the groundwork for the talk.
5. Our Christmas packages were so heavy, we (laid, lay) them down as soon as we entered the house.

7f(2)

Be sure to use the correct forms of *set* and *sit*.

Set means "arrange" or "put in place."

WHEN WRITING ABOUT	USE	EXAMPLES
the present:	set	Please *set* the flowers here.
with a helping verb:	setting	The committee *is setting* guidelines.

the past:	set	He *set* the time for the meeting.
with a helping verb:	setting	They *were setting* the chairs in a row.
	set	She *has set* the books down.

Sit means "rest in a sitting position" or "occupy a place."

WHEN WRITING ABOUT	USE	EXAMPLES
the present:	sit	They *sit* here every day for lunch.
with a helping verb:	sitting	He *is sitting* in the car.
the past:	sat	The cat *sat* in the warm sunshine.
with a helping verb:	sitting	The boys *were sitting* on the fence.
	sat	They *have sat* there each evening.

Present

Set (or *setting*) in the present means "arrange in place." It needs an object (the thing receiving the action). When you set something down, you are doing something to that thing.

> We *set* down certain rules each year. (rules = the object)
> The girls *are setting* their hair. (hair = the object)
> She *sets* the timer for the roast. (timer = the object)
> *Set* your priorities. (priorities = the object)

Sit (or *sitting*) in the present means "rest in a sitting position" or "occupy a place." When you sit, you do not do something to anything.

> Are you going to *sit* around and do nothing?
> She *is* always *sitting* in the same spot.

Past

Set (or *setting*) in the past means "arranged" or "put into place." When you set something down, you were doing something to that thing or object.

> Last week we *set* up a summer schedule. (schedule = the object)
> My mother and sister *were setting* out tomato plants. (plants = the object)

Sat (or *sitting*) in the past means "rested" or "occupied a seat."

> My grandmother often *sat* for hours, rocking back and forth.
> My boyfriend and I *were sitting* on the sofa when my father entered the room.

Set *and* sat *with helping verbs*

Set with a helping verb means "arranged."

> I *have set* the alarm for 6:00 A.M.
> The time *is set* for the match.

Sat with a helping verb means "occupied a seat."

> How long *have* you *sat* in that position?

EXERCISE 32

In the following sentences, underline the correct form of *set* and *sit* in parentheses.

1. While I was (setting, sitting) on the porch, I was trying to figure out what happened.
2. There is a house (sitting, setting) on that land across the river.
3. You should have (set, sat) down and drawn the object you wanted to build.
4. Paul often comes over and (sits, sets) awhile with me.
5. (Set, Sit) that package down over there on the table.

7g
Use verbs to help you tell time.

Whenever you use a verb, you are telling time. This is true because verbs give you an idea of when something is happening. They can tell you that something is happening now.

I *surrender*.
He *surrenders*.
We *are surrendering*.
They *do surrender*.
It *is being surrendered*.

They can tell you that something happened in the past.

I *surrendered*.
We *did surrender*.
We *have surrendered*.
It *was surrendered*.
They *had* all *surrendered*. [before the fighting stopped]
It *had been surrendered*. [before we realized it]

They can tell you that something will happen in the future.

I *will surrender*.
He *is going to surrender*.
We *are surrendering*. [tomorrow]
They *will* all *have surrendered*.

There is another way that verbs tell time. They tell you whether something happened all at once or continues to happen.

ALL AT ONCE	I *hid* from the pirates.
ALL AT ONCE	He *has hidden* all his money.
CONTINUING	We *are hiding* from the pirates.
CONTINUING	We *would hide* whenever the pirates approached.

To tell time accurately, English uses six tenses. (The word *tense* refers to the time expressed by the verb.) The tenses are formed from the four principal parts of the verbs. Below is a chart showing the six tenses for a regular and an irregular verb. For each of these four tenses, there is an *-ing* (progressive) form listed. This form, like the others, not only tells the reader whether the time is present, past, or future, but it also suggests that the action is continuing rather than completed all at once.

REGULAR VERB (*finish*)		IRREGULAR VERB (*begin*)	
Singular	*Plural*	*Singular*	*Plural*

Present tense (one-word verb)

I finish	we finish	I begin	we begin
you finish	you finish	you begin	you begin
he, she, it finishes	they finish	he, she it begins	they begin

Present progressive (*am, is,* or *are* + present participle)

I am finishing	we are finishing	I am beginning	we are beginning
you are finishing	you are finishing	you are beginning	you are beginning
he, she, it is finishing	they are finishing	he, she, it is beginning	they are beginning

Past tense (one-word verb)

I finished	we finished	I began	we began
you finished	you finished	you began	you began
he, she, it finished	they finished	he, she, it began	they began

Past progressive (*was* or *were* + present participle)

I was finishing	we were finishing	I was beginning	we were beginning
you were finishing	you were finishing	you are beginning	you are beginning
he, she, it was finishing	they were finishing	he, she, it was beginning	they are beginning

Future tense (*will* + present)

I will finish	we will finish	I will begin	we will begin
you will finish	you will finish	you will begin	you will begin
he, she, it will finish	they will finish	he, she, it will begin	thcy will bcgin

Future progressive (*will* + *he* + present participle)

I will be finishing	we will be finishing	I will be beginning	we will be beginning
you will be finishing	you will be finishing	you will be beginning	you will be beginning
he, she, it will be finishing	they will be finishing	he, she, it will be beginning	they will be beginning

Present perfect tense (*has* or *have* + past participle)

I have finished	we have finished	I have begun	we have begun
you have finished	you have finished	you have begun	you have begun
he, she, it has finished	they have finished	he, she, it has begun	they have begun

REGULAR VERB (*finish*)		IRREGULAR VERB (*begin*)	
Singular	*Plural*	*Singular*	*Plural*

Present perfect progressive (*has* or *have* + *been* + present participle)

I have been finishing	we have been finishing	I have been beginning	we have been beginning
you have been finishing	you have been finishing	you have been beginning	you have been beginning
he, she, it has been finishing	they have been finishing	he, she, it has been beginning	they have been beginning

Past perfect tense (*had* + past participle)

I had finished	we had finished	I had begun	we had begun
you had finished	you had finished	you had begun	you had begun
he, she, it had finished	they had finished	he, she, it had begun	they had begun

Past perfect progressive (*had* + *been* + present participle)

I had been finishing	we had been finishing	I had been beginning	we had been beginning
you had been finishing	you had been finishing	you had been beginning	you had been beginning
he, she, it had been finishing	they had been finishing	he, she, it had been beginning	they had been beginning

Future perfect tense (*will* + *have* + past participle)

I will have finished	we will have finished	I will have begun	we will have begun
you will have finished	you will have finished	you will have begun	you will have begun
he, she, it will have finished	they will have finished	he, she, it will have begun	they will have begun

Future perfect progressive (*will* + *have* + *been* + present participle)

I will have been finishing	we will have been finishing	I will have been beginning	we will have been beginning
you will have been finishing	you will have been finishing	you will have been beginning	you will have been beginning
he, she, it will have been finishing	they will have been finishing	he, she, it will have been beginning	he, she, it will have been beginning

These are the most common uses of the six tenses:

Present

1. The present tense tells the reader that something is happening now.

   He *begins* his work cheerfully.
   He *is finishing* his work now.

2. It tells that something happens on a regular basis.

   He usually *begins* his work early.
   He always *finishes* on time.

3. It emphasizes the present action by using *does* or *do*.

   He *does finish* on time.

Past

1. The past tense tells that something happened; it does not suggest that the action is still going on.

   I *finished* at 7:30.
   I *was finishing* that book when you *arrived*.

2. The past form *did* emphasizes something the subject did.

   I *did finish* the book.

3. The past form *used to* tells that the subject did something on a regular basis.

   I *used to finish* on time.

Future

The future tense tells that something will happen.

   She *will finish* at 7:30.
        OR
   She *will be finishing* at 7:30.
        OR
   She *is going to finish* at 7:30.

Present perfect

The present perfect tense tells about something that happened in the past and is or may be still continuing.

You *have begun* to improve. [You may still be improving.]
You *have been finishing* your chores for hours now. [You still are.]

Past perfect

The past perfect tense tells about a past action that took place before another action that happened in the past.

We *had finished* the inventory before the manager arrived.
We *had been finishing* our chores when our mother made an untimely appearance.

Future perfect

The future perfect tense describes something that will happen in the future before something else that will happen.

By the time you get here, I *will have finished* the project.
When 4:00 arrives, I *will have begun* my homework.

7g(1)
Be accurate in telling your reader when something happened. Do not shift tenses.

As you know, a sentence can be very simple:

My raccoon bit me.

or it can be involved:

When he became frightened, my raccoon bit me.

In the first sentence time or tense is no problem. (My raccoon bit me at some time in the past.) In the second sentence there are two verbs (*became* and *bit*). When you write a sentence with more than one verb, it is important to be accurate in telling time—that is, in telling the reader whether something has happened, is happening now, will happen in the future, or happened before something else that has already happened. Otherwise you will confuse the reader.

It is confusing to write:

> When he becomes frightened, my raccoon bit me. [Does he bite you whenever he becomes frightened, or did he bite you that one time?]

It is better to write:

> When he *becomes* frightened, my raccoon *bites* me.
>
>   OR
>
> When he *became* frightened, my raccoon *bit* me.

Here are some other examples that show how important it is to tell time correctly.

CONFUSING	I notice there were some buses full of people. [Do you notice now that there are buses full of people?
	OR
	Did you notice yesterday that there were buses full of people?]
CLEAR	I *noticed* that there *were* some buses full of people.
	OR
	I *notice* that there *are* some buses full of people.
CONFUSING	I knew I would not be able to get the job I want. [Did you know you would not be able to get the job you wanted?
	OR
	Do you know now that you will not be able to get the job you want?]
CLEAR	I *knew* I *would* not *be able* to get the job I *wanted*.

When you are telling a story, do not get so caught up in the experience of telling it that you think something is really happening while you tell it.

WRONG	I saw him cross the street. I knew he wanted to talk to me, so I stop right in front of him.
RIGHT	I *saw* him cross the street. I *knew* he *wanted* to talk to me, so I *stopped* right in front of him.

EXERCISE 33

Clear up your reader's confusion. Change one of the verbs in each of the following sentences to make clear whether you are talking about past, present, or future time.

1. Blow into the victim's mouth or nose until you see his chest began to rise.

2. Howard doesn't like to take orders because he wants to live as a free man, able to do what he wanted.

3. I saw a red light flashing behind me, so I pull my car to the side of the road.

4. Shoplifting can be prevented if everyone recognized the problem as a major one.

5. When Carl was away from home for a week, he starts to get homesick.

6. If Nancy told him to stop seeing a girl he likes very much, he will do it.

7. The reason I enjoy the job so much was that I could make fifty dollars a day.

7g(2)
Use *would* or *would have* to suggest that it is possible for something to happen.

a. Use the simple past in the dependent (*if*) clause and *would* in the main clause when you want to say that if something happened, something else would happen.

   If I saw him, I *would* tell him the truth.

   Notice that the above example has two parts:

   1. *If* something happened (dependent clause),
   2. something else *would* happen. (main clause)

Be sure not to use *would* in the dependent clause after *if*; use the past instead.

> **WRONG** If they would be able, they would visit him. [You want to say that if they *really were* able, they would visit him.]
>
> **RIGHT** If they *were* able, they would visit him.

b. Use the past perfect (*had* + past participle) in the dependent clause and *would have* in the main clause when you want to say that if something had happened, something else would have happened.

> **WRONG** If they would have known that he was sick, they would have visited him. [You want to say that if they *had really known* that he was sick, they would have visited him.]
>
> **RIGHT** If they *had* known that he was sick, they would have visited him.

Sometimes the main clause comes before the dependent (if) clause.

> They *would* visit him *if* they were able.
> They *would* have visited him *if* they had known that he was sick.

EXERCISE 34

Copy the first sentence of each of the following pairs of sentences. Then complete the second sentence with words of your own, using *if* and the part of the sentence you are given.

■ **Examples** If *we touched the dog's bowl while he was eating,* he would really snap at us.

If *she learned the truth*, she would be furious.

We would have told you the answer if *we had known it.*

We would have called you last week if *there had been time*.

1. If Ed *played the game at all,* he would try to do his best.

If Ed _____ , he would always follow through on his promise.

2. If you *had worn your safety belt*, you would not have been thrown against the windshield.

   If you _____ , you would not have gotten into trouble.

3. If I *had a free throw right now*, I would probably make it.

   If I _____ , I would find one somewhere.

4. I would have done better on my finals if *I had just relaxed*.

   I would have made a million dollars if _____ .

5. If I *had called my brother*, he wouldn't have heard me.

   If I _____ , they wouldn't have listened.

7g(3)
Use *would have* + an infinitive to suggest something you wanted to do or thought about doing.

> I *would have* liked to see her. [but I didn't see her]

Be sure to express this idea clearly. Do not make the mistake of writing:

> **WRONG**   I would have liked to have seen her.

That sentence suggests that you would have liked yesterday to have seen her a month earlier. What you mean is that you would have liked yesterday to see her yesterday.

> **RIGHT**   I would have liked *to see* her.

Here is another example.

> **WRONG**   I would have wanted to have gone.
> **RIGHT**   I *would have* wanted to *go*.

7g(4)
Distinguish between *will* and *would* in telling time.

In addition to suggesting possibility, *would* also shows that something was done often or regularly.

> After church we *would* visit my grandmother.
> On Saturday mornings, my father and I *would* pick up our fishing rods and head for the lake.

Do not use *would* instead of *will* to describe something that is going to happen in the future.

> **WRONG**   Next Sunday Joe would definitely be at her house.
> **RIGHT**   Next Sunday Joe *will* definitely be at her house.

7g(5)
Use the past perfect (*had* + past participle) to show that one past event happened before another past event.

> I knew that I *had been* wrong.
> She *had known* for years that a disaster was going to occur.

EXERCISE 35

In the following sentences, change the italicized verbs if they are incorrectly used. Write C next to any sentence in which the verb is used correctly.

1. If I *wouldn't have known* what to do, it would have been a tragic accident.
2. We knew you would have wanted *to have visited* Elaine then.
3. Whenever I *called* her, she always found an excuse.
4. If you *had studied* the map, you would have known what trails to take.
5. Use great caution in working underneath your car, so you *would* not let it fall on you.

6. If I had known you were going to be there, I would have wanted *to have gone* too.

7. Roger certainly would not have been able *to have known* my address.

8. I would have helped him if they *would have* let me.

EXERCISE 36

In the following sentences, underline the correct form of the verb in parentheses.

1. If there were no trust in marriage, just think of all the suspicions that (will, would) arise over the most insignificant things.

2. Laura's dream (ended, has ended), so she returned to her own world again.

3. If the original inhabitants of the house (returned, had returned), they would have found many changes.

4. He had the reputation of being unscrupulous because in the past he (forged, had forged) some documents.

5. If Mr. Judson had known of the existence of the children, their mother (would not inherit, would not have inherited) his fortune.

6. The criminals threatened that if they heard one word from a single individual, he (will, would) be sorry.

7. Some people become hostile or upset when they (miss, would miss) their favorite programs.

8. If everything is in proper working order, you (would, will) have found a good used car.

9. If you (had, would have) used a CB radio, you would have known that Williamsburg was a speed trap.

10. You should have called your mother. She would have wanted to (see, have seen) you.

7h

Recognize words that only look like verbs.

Some words masquerade as verbs. They come from verbs, and they look like verbs, but these words have other important uses.

7h(1)
Recognize *-ing* words that are not verbs.

Words like *buying, being, singing,* and *running* can be verbs when they appear with helping verbs. They say something about a subject.

> She *is buying* a new car.
> He *is being* stubborn.

Sometimes, however, they only masquerade as verbs. Besides appearing with helping verbs to say something about the subject, words ending in *-ing* have other uses.

A word ending in *-ing* can be a noun; it can name a person or thing.

> *Eating* is my uncle's favorite pastime. [*Eating* names a thing; it names my uncle's favorite pastime.]
> Unhappiness can cause *overeating*. [*Overeating* names a thing; that thing is caused by unhappiness.]

A word ending in *-ing* can also be an adjective.

> My brother Billy reminds me of a *laughing* hyena. [*Laughing* tells what kind of hyena my brother reminds me of.]
> *Being stubborn*, my father wouldn't listen to my explanations. [*Being stubborn* describes my father.]

There are some things to remember about *-ing* words when they are not used as verbs.

1. Do not write an *-ing* fragment.
   > **WRONG** Driving carefully.
   > **RIGHT** *Driving carefully*, I made my way home.

2. The *-ing* ending suggests that something is going on or continuing. (See **7c**.) Be sure to add this ending to a word expressing continuing action.
   > **WRONG** She often eats a snack while watch the news on TV.
   > **RIGHT** She often eats a snack while *watching* the news on TV.
   >
   > **WRONG** Charlie finally went home, have no other place to go.
   > **RIGHT** Charlie finally went home, *having* no other place to go.

7h(2)
Use infinitives like *to swim, to walk,* or *to find* correctly.

A word used after *to* in an expression like *to swim, to walk,* or *to find* also masquerades as a verb. This kind of expression is called an *infinitive.* It looks like a verb, but it usually serves as the subject or object of a verb.

> *To swim* well demands much practice. [*To swim* is the subject of the sentence.]
> A baby tries *to walk* at the age of six months. [*To walk* is the object; it tells what the baby tries to do.]

Sometimes an infinitive like *to swim, to walk,* or *to find* appears first in a sentence. Do not separate the infinitive or infinitive phrase from the rest of the sentence with a period; since it is not a sentence, it cannot stand by itself.

> **WRONG** To find your errors.
> **RIGHT** *To find* your errors, read your paper carefully.

Be sure not to add an *-s* or an *-ed* ending to an expression like *to swim, to walk,* or *to find.*

> **WRONG** In basketball you need four people to assists you in a fast-break execution.
> **RIGHT** In basketball you need four people *to assist* you in a fast-break execution.

Caution: In some infinitive expressions the *to* is omitted because the verbs that come before these infinitives do not require *to.*

> *Contrast*
>
> Sam allows Linda *to help* him.
> WITH
> Sam lets Linda *help* him.

In both cases, *help* is an infinitive, but *to* is omitted in the second example because *let* does not require the use of *to*. Here are some other verbs that do not require *to* when followed by an infinitive.

help He *helps* me *work*. [OR He *helps* me to *work*.]
make She *makes* me *laugh*.

EXERCISE 37

In the following sentences, decide whether the italicized word is a verb or a word masquerading as a verb. Write *v* above all verbs and *m* above all words masquerading as verbs.

■ **Examples**
                         v
Everyone is always *talking* about the good old days.
        m
To forget my lines during the play would be a great embarrassment.

1. You are just *being* modest about your accomplishments.
2. *Wishing* for the telephone to ring is no way to *spend* your life.
3. To *have* all the money in the world is my fondest desire.
4. All of us are *going* to my grandmother's house tomorrow.
5. It is impossible to *find* a clean shirt in that closet.
6. *Slamming* the garage door, my brother ran toward the car.
7. Our dog Trixie, *barking* constantly, followed the mail carrier back to her truck.

EXERCISE 38

In the following sentences, underline the correct form in parentheses.

1. I have to (use, used) a good shampoo.
2. A walk will help a person (get, gets) some exercise.

3. Just to (show, showed) how well-educated Clyde is, I will give an example.

4. I felt that all those parades and street lights only helped to (commercialize, commercialized) Christmas.

5. My sister (use, used) all her free movie coupons last week.

6. Inflation has caused prices to (double, doubled) in the last five years.

7. The first thing Ellen does is to (mark, marks) the card to show how long she has (work, worked).

8. By (read, reading) the directions carefully, you will be less likely to make a mistake.

9. (Go, Going) to school on time is a good idea.

10. My brother usually helps me (vacuum, vacuumed) the rug.

CHAPTER EIGHT

Making Sense of Sentences

> *Learn to recognize and correct mixed-up and nonsense sentences.*

8a
Avoid the mixed-up sentence.

Sometimes you know that something is wrong with a sentence, but you cannot figure out what it is. In this section we are going to look at some sentences that are mixed up and try to see how they can be corrected. You will see several kinds of sentence mistakes that you will not find explained anywhere else in this handbook.

8a(1)
Avoid falling into the *in which, for which,* or *of which* trap.

Suppose you write:

> He had been told to obey the last orders from his superiors in which he had received that morning.

If you were trying to say that he obeyed the orders *which* he received, the *in* has no place in the sentence. You probably also had in the back of your mind that he had been told to obey orders *in which* certain instructions appeared. You meant to say, then,

> He had been told to obey the last orders from his superiors, *which* he had received that morning.
>
> OR
>
> He had been told to obey the last orders from his superiors, *in which* he had been instructed to prepare for an invasion.

Here are other examples of sentences in which the writer needlessly uses *in, on, for,* or *of* and, therefore, writes a mixed-up sentence.

WRONG	I have had much experience in that type of job in which you will see in my personal data sheet.
RIGHT	I have had much experience in that type of job, *which* you will see in my personal data sheet.
WRONG	Love is a feeling of which is developed from a friendship into a meaningful and happy affection.
RIGHT	Love is a feeling *which* is developed from a friendship into a meaningful and happy affection.

EXERCISE 1

Correct the following sentences, crossing out *in, on,* and *of* when they are not needed.

1. Bobby finally caught the basketball in which he was trying to get the whole second quarter.
2. A dealer will give you a high price in which is more than the true value of the car.
3. Jealousy is a powerful emotion of which most people feel at some time.
4. The handle is the wooden part on which the blade is attached to.
5. Eddie likes the school in which he is enrolled.

8a(2)
Avoid using *who, which,* or *that* when it serves no purpose in the sentence.

The words *who, which,* and *that* are commonly used to refer to words that you have just used. It is correct to say:

> This is the actress *who* broke a million hearts in the movies of the 1930s. [*who* refers to the actress.]

It is also correct to say:

> Here are the keys that I have been looking for all day. [*that* refers to the keys.]

a. *Who, which,* or *that* cannot be used as a joining word in place of *and*.

When you write:

> He is very bright which he is always telling me about his accomplishments.

you probably meant to use *and* instead of *which* because you have joined two complete thoughts or finished sentences. You should have written:

> He is very bright, *and* he is always telling me about his accomplishments. [*and* used as a joining word]
>
> OR
>
> He is very bright, a fact *that* I never realized. [*that* used as a referring word]

Here are some other mixed-up sentences in which the writer should have decided whether to use *and* as a joining word (conjunction) or *who, which* or *that* as a referring word (pronoun).

WRONG	I have a friend that I enjoy everything he does.
RIGHT	I have a friend, *and* I enjoy everything he does.

OR

I have a friend *who* does things that I enjoy.

WRONG	The men have been drinking which they knew they were not supposed to drink.
RIGHT	The men have been drinking, *and* they knew they were not supposed to drink.

OR

The men have been drinking something *that* they were not supposed to drink.

b. Do not use *which* or *that* when you really need a clause introduced by *in which*, *to which*, *on which*, or *of which*.

WRONG	He is content to get a job that he has no room for advancement.
RIGHT	He is content to get a job *in which* he has no room for advancement.

EXERCISE 2

If the word *which* or *that* is incorrectly used in any of the following sentences, change it to a comma plus *and* or use it in a clause introduced by *in which*, *to which*, *on which*, or *of which*. Do not change any correct sentences.

■ **Examples**   I found his notebook which I carefully put it away for him.
              I found his notebook, *and* I carefully put it away for him.

              Word Search is a magazine that you find word associations.
              Word Search is a magazine *in which* you find word associations.

1. My cousin is always buying expensive clothing which she can't really afford it.
2. There is a black and white clock to the right of the sign which the time on it says ten minutes to three.
3. I looked through the rack until I found a dress that I really liked.
4. The cabinets are brown which we keep our glasses, cups, toothpicks, hot sauce, sugar dish, and other things we need in the dining room.

5. It is a break in the dream world that the family is living.

6. There is a high shelf in the garage which my power tools are located.

7. *Rolling Stone* is the magazine that the information you are looking for can be found.

8. Antigone says Creon does not believe in the gods which she is right.

9. In my room are many hiding places that only I know where they are.

10. Keep straight ahead until you get to the gas station which is located near the bend in the road.

8a(3)

Avoid mixing up a statement and a question in the same sentence without meaning to do so.

When you say:

He asked me did I want to go.

you are mixing two things. You meant to say:

He asked me if I wanted to go.
> OR
He asked me, "Do you want to go?"

WRONG	I asked him one day how does it feel to be his size.
RIGHT	I asked him one day how it felt to be his size.
	OR
	I asked him one day, "How does it feel to be your size?"
WRONG	The mechanic asked me did I keep my car tuned up nicely.
RIGHT	The mechanic asked me whether I kept my car tuned up nicely.

Notice that each of these sentences contains two parts: (1) the asking or wondering part and (2) the thing the person asked or wondered or wanted to know. When both of these parts are written in statement form, the subject should come before the verb in both parts.

She wondered if I would wear my new ring.
He asked her where she had put the extra cookies.

EXERCISE 3

Change the following direct questions to statements by following these five steps.

1. Put the asker or wonderer first.
2. Write *if* or *whether*.
3. Write the thing being asked.
4. Make sure you put the subject before the verb in Step 3.
5. You may need to change the second verb. For example, *will* may become *would*.

■ **Example**   My brother asked me, "Will you be home at 4:00?"
        My brother asked me *if I would be home at 4:00.*

1. John asked my sisters, "Are you going home?"
2. Lisa asked, "Will he be at the party?"
3. Sarah wondered, "Will there be a meeting at the recreation center?"
4. We all wondered, "Will we get home in time for dinner?"
5. I asked her, "Did you have to go to court on Tuesday?"

EXERCISE 4

Correct the following sentences by putting the subject before the verb in each of the two parts. Add *if* or *whether* and change the verb form when necessary. Take out any unnecessary words.

■ **Example**   She wanted to know why was I always giving her a smart
        answer.
        She wanted to know why *I was always giving her a smart*
        answer.

1. Her aunt asked her what was she really looking for in life.
2. They will soon see do you have the qualifications for the job.
3. I asked her could we study together.

4. I asked my friend when was the last time this place had been raided.

5. They wanted to know which room did we see the fire in and how bad was it.

8a(4)
Avoid writing a mixed-up sentence when you are trying to give someone a definition of a word you are using.

It is hard to define something, so instead of telling the reader what a word means, you may find yourself giving an example of when or where it happens. When you say:

> A *hassle* is when a police officer searches someone for no reason.

you are forgetting that a *hassle* is not *when* a person gives another a hard time; it is the hard time itself. You should have said:

> A *hassle* is a hard time or run-around one person gives another.
>   OR
> When a police officer searches someone for no reason, he is *hassling* him.

Often the best way to define a word is to decide to what class or general category the word belongs and to make that class the first part of the definition.

WORD	CLASS	DEFINITION
clutch	device	A *clutch* is a device used for holding an object firmly.
home run	hit in baseball	A *home run* is a hit in baseball that allows the batter to touch all the bases and score.

EXERCISE 5

Copy the following sentences. Under each sentence, write one of your own, giving a definition of something. Remember to make the class the first part of the definition.

1. The *four corners* is a strategy used by some college basketball teams when they are ahead in a game, to keep the basketball from their opponents.

2. *Cool* is a word that describes people who run their affairs in a very capable way.

3. A *pop rivet tool* is a device used to fasten parts made of thin metal.

4. *Jealousy* is a feeling that makes you dislike someone who has something you would like to have yourself.

EXERCISE 6

Correct the following definitions by saying *what* something is, not when or where it is.

1. *Greed* is when you want something that you don't need.

2. *Love* is when two people want to be together.

3. A *carburetor* is where you mix air and gasoline.

4. A *field goal* is where a team tries to score three points by kicking the football between the opponents' uprights.

8a(5)
Avoid writing a mixed-up sentence that has no subject.

If you are trying to say two different things in the same sentence, you sometimes write a sentence without a subject (the person or thing you are talking about in the sentence). For example, suppose you say:

> After finishing your education will assure you of a job in the future.

What will assure you of a job in the future? You have not answered that question. You meant to say:

> After finishing your education, *you* will be assured of a job in the future.
>
> OR
>
> *Finishing* your education will assure you of a job in the future.

Here is another example:

WRONG   To pull a cart needs twice the strength of a pony.
RIGHT   To pull a cart, a *person* needs twice the strength of a pony.

EXERCISE 7

Correct the following sentences by giving the sentence a subject.

1. After knowing police officers in Portsmouth and Suffolk agree they are very different.
2. For students living away from home have to decide what kind of housing is best suited to them.
3. When people feel that everything they say or do is right because of what they believe or have been taught is a wrong attitude to take.
4. Underneath the hood consists of many parts.
5. In the typing class has enough machines for all the students to use.
6. By singing in a church choir helped Bessie Smith become a great blues singer.

8a(6)
Avoid mixing two thoughts so completely that the reader cannot tell which of the two ideas you are trying to get across.

Sometimes your problem is not the absence of a subject. Suppose you write:

> Once you become used to driving, the hard part is over except when you drive on the highway with other cars you feel as if you can't cope with it.

You have two ideas here. One idea is:

> Once you become used to driving, the hard part is over except when you must drive on the highway with other cars.

The other idea is:

> When you drive on the highway with other cars, you feel as if you can't cope with the situation.

Here are some other examples of this problem.

WRONG   The first thing to do to bake a cake you will need two eight-inch cake pans.

RIGHT   The first thing to do to bake a cake is to get out two eight-inch cake pans.

OR

To bake a cake, you will need two eight-inch cake pans.

WRONG   She is too nice a person until people like to take advantage of her.

RIGHT   She is such a nice person that people like to take advantage of her.

OR

She is a nice person until people take advantage of her.

EXERCISE 8

Correct the following sentences by rewriting them, after deciding which idea you want to emphasize.

1. The way to make a jumper is first you have to lay your pattern out.

2. After about an hour had passed before he decided to let me go.

3. In the other corner there is a closet where you can put your clothes in it.

4. Football games last anywhere from a half-hour to three or four hours long.

5. If going on a trip, you will enjoy it more if it has been planned in advance about where you are going, what you are taking, and how long you are going to stay.

6. Buying items that you can't afford or don't need are unnecessary problems.

7. Of all the people I didn't want to see was the man next door.

8. We finally realized that when our son left home that we had neglected him.

EXERCISE 9

This exercise contains all of the types of mixed-up sentences described in 8a. Correct each of the sentences.

1. Turn the engine off, turn the emergency flasher on, and apply the emergency brake are the next three things to do.

2. A lazy person is when you always wait for other people to do your work for you.

3. After Burt finished, I asked him how did it taste.

4. Mrs. Howard is one woman that you would not forget her after you had met.

5. To be a maid, she seems to be head of the house all the time.

6. Rudeness is a trait in which everyone needs to think about.

7. My cousin Stella is one of the most ignorant girls of which I have ever met.

8. Then I just thought about it was payday, and I had just been paid.

9. Ann's letter was very well-written which I feel it showed much planning.

10. When you see the happy look on the face of someone you have just given a gift is a good feeling.

8b

Cure your seriously mixed-up sentences.

Be your own doctor. *Diagnose the illness in your mixed-up sentences, and cure them by saying what you meant to say.* In the last section, you looked at some mixed-up sentences and saw how easy it is to mix two thoughts in the same sentence so that neither thought comes across clearly. Sometimes a mixed-up sentence can get so out of hand that it is hard to make just one single correction. When that happens, about all you can do is resort to drastic surgery. Look at the sentence again, decide what you wanted to say, and say it. Then delete everything that does not relate to your main point.

> **MIXED-UP**   You try to be alert for additional game, whether it be rabbit, quail, or squirrel, not so much to bag it, but to acquaint ourselves with what the natures of many woodland creatures look like for the purpose of passing this knowledge on to our children.

There are at least four different things the writer might have been saying in this sentence:

1. You (or we) need to be alert for game.
2. We need to acquaint ourselves with the natures of woodland creatures.
3. We need to acquaint ourselves with what woodland creatures look like.
4. You (or we) need to pass on the knowledge of woodland creatures to your (our) children.

It is best to start over with this sentence. Its main point seems to be the importance of gaining and passing on the knowledge of wildlife.

> **BETTER**   We try to acquaint ourselves with rabbit, quail, and squirrel so we can pass on our knowledge of these creatures to our children.

> **MIXED-UP**   Not like soul music, which is slow and meaningful, rock is a fast-moving age in the years before me, the present years and the years to come.

It is difficult to be sure, but the writer might have been saying one of three things:

1. Unlike soul, rock is fast-moving.
2. Rock is part of a fast-moving age.
3. Rock has its own place in history.

Let us say that the writer is talking about the place of rock music in this age.

BETTER   Unlike soul—which is a slow, meaningful form of music—rock is part of a fast-moving age.

You can see that it is impossible to give a prescription to cure all mixed-up sentences. You must be your own doctor. Make a diagnosis of why the sentence is mixed up, and cure it. It will be easier to make this diagnosis if you ask yourself what one thing you meant to say in the sentence and eliminate anything that gets in the way of saying it.

EXERCISE 10

Cure the following sentences. Decide what the writer meant to say. Then rewrite the sentence, eliminating anything that does not help the writer make the point.

1. The beach is very beautiful with its light-blue water floating with large and small waves are seen from afar.
2. I feel that since I am the first of all my brothers who really had a hard time, I should be the first of which to get ahead, but I learned that's not true.
3. The students of today will have to run this country one day, and it's going to be in bad shape when the student who breaks his back to pass the exam and others break theirs to see the other's paper.
4. The Midway Shopping Center, which is found in the middle of town, and there you will find several stores that may be convenient to anybody that likes to shop can shop there.
5. Behind that man was a tree on shore with grass, bark, and is split with a tree stump.
6. There are several vines hanging from this tree in which there is one on the man's left side of the boat.
7. That's another example of how visual aids and other communication forms he uses, stating that they are a cause of violence.

8c
Think about what you are saying. Make your sentences make sense

Some sentences seem to make sense, but the more you think about them, the more you realize that they do not. A group of words may have a subject and a verb and it may sound like a sentence, but unless it says something, it is not really a sentence. The words

> I am going to ambition a muskrat.

contain a subject and a verb, but the resulting sentence does not mean anything. Although you have probably never written anything that silly, it is easy to write a sentence which sounds all right technically but which does not say anything. You need to consider both the way a sentence is put together and what it says.

> NONSENSE   I believe the views of society are that a woman is not liberated and she should not work because she should slave at home and should not own her own business.

The writer has not really made a clear statement about society's view on women's liberation. Slaving at home and owning a business do not *cause* a woman to be liberated or not liberated. They do not *cause* a woman to work or not to work. Writers are entitled to express any opinion they wish, but they must make sure that their readers understand what that opinion is. After thinking about the intended meaning, this writer might have written:

> BETTER   In our society no woman is truly liberated.

Another type of nonsense sentence is this:

> Women's liberation is widely known among Americans.

This sentence makes sense from the standpoint of structure, but the writer is not saying anything. The sentence simply states an obvious

152   *Sentence Basics*

truth like "Bread is a type of food" or "Lollipops taste good." Saying these things does not contribute to the world's storehouse of knowledge. Perhaps the writer really wanted to say:

> Women's liberation has gained respectability among Americans during the last ten years.

EXERCISE 11

Rewrite the following nonsense sentences so they make sense.

1. Night driving takes place after the sun goes down.
2. Although my wife and I do not need to agree on every issue, her opinions should be the same as mine.
3. When a woman marries, she should take care of her home and children if she has children.
4. Even though women act as if they are liberated, they are not really liberated, and they do accept responsibilities with great pride.
5. We are not aware of what our dreams mean when we're not asleep because of the existence of day-to-day living.
6. Nobody can do anything about the high cost of living because the problem hasn't been found. Maybe one day everything will come to an end, but until then, we'll have to take life as it comes.
7. She's short and stocky, which to me makes her age unbelievable.
8. No honor or responsibility conferred on the students by the faculty excels that which the National Honor Society represents.

PART TWO

MORE ABOUT SENTENCES

CHAPTER NINE

Sentences with Misplaced and Dangling Parts

> *Improve your sentences by eliminating misplaced and dangling parts.*

9a
Relocate the misplaced parts in your sentences.

Sometimes a sentence will sound awkward because one or more words are out of place. These words have to be relocated or placed next to the person or thing they are describing.

OUT OF PLACE   I see a boat beside this man that is green and looks as if it is tied to a tree. [The man is not green or tied to a tree; to make this sentence clear, put the words describing the boat next to the word *boat*.]

BACK IN PLACE   Beside this man I see a boat *that is green and looks as if it is tied to a tree.*

OUT OF PLACE   Television coverage puts the president on the air anytime he suggests which includes all available channels. [It is the television coverage that includes all available channels.]

BACK IN PLACE   Television coverage, *which includes all available channels,* puts the president on the air anytime he suggests.

EXERCISE 1

Relocate the italicized misplaced parts so that the following sentences will be clear.

■ **Example**   My aunt bought an antique clock at the auction last week *and an old steamer trunk.*
My aunt bought an antique clock and an old steamer trunk at the auction last week.

1. Most of the time when a team is playing on TV *that we like,* we watch the game together.

2. I saw your advertisement in the *Los Angeles Times* of November 28, 1983, *for a clerk-typist.*

3. I would describe this place as being very warm and cozy *which is my bedroom.*

4. One thing you can do in your home is to keep all lights turned off *that are not necessary.*

5. Love of money has gotten people killed *such as robbers and gamblers* over the years.

6. In the 1930s she became chief clerk and knew all the farmers in our county by name *and most of the businesspeople.*

7. Hand tools are used for doing the required work *such as pliers, side cutters, screwdrivers, and wrenches.*

8. Remove all the equipment from the trunk *that was mentioned in the previous paragraph.*

9b

Give any dangling part in your sentences something to describe.

Sometimes, without really wanting to, you can make your reader laugh. Suppose you had written the sentence:

When thoroughly stewed, the patients will enjoy our prunes.

A reader would probably have found this sentence funny because it certainly does not mean what it seems to mean. You do not want to suggest that the patients have to be stewed in order to enjoy the prunes. The words *when thoroughly stewed* are dangling in the sentence like a loose part. Make it clear that they refer to the prunes instead of to the patients by giving them a subject to describe. The sentence should read:

When the prunes are thoroughly stewed, the patients will enjoy them.

Here are some other sentences with dangling parts. Notice in each case that the corrected sentence supplies a clear subject for the dangling part to describe.

DANGLING	Driving to the lodge, the car's transmission started acting up. [Who is doing the driving?]
CLEAR SUBJECT	*When we were driving to the lodge,* the car's transmission started acting up.
DANGLING	In order to clean, the bathroom door must stand open. [Who is doing the cleaning?]
CLEAR SUBJECT	*When you are cleaning,* the bathroom door must stand open.
DANGLING	Passing through the door on my right, bizarre posters showing a lion, the Taj Mahal, a dog with suitcases, and a sign saying "I Won't Stay in a World Without Love" can be seen. [Who is passing through the door?]
CLEAR SUBJECT	*A person passing through the door on my right* can see bizarre posters showing a lion, the Taj Mahal, a dog with suitcases, and a sign saying "I Won't Stay in a World Without Love."

Be careful not to allow a group of words to dangle without a subject for it to describe.

EXERCISE 2

In each of the following sentences, the dangling part is italicized. Correct the sentences so that there is no longer a dangling part by supplying a clear subject for that part to describe.

■ **Example**   *Hoping to keep awake in class,* a lot of coffee was consumed.
Hoping to keep awake in class, we consumed a lot of coffee.

1. *By trying to remember my speech,* some of the contents were twisted.
2. The new oil filter needs oil around the gasket *before putting it on.*
3. *By having this extra room,* the kitchen cabinets can be easily installed.
4. *Desiring to have a perfect evening,* how can it turn out any other way?
5. *By doing this,* it will avoid an argument later on.
6. *By forgetting any essential steps,* a paragraph can be confusing.
7. *After searching over an hour for a used separator,* the snow began to pile up on the ground.
8. Similarities between the two cars come in handy *when trying to get parts.*

EXERCISE 3

Find the dangling part in each sentence. Then rewrite the sentence, giving the part something to describe.

1. In trying to locate the store you want, it is never there.
2. Driving to California, the roads were crowded with noisy tourists.
3. By trying to get started on time, it will avoid a later argument in the event that they miss out on something.
4. After leaving the highway at the Effingham Street off-ramp, the street is brightly lit.
5. By using government enforcement of gasoline rationing regulations, gasoline can be conserved and distributed evenly to all citizens.

CHAPTER TEN

Nonparallel and Rambling Sentences

> *Write parallel sentences and give sentences direction.*

10a
Make the parts of your sentences parallel.

A sentence with nonparallel parts does not say what you want it to say. For example, a student wrote about trick-or-treating:

> Parents don't want to see their children robbed of candy bags, hit by cars, and consumption of doped candy by their children.

You can easily see that the above sentence is not parallel. In the list of the hazards of trick-or-treating, the third item is clearly not the same as the others. The writer should have corrected the sentence by making the third item like the other two. A verb form was needed to balance the other verbs.

	NOT PARALLEL
Parents don't want to see their children	robbed of candy bags
	hit by cars
	consumption of doped candy by their children

	PARALLEL
Parents don't want to see their children	robbed of candy bags
	hit by cars
	given doped candy

Parents don't want to see their children *robbed* of candy bags, *hit* by cars, and *given* doped candy.

In the following sentences, two or more things are not parallel. In each case, making the things like one another helps the writer say what he or she wants to say.

The park is a place where everyone can have a good time or just to be sitting around doing nothing.

	NOT PARALLEL
The park is a place where everyone can	have a good time
	just to be sitting around doing nothing

	PARALLEL
The park is a place where everyone can	have a good time
	sit around doing nothing

The park is a place where everyone can *have* a good time or just *sit* around doing nothing.

You can use landmarks such as houses, streams, or even cutting notches on trees.

	NOT PARALLEL
You can use landmarks such as	houses
	streams
	cutting notches on trees

You can use landmarks such as   **PARALLEL**
houses
streams
notches cut on trees

You can use landmarks such as *houses, streams,* or even *notches* cut on trees.

The more options a car has and the larger it is, it will cost more and its maintenance will be greater.

The more options a car has   **NOT PARALLEL**
the larger it is
it will cost more
its maintenance will be greater

The more options a car has   **PARALLEL**
the larger it is
the more it will cost
the more maintenance it will require

The *more* options a car has and the *larger* it is, the *more* it will cost, and the *more* maintenance it will require.

Sometimes you will have to eliminate one or two items from your sentence because they cannot be made like the others. If you want to mention these items, you will have to put them into a new sentence.

She is medium-sized, 5′5″ tall, wears glasses, dresses neatly, and very attractive.

She is   **NOT PARALLEL**
medium-sized
5′5″ tall
wears glasses
dresses neatly
very attractive

Nonparallel and Rambling Sentences   **163**

	PARALLEL
She is	medium-sized
	5′5″ tall
	[eliminate item]
	always neatly dressed
	very attractive

She is *medium-sized, 5′5″ tall, always neatly dressed,* and *very attractive.*

Sometimes, just correcting an item on a list is not enough to make the sentence make sense. In the example

> Her eyes are dark brown, thin eyebrows, a smooth complexion, and a thin mouth.

not all the things listed describe that person's eyes. In this case, the items themselves are balanced, but the writer has to decide what he or she is listing. In this case, the writer is really describing a person's features.

	CONFUSING
Her eyes are	dark brown
	thin eyebrows
	a smooth complexion
	a thin mouth
	CLEAR AND PARALLEL
She has	dark-brown eyes
	thin eyebrows
	a smooth complexion
	a thin mouth

She has *dark-brown eyes, thin eyebrows, a smooth complexion,* and *a thin mouth.*

EXERCISE 1

Make the items parallel in each of the following sentences. Decide what you are listing, and make a chart like the one in the example. Change wording if necessary.

■ **Example**   He has thick eyebrows, long eyelashes, side-burns, and has
a few strands of hair under his chin.

He has (1) thick eyebrows
(2) long eyelashes
(3) sideburns
(4) a few strands of hair under his chin.

1. If you are careless when you work with electricity, you may get shocked, burned badly, or loss of life.

2. Some people go to college to play football, get married, and for many other reasons.

3. John has more money for movies, to take trips, buying clothes, and to spend on records now that he has a job.

4. The first thing Mrs. Johnson did was to introduce herself and that she is the librarian.

5. The acetylene torch is used to heat metals, free bolts, bend steel pipes, and numerous other things in workshops.

6. Sometimes I can't find any shoes, my car keys, or the phone rings as I am about to slam the door.

EXERCISE 2

Rewrite each of the following sentences, being sure that the items in them are parallel.

■ **Example**   I'm glad I am young, handsome, and never been married.
I'm glad I am young, handsome, and *unmarried*.

1. I told him I had just arrived in town and to call and ask my mother.

2. Mike is 5'11", broad shoulders like a football player, bulging muscles, and is rough in his actions.

3. Tom has complete control over his emotions, whether love, friendship, or even someone he dislikes.

4. A husband forgets that there are bills to pay, food to buy, and that the rent has to be paid.

5. We talk about things like buying clothes, shoes, what style someone is going to wear, and how to make clothes.

6. When you vote, consider the candidate's political background, his point of view on different issues, and if you think he will get the job done.

7. Mrs. Linde listens, gives advice, and she makes Nora face reality.

8. My father never gets upset about our grades or when we make mistakes.

9. Larry Bird uses his size well in rebounding, jump shots, blocking shots, and keeping up with the other players.

10. The following are advantages of having a 40-channel CB: being able to talk to more people, able to find a channel to talk on, and a better chance of finding help.

10b
Give your sentences direction.

A rambling sentence seems to go nowhere. Perhaps you have forgotten what you wanted to say, yet you feel the need to fill space on the paper. When you find a rambling sentence in your writing, rewrite it so that it takes you somewhere. Decide what you meant to tell the reader in the first place.

> Carelessness is shown when children leave their toys on a stairway or sidewalk where others can trip over them and be seriously injured, which may result in a tremendous loss of income.

The direction of this sentence is not clear because it is difficult to decide whether the writer is listing the results of carelessness, worrying about a possible lawsuit, or warning a potential victim. The writer has to decide where the sentence is going, and then eliminate what is not needed or put it into another sentence.

> Carelessness is shown when children leave their toys on a stairway or sidewalk where others can trip over them. (An injury resulting from such carelessness can lead to disability and possible loss of income.)

The following sentence has too much unnecessary information at the beginning.

> Since I was a technical consultant on diesel electric power plants to the Turkish Air Force, which had fifteen radar sites and thirty air force bases with this type of equipment, I traveled most of the time.

The writer does not need all the information about radar sites and bases to make the point.

> Since I was a technical consultant to the Turkish Air Force on their many diesel electric power plants, I had to travel most of the time.

EXERCISE 3

Give these sentences direction. Decide what the writer is telling you, and eliminate all unnecessary information or put it into another sentence.

1. It may have been a busy day or my uncle may have gotten on his nerves, but sometimes my father can be an understanding man as long as nothing goes wrong.

2. For a woman who is already neglected because she is the wife of a successful lawyer and the member of a prominent family and has many family problems, the time spent playing golf when he could be at home would make the situation even worse.

3. In the area of the house where my son's bedroom is, the wall sticks out, making a corner on the house where the wall changes levels, making the wall wider where my son's and my mother's rooms connect.

4. Kevin doesn't allow anybody to enter his garage because after he finishes cleaning it up and putting his tools in place, he doesn't want people coming in here because they may knock things out of place.

CHAPTER ELEVEN
Guiding Readers

> *Guide your readers so that they will not feel puzzled.*

Your readers should not have any doubts about when things are taking place or whether what you have written is intended to be serious, funny, sad, or exciting. You, the writer, should be clear in your own thinking and should make it clear to the reader:

> *when* things are happening,
> *who* is telling about events,
> *what* emotion, or feeling, is expressed,
> and
> *who* is referred to when short substitute words are used.

11a
Guide your readers so that they will know when events are happening.

If you are writing about things that are happening now, the verbs you use should tell about the present. If you are writing about things that happened at some time in the past, let the reader know. Do not confuse the reader by mixing the time of the verbs.

CONFUSING   My previous employers always asked for references when I apply for a job.

CLEAR   My previous employers always asked for references when I *applied* for a job.

Caution: When you write about a story, a play, or another work of literature, you usually use the present tense. Avoid shifting from the present to the past tense unless you want to show that one event takes place before another.

CONFUSING   In *Hamlet,* Shakespeare gives us a memorable hero who cannot decide to avenge the death of his father even though he realized that he had a responsibility to do so.

CLEAR   In *Hamlet,* Shakespeare *gives* us a memorable hero who cannot decide to avenge the death of his father, even though he *realizes* that he *has* a responsibility to do so.

EXERCISE 1

Read the following sentences. In each sentence one verb should be changed so that the time of the action is clear. Decide on the changes to be made and correct the sentences.

1. She raised many foster children but never has any of her own.
2. The wind was blowing, and the sun was shining; the children are digging in the sand while I played volleyball with my friends.
3. As Eileen entered the shop, she sees the different colors of wax and the various sizes and shapes of candles.
4. I remember the good times I have as a child, but I am happy to be old enough now to decide things for myself.
5. Books were checked out at the circulation desk, and assistance can be found there.

6. My Army written examination went smoothly, but the physical seems to take all day.

7. Finally, realizing he was too old to be uprooted, Knute decides to return to his native soil.

11b

Guide your readers so that they will understand the point of view. Be sure that they know who is telling about events and to whom the writer is speaking. Avoid shifting person.

Many of your papers will be about personal experiences, and you will make frequent use of the words *I* and *we*. Some papers may give directions for doing something or may ask for some action and will be directed to *you*. Other papers may be stories, or narratives, which are about someone else, and you will use the words *he, she, it,* or *they*.

These pronouns suggest a focus for your paper. If you are telling things from your point of view, you are using first person (*I, we,* and so on). If you are writing to someone, you are using second person (*you, your, yours*). If you are writing about someone, you are writing about a third person other than *I* or *you*. In that case you use the pronouns *he, she, it,* and so on. Here is a chart suggesting the appropriate pronouns to use, depending on whether you are writing about yourself, to others, or about others.

	SUBJECT PRONOUNS	POSSESSIVE PRONOUNS	OBJECT PRONOUNS
First person (*writing about yourself*):	I, we	my, our, mine, ours	me, us
Second person (*writing to others*):	you	your, yours	you
Third person (*writing about other persons or things*):	he, she, it, they	his, her, hers, its, their, theirs	him, her, it, them

Before beginning your paper, decide whether you are writing about yourself, to others, or about other persons and things, and use the correct pronouns throughout your paper. Do not shift person.

CONFUSING	I went to the mountains for my vacation. You certainly learn to drive carefully on the steep roads.
BETTER	I went to the mountains for my vacation. *I* certainly learned to drive carefully on the steep roads. [The reader sees the experiences through the eyes of the writer (*I*).]
CONFUSING	Remove the globe or shade before you take out the bulb that doesn't work. Then he screws the new bulb firmly in place.
BETTER	Remove the globe or shade before you take out the bulb that doesn't work. Then screw the new bulb firmly in place. [The reader (*you*) is receiving directions from the writer.]
CONFUSING	John and Toby went down the river in a canoe. You need to pull the canoe onto the grass at your campsite.
BETTER	John and Toby went down the river in a canoe. *They* remembered to pull the canoe onto the grass at the campsite. [The writer and the reader are watching what happens to others (*they*).]

EXERCISE 2

Edit the following paragraph, correcting any shifts in person.

When I make a dress, I go to one of my favorite shopping centers and pick out some material and accessories. Then I find a pattern that is simple yet attractive. When you finish selecting the material and pattern, take your pattern and lay it on the material, pinning it carefully. I try to be careful when cutting the pattern so I won't cut the wrong side of the material. Pin the dress before sewing it so that you won't make any mistakes. After you have finished sewing it, you will be pleased with the money you have saved.

EXERCISE 3

Rewrite the following paragraph eliminating all shifts in person.

> When a person has had a particularly hectic or disastrous day trying to juggle a school load of fifteen credit hours, a forty-hour work week, and the needs of a family, she may ask herself what she is doing in college. What has possessed you to sit in classes, often with students just a few years older than your children, and pursue a degree? The answer is often not simple. I have always enjoyed being a student. My school career during grade school and high school was particularly satisfying and happy. School work seems easy for people who like the discipline and challenges it brings them. In school you are always someone special.

11c
Guide your readers so that they will know whether your writing is serious, funny, sad, or exciting.

Do not confuse your reader by mixing two writing styles.

CONFUSING	In the corner of the room stood an elegant velvet-upholstered sofa with a bunch of funny-looking pillows at one end. [The reader probably does not know whether the writer is admiring or making fun of the sofa.]
BETTER	In the corner of the room stood an elegant velvet-upholstered sofa with *several unusual pillows* at one end.

CONFUSING	The smoke drifted gently from the chimney; there was a warm haze of sunlight, and everything was totally awesome. [The slang expression at the end of the sentence is not in the same style as the dignified description at the beginning.]
BETTER	The smoke drifted gently from the chimney; there was a warm haze of sunlight, and *everyone felt calm and relaxed.*

Do not confuse your reader. Before you begin to write, decide on the feeling you wish to express and be sure that each sentence contributes to it.

11d
Guide your readers so that pronoun references are clear.

Most of the time, when writers want to refer to a person or thing they have just named, they use a pronoun to avoid using the same word or group of words again. For example, writers would not say:

My friends laughed because my friends thought I was cute.

Writers would almost certainly use the word *they* in place of the second *my friends.* When pronouns like *they, he, she, it,* and *this* are used in place of other words, it is important that they refer clearly to definite persons or things coming before them.

UNCLEAR	Several teachers complained about those noisy students. We thought they were being unreasonable. [Did we think the teachers or the students were being unreasonable?]
CLEAR	Several teachers complained about those noisy students. We thought *those teachers* were being unreasonable.
UNCLEAR	Snow on a highway gives drivers steering problems. This can be a major cause of accidents. [What can be a cause

of accidents? Snow? Bad steering? The dangerous situation itself?]

CLEAR Snow on a highway gives drivers steering problems. *These problems* can be a major cause of accidents.

11d(1)

Be sure that when you use a pronoun like *it, they, them,* or *that,* you have already given your readers a clear reference for this word.

Do not expect your readers to guess something that you have not told them.

UNCLEAR My paper looks okay, but my teacher with her 20/20 vision will spot them every time. [You know that *them* refers to the mistakes in your paper, but you should not expect your readers to guess this fact.]

CLEAR My paper looks okay, but my teacher with her 20/20 vision will spot *my mistakes* every time.

UNCLEAR In high school they want a note for every day a student is late or absent. [Tell your readers who *they* are.]

CLEAR In high school *the principal's staff* wants a note for every day a student is late or absent.

UNCLEAR The steering wheel is small, but it is easy to steer. [*It* cannot refer to the steering wheel; it must be the unnamed car.]

CLEAR The steering wheel is small, but *the car* is easy to steer.

11d(2)

Use *this* and *that* to refer to specific persons or things.

Do not use the words *this* and *that* when you mean *a, an,* or *the.* When you are describing or referring to a person or thing that you have not previously mentioned to the reader, write *a* boy or *the* boy instead of *this* boy. Never use the incorrect expressions *this here* or *that there.*

WRONG	I met this here girl I liked in Knoxville.
RIGHT	I met *a* girl I liked in Knoxville.
WRONG	I walked into this store, and I saw this really great bargain.
RIGHT	I walked into *a* store, and I saw *a* really great bargain.

11d(3)
Be sure to give no more than one possible reference for a pronoun.

Sometimes *this, it, they, he, she, his, her, them,* or *their* can refer to more than one person or thing that comes before it. Do not force your reader to guess which reference you intend. When necessary, rewrite the sentence, removing the incorrect reference.

UNCLEAR	Citizens need to conserve their coupons so that they will last through a long and difficult rationing period. [It is not entirely clear whether the citizens or the coupons will have trouble lasting through the rationing period.]
CLEAR	*Coupons* need to be conserved so that *they* will last through a long and difficult rationing period.
UNCLEAR	I don't need music to start dancing that step. I can feel it in my bones. [Can I feel the music or the step?]
CLEAR	I don't need music to start dancing that step. I can feel *the music* in my bones.

EXERCISE 4

In each of the following sentences, the italicized pronoun should refer to a person or thing already named. If there is no clear reference for the italicized pronoun or if the pronoun could refer to more than one person or thing, correct the sentence to clear up the confusion.

■ **Example** This is a badly written article. Instead of giving the readers more specifics, *they* avoid the issue.

This is a badly written article. Instead of giving the readers more specifics, the authors avoid the issue.

1. Nowadays people buy new appliances as if *it* were no more than writing a check.
2. The carburetor is not very large. *It* has power steering and power brakes.
3. It is dangerous at night because *they* have not turned on the street lights.
4. The first thing you notice about the roads is the gravel. *This* can be a hazardous situation.
5. We could only see the rice paddies move as *they* got close to us.
6. We were shown the microfilm section and the order in which *they* were filed.
7. If you were in one of those large cities in Germany, it would remind you of New York because of *their* fast driving and walking.
8. There are many ruts and holes in the road. *This* makes it impossible to stay on your side of the road.
9. *They* should give more benefits to the elderly and the unemployed.
10. When a police officer stopped us, this was the third time *they* had stopped us that night.

11d(4)

Use a singular pronoun like *he, she, his, its,* or *him* to refer to one person or thing. Use a plural pronoun like *we, they, their,* or *them* to refer to more than one person or thing. See **6b.**

> **WRONG**   The wise shopper looks inside the garment to see that they have adequate seams.
>
> **RIGHT**   The wise shopper looks inside the garment to see that *it* has adequate seams.

11d(5)

Use a singular noun to refer to a person or thing you have already written about; use a plural noun to refer to more than one person or thing.

> **WRONG**   Some husbands are not the sole provider in a household.
>
> **RIGHT**   Sometimes *a husband* is not *the sole provider* in a household.

In guiding your readers, remember to

1. be sure you have already given a clear reference for words like *it*, *they*, and *them*.
2. be sure that words like *he*, *she*, and *their* have only one possible reference.
3. use a singular word to refer to one person or thing; use a plural word to refer to more than one person or thing.

EXERCISE 5

Rewrite the following sentences so that the italicized words refer clearly and correctly to one particular word coming before it.

1. Every viewer of pay TV receives a TV guide so *they* don't need previews to keep the viewers informed of upcoming programs.
2. We became familiar with the play index. *They* listed books and plays and their location.
3. Most librarians help the student look for the books *they* need.
4. Time schedules should be posted at bus stops. *It* should be protected from the elements and the graffiti artists.
5. A person must be able to use *their* hand to signal if *they* are going to turn right.
6. In Washington I saw a really pretty girl from the West Indies. There were many of *them* walking around.
7. High-class people eat as though *he* does not care whether *he* is eating his dinner.
8. Hunting dogs are different from *the guard dog*.

PART THREE

SPELLING AND PUNCTUATION

CHAPTER TWELVE
Spelling

Spell the words in your papers correctly. Learn to use hyphens when needed. Separate words into syllables to avoid misspelling.

12a
Learn the simple rules of spelling.

To write acceptable papers, you must spell correctly. If you have trouble with spelling, the words that give you the most trouble are probably not particularly long or unusual but actually short and familiar—so familiar that you do not think it is necessary to look them up in your dictionary. But use a dictionary whenever you are in doubt about the spelling of a word. There are some rules you can use to help you remember the spelling of some of the familiar words that might cause you trouble.

12a(1)
Change the -y at the end of a word to -i before you add an ending, except when you add the ending -ing.

happy + ness = happiness	pretty + est = prettiest
study + es = studies	party + es = parties
study + ed = studied	party + ed = partied
study + ing = studying	party + ing = partying

Exceptions: When -*y* is preceded by a vowel, do *not* change -*y* to -*i*.

enjoy + able = enjoyable	employ + er = employer
enjoy + s = enjoys	employ + s = employs
enjoy + ed = enjoyed	employ + ed = employed

EXERCISE 1

Add the endings indicated to the following words and write the words correctly with the added endings.

1. sloppy + ness	5. vary + es	9. happy + er
2. marry + ing	6. marry + ed	10. enjoy + ing
3. easy + est	7. duty + ful	11. vary + ed
4. employ + able	8. carry + ed	12. greedy + est

12a(2)
Write *i* before *e*

field	grief	belief
relieve	niece	friend

except after *c*

ceiling	deceive	receipt
receive	conceit	conceive

or when sounded like *ā* as in n*ei*ghbor and w*ei*gh.

Exceptions:

seize	neither	height
weird	either	foreign

Note: These are not the only exceptions to this rule. Look in your dictionary if you are not sure about the spelling of a word.

EXERCISE 2

Fill in the blanks with *ie* or *ei* to complete the following words.

1. p _____ce
2. th _____f
3. bes _____ge
4. dec _____t
5. w _____ght
6. perc _____ve
7. s _____ge
8. rel _____f
9. ch _____f
10. bel _____ve

12a(3)
Learn the different ways to make words plural.

You usually add *-s* to a singular noun to make it plural.

> fence + -s = fences   chair + -s = chairs

If a singular noun ends in *-s, -ch, -sh,* or *-x,* add *-es* to make the word plural.

> classes + -es = classes   brush + -es = brushes
> church + -es = churches   box + -es = boxes

If a singular noun ends in *-y* preceded by a consonant, change the *-y* to *-i* and add *-es* to make the word plural.

> candy + -es = candies
> party + -es = parties

If a singular noun ends in -*y* preceded by a vowel, keep the -*y* and add -*s* to make the word plural.

> joy + -s = joys
> key + -s = keys

If a singular noun ends in -*fe,* change the -*fe* to -*ve* and add -*s* to make the word plural.

> life + -s = lives
> knife + -s = knives

Exceptions: safe + -s = safes
café + -s = cafés

If a singular noun ends in -*f,* change the -*f* to -*v* and add -*es* to make the word plural.

> half + -es = halves
> leaf + -es = leaves

Exceptions: belief + -s = beliefs
dwarf + -s = dwarfs
OR
dwarf + -es = dwarves

Add -*es* to some singular nouns that end in *o* to make them plural.

> hero + -es = heroes
> potato + -es = potatoes

Note: Not all singular nouns that end in *-o* take *-es* to make them plural. Look in your dictionary if you are not sure about the plural form of a word.

Exception: Add *-s* to the first word of singular combination words to make them plural.

> mother-in-law + *-s* = mothers-in-law
> head of state + *-s* = heads of state

Some singular nouns change their spelling without adding *-s* to make them plural.

> woman = women
> child = children

Some singular nouns do not change at all in the plural.

> A *deer* jumped into the clearing.
> I saw three *deer* beside the road.

EXERCISE 3

Make the following singular nouns plural.

1. study
2. noise
3. man
4. pass
5. valley
6. match
7. stereo
8. sister-in-law
9. industry
10. business
11. tomato
12. mix
13. foot
14. child
15. belief
16. sheep

12a(4)

Learn the difference between words ending in *-ent* and *-ence* and between words ending in *-ant* and *-ance*.

Some words may sound the same when you say them quickly, but they do not mean the same thing.

ADJECTIVES	ADJECTIVES USED WITH THE NOUNS THEY DESCRIBE
different	That is a *different* idea.
important	This is an *important* letter.
convenient	That is a *convenient* restaurant.
patient	He is a *patient* teacher.
present	All students are *present* today.

NOUNS	NOUNS USED BY THEMSELVES
difference	That is the *difference*.
importance	This letter has *importance*.
convenience	A dishwasher is a kitchen *convenience*.
patience	He has little *patience*.
patients	The emergency room was full of *patients*.
presents	Put the *presents* under the tree.
presence	I sensed the *presence* of my father in the room.

WRONG WORD	Another different between these two restaurants is the hours they are open.
RIGHT WORD	Another *difference* between these two restaurants is the hours they are open.
WRONG WORD	J. J. is a very intelligence dog.
RIGHT WORD	J. J. is a very *intelligent* dog.
WRONG WORD	Don has more patient that I have.
RIGHT WORD	Don has more *patience* than I have.

Note: If you are in doubt about the way to spell the form of the word you need, it is best to find the word in your dictionary. For example, your dictionary can show you that *evident* and *evidence* are two different words.

ev·i·dence (ev ə dent[t]s) *n*: an outward sign; something that furnishes proof

ev·i·dent (ev ə dent) *adj*: clear to the vision or understanding

EXERCISE 4

Correct the following sentences by changing the spelling of any word forms spelled incorrectly.

1. No one is going to strike my neighbor in J. J.'s present.
2. Probably the main different between Mary and Elmer is their personalities.
3. The detective has found no evident to support his suspicions.
4. A nurse's aide has to be patience.
5. They are from two difference faiths.
6. The new shopping center in the middle of town is the most convenience place to shop.
7. I don't understand the significant of what you are saying.
8. Living in Germany is much difference from living in the United States.
9. It takes a lot of intelligent to get a college degree.
10. In the nursing home there are many patience to help.

12a(5)

After a word ending in silent -*e*, drop the -*e* when you add an ending beginning with a vowel. Keep the -*e* when the ending begins with a consonant.

state + -ed = stated
hope + -ing = hoping
BUT
state + -ment = statement
hope + -less = hopeless

EXERCISE 5

Add the endings indicated to the following words, and write the resulting words correctly.

■ **Example** rake + -ing *raking*

1. hope + -ful _____
2. taste + -ed _____
3. use + -less _____
4. come + -ing _____
5. phone + -ed _____
6. bite + -ing _____
7. bone + -less _____
8. dine + -ing _____

12a(6)

Double the consonant before adding an ending when you hear a short vowel sound; do not double the consonant when you hear a long vowel sound.

You can hear some vowels say their name. A short vowel does *not* say its name: *quĭt*. A long vowel *does* say its name: *quīte*.

SHORT	LONG
can	cane [You hear ā.]
bit	bite [You hear ī.]

When you must add an ending that begins with a vowel to a word, listen to the vowel before the ending. If it is short, you usually double the consonant before adding the ending; if it is long, you do *not* double the consonant.

> begin (short) + -ing = beginning
> dine (long) + -ing = dining
>
> hop (short) + -ed = hopped
> hope (long) + -ed = hoped

EXERCISE 6

Write long or short next to each of the following to indicate the sound of the italicized vowel.

1. later _____
2. latter _____
3. spiting _____
4. spitting _____
5. cutting _____

6. roped _____
7. pod _____
8. lane _____
9. sitter _____
10. sited _____

EXERCISE 7

Put a check mark in column **A** or **B** to indicate the correct spelling of the following.

A	**B**
1. brakeing _____	braking _____
2. hamer _____	hammer _____
3. writing _____	writting _____
4. equiped _____	equipped _____
5. dining _____	dinning _____
6. ripened _____	rippened _____
7. tripping _____	triping _____
8. skinned _____	skined _____

12b

Use a hyphen (-) to join words and numbers.

12b(1)

Use a hyphen to join two or more words that work together as one word to describe another word, except when the words follow the word they describe.

middle-aged woman
well-known writer

The woman was *middle aged.*
The writer was *well known.*

If you are in doubt, look in your dictionary to find out when to use a hyphen between two words joined to describe another word.

12b(2)
Use a hyphen when you spell out compound numbers from twenty-one to ninety-nine.

> sixty-eight
> seventy-three

12b(3)
Use a hyphen with fractions.

> one-fourth
> three-fifths

12b(4)
Use a hyphen to join *self-*, *all-*, and *ex-* to a word in order to make a single word.

> self-control
> all-powerful
> ex-husband

12b(5)
Use a hyphen to divide a word at the end of a line.

There are definite places where a long word may be divided when you cannot put it all on one line of your paper. Your dictionary uses dots between the syllables of a word to show you where these places are:

> soph·o·more

See **20b(1)** for more information on dividing words.

EXERCISE 8

Add hyphens if they are needed in the following sentences.

1. All night study sessions soon become a way of life for many students.
2. I will be twenty seven on my next birthday.
3. All new employees have six weeks of on the job training before they are expected to work alone.
4. I was in Vietnam on a search and destroy mission.
5. Three fourths of my paycheck is spent before I even get it.
6. The surprisingly mild mannered nurse was a relief after the quick tempered doctor.
7. Many gas stations now have self service only.
8. We used to live in a five room apartment with orange shag wall to wall carpeting.
9. The party is a once a month affair.
10. The middle class neighborhood has changed a lot since I moved away.

12c
Avoid writing extra letters or omitting letters by counting syllables in the words you write.

Every syllable has a separate vowel sound. You can sometimes avoid misspelling words you are uncertain about by counting the syllables in those words.

Remember: Just count the vowel sounds, not the vowels themselves.

> su·per (two vowels and two vowel sounds)
> cool (two vowels yet one vowel sound)

Counting syllables can avoid some common misspellings.

WRONG	RIGHT
garabage (three syllables)	garbage (two syllables)
ingridents (three syllables)	ingredients (four syllables)

EXERCISE 9

Count the number of vowel sounds that should be in each word. Then check the correct spelling.

A	B
1. convient _____	convenient _____
2. interest _____	intrest _____
3. experince _____	experience _____
4. a quite room _____	a quiet room _____
5. flor _____	flower _____
6. The world was created. _____	The world was crated. _____
7. materal _____	material _____
8. rember _____	remember _____

CHAPTER THIRTEEN

Commas and No Commas

> *Use a comma when you need it.*

Some students feel that the comma was invented only to cause problems in writing. Others decide where commas go in a sentence by reading the sentence aloud and placing commas wherever they pause or vary their tone of voice. Both groups of students could manage the comma correctly and easily if they would learn the reasons for using commas and use commas only when there is a reason.

13a
Use a comma and a coordinating conjunction (*and, but, or, nor, for, so,* or *yet*) to separate two main clauses.

As you know, two main clauses cannot be correctly separated by a comma alone (see **3c**), but when these clauses are joined by a *coordinating conjunction,* the comma gives the slight separation needed.

> There was a steady rain the day that I arrived home, *and* I had the impression that it would never stop.
> It was almost too late to get a ticket for the Stones concert, *but* I do not give up easily.

13b
Use a comma between a dependent and a main clause when the dependent clause comes first in the sentence.

A dependent clause is commonly introduced by a *subordinating conjunction* like *when, after, before, if, although, unless, because,* and *since.* When the dependent clause comes before the main clause, use a comma between the two clauses.

DEPENDENT CLAUSE	Because it rained every day for a week
MAIN CLAUSE	We could not go on the camping trip.
WITH COMMA	*Because* it rained every day for a week, we could not go on the camping trip.

Notice that if the dependent clause comes last, a comma is *not* used.

WITHOUT COMMA	We could not go on the camping trip *because* it rained every day for a week.
DEPENDENT CLAUSE	When the wind blows from the north
MAIN CLAUSE	The house creaks and groans.
WITH COMMA	*When* the wind blows from the north, the house creaks and groans.
WITHOUT COMMA	The house creaks and groans *when* the wind blows from the north.

EXERCISE 1

Correct any errors in the use of commas in the following sentences by adding or omitting a comma when necessary.

■ **Example**   We felt much more intelligent after we received our diplomas, but I'm not sure we really were.

1. Changes in women's roles became evident, when women entered more demanding fields of study.

2. Zaroff saw Rainsford as a challenge, because he was a well-known hunter and was very different from sailors he had hunted previously.

3. When Henry VIII challenged the authority of the pope, he was taking an important step in the history of the English church.

4. Amanda wanted Tom to bring home a gentleman caller for Laura so she did not stop nagging him until he produced one.

5. Although there are many requirements for the ideal husband I will list only a few.

6. I like to cook all the time, when I am at home.

7. When it was time to leave for the day my car wouldn't start.

8. While you are driving, keep my directions handy to avoid making the wrong turn.

EXERCISE 2

Edit the following paragraph, correcting any errors in the use of the comma between clauses.

> There is one important difference between the water-skier and the snow-skier, and that difference is the amount of physical exertion an individual uses. Although the water-skier is being pulled while skiing, he usually has to lean back on his skis and hold on to the tow rope. Because of his position on the skis, he uses many leg, arm, and back muscles to maintain his balance, he can tire easily due to the strenuous effort required. The snow-skier positions himself forward on his skis and his boots help to support his leg and ankle muscles to help him maintain good body control. His ski poles help him keep his balance. The snow-skier doesn't use the same muscles as the water-skier so he can set his own pace and ski for longer distances than the water-skier.

13c
Use commas between the words or groups of words in a series or list. (See also 14b.)

Notice how the commas are used in the following sentences.

> The room was small, dingy, and cold.
> Make your breakfast table beautiful with a bowl of apples, oranges, bananas, and pears.
> Pearl ran down the stairs, threw her books on the table, grabbed her coat, and started toward the door.

If you are not sure about the use of the comma in the last sentence, look at the series or list of things that Pearl did:

Pearl {
ran down the stairs,
threw her books on the table,
grabbed her coat,
    and
started toward the door.

13d

Use commas between adjectives such as *large, small, dark, beautiful, exciting,* and *noisy* in place of the word *and.* If *and* cannot be used, a comma is not needed.

Either the comma or *and* shows that both of the adjectives refer to the person or thing being described.

Study the following sentences, which use either a comma or the word *and* between adjectives.

She came running into the large, empty room.
She came running into the large *and* empty room.

It was a noisy, exciting race.
It was a noisy *and* exciting race.

The only clue was a small, dark stain on the carpet.
The only clue was a small *and* dark stain on the carpet. [The words *small* and *dark* both describe *stain.* The word *and* can substitute for the comma.]

Study the following sentences, which do not need either a comma or the word *and* between the adjectives.

He wore a bright blue sweater.
He wore a bright and blue sweater. [*Blue* describes *sweater,* and *bright* describes the color *blue.* Neither a comma nor *and* is needed.]

Both of the girls had dark brown hair.
Both of the girls had dark and brown hair. [*Dark* describes *brown,* and *brown* describes *hair.* Neither a comma nor *and* is needed.]

13e
Use commas to set off, or separate, the name of a person to whom you are speaking.

If the name of a person is simply mentioned in the sentence, the commas are not needed.

> Jim, take the books to the library. [A comma is used because someone is speaking *to* Jim.]
> Jim will take the books to the library. [Someone is speaking *about* Jim, and no comma is needed.]
>
> Wait, Angie, and I will go with you. [Angie is spoken *to*.]
> The two girls asked Angie to wait for them. [Angie is spoken *about*.]

13f
Use commas to separate the names of speakers from their exact, or quoted, words.

> Earlene said, "The books must go the library before Tuesday."
> "The books," Earlene said, "must go to the library before Tuesday."
> "The books must go to the library before Tuesday," Earlene said.

See Section **16a** for a more complete discussion.

EXERCISE 3

Add commas where they are needed in the following sentences. Look back at **13c, 13d, 13e,** and **13f** if you need help.

1. You will need a bowl two spoons a cup and a plate.
2. A twisted rotten tree crashed through the porch roof.
3. Melinda had small delicate hands and narrow feet.
4. Did you see Sylvia last night?
5. Catch the ball Sally.
6. Joe's car had a flat tire a broken headlight two dented fenders and a cracked windshield.

7. The boys ran and jumped and yelled all afternoon.

8. Wilbur asked "Where are the papers and cans for collection?"

9. Irene wore a beautiful emerald bracelet.

10. "The meeting will be held tomorrow" said Mr. Mason.

13g

Use commas to separate the parts of names of places, dates, and addresses.

If only one item in a place name, date, or address is used, it is not separated by commas from the rest of the sentence.

> Norfolk, Virginia, is the location of the famous Azalea Gardens.
> The Azalea Gardens are located in Norfolk. [name of city only]
> Virginia has many beautiful flowers in the spring. [name of state only]

> Please send the package to Mrs. C. R. Chesterton, Lyman, Wyoming 82937. [The zip code is not separated by a comma from the name of the state.]
> Please send the package to Mrs. C. R. Chesterton in Wyoming. [Only the name of the state is given. A comma is not needed.]

> The main office is located at 317 Palm Avenue, Summerfield, Oklahoma 74966.

> We will arrive on Sunday, July 17, 1977.

If the day of the month is not given, the comma may be left out.

> He will start his new job in August 1977.

EXERCISE 4

Add commas where they are needed in the following sentences.

1. My sister moved to Lewisville Texas in June 1969.

2. Dave's new address is 21786 Hallwood Drive Walnut Creek California 94595.

3. The celebration was scheduled for the last Friday in September.

4. Plainfield Kansas is a small town where all of the people know each other.

13h
Use commas to separate a word or a group of words that may add information but are not essential to the meaning of the sentence.

13h(1)
Use commas around a phrase that gives nonessential information about a person or thing.

Sometimes a person or thing is renamed or described, but the word or group of words that is used is not necessary to the meaning of the sentence.

> Mary, *the girl in the red dress,* will be the first one in the talent show.

The words *the girl in the red dress* help to describe Mary, but the meaning of the sentence does not depend on them. The group of words is properly separated from the rest of the sentence by commas.

> Mary will be the first one in the talent show.

> Barbara has a wonderful job as a model.
> Barbara, *my sister,* has a wonderful job as a model. [The words *Barbara* and *my sister* describe the same person, but the fact that Barbara is someone's sister is not a necessary part of the sentence.]

13h(2)
Use commas around a *who* or *which* expression (relative clause) when it is not essential to the meaning of the sentence.

When a clause beginning with *who* or *which* does not restrict or limit the person or thing it describes, you should put commas around it.

These commas suggest that you could separate it from the sentence without changing your meaning.

> Joe Greene, *who studies hard,* can get good grades.

Here the relative clause *who studies hard* is not essential to the meaning of the sentence. The important thing is that Joe Greene can get good grades. Contrast this sentence:

> Any student *who studies hard* can get good grades.

Here the relative clause *who studies hard* is essential because you are not saying that any student can get good grades—only a student who studies hard.

13h(3)

Use commas to separate parenthetical expressions such as *however, therefore, for example, as a result, in fact,* and *in that case* from the rest of the sentence. They are called parenthetical because they are not emphasized. They could be put in parentheses or omitted.

These words may be used at the beginning, in the middle, or at the end of the sentence. They are called *transitional* because they take the reader from one point to another.

> *As a result,* air and water pollution are increasing every day.
> The tire, *however,* will need to be balanced before it is used.
> They knew, *in fact,* that a mistake had been made.
> Not all dogs get along with small children, *for example.*

Caution: When words such as *however, therefore, for example, as a result, in fact,* and *in that case* are used between main clauses, a semicolon is used before the word or words, and a comma is used after them. (See also **3b** and **14a**.)

The score was forty-two to six at the half; *therefore*, the coach gave everyone on our team a chance to play.

13h(4)
Use commas to separate introductory expressions containing participles or infinitives from the rest of the sentence.

Much embarrassed, Mr. Martin left the room.
Moving rapidly, the last runner began to catch up with the rest of the group.
After selecting the lettuce and radishes, wash them carefully and chill them before it is time to make the salad.
To remove any lint, clean each windowpane with a paper towel.

13h(5)
Use commas after words such as *first, next, last, finally*, and *in conclusion* when these words begin a sentence.

These words show the time order of the events you are writing about and should be separated from the rest of the sentence by a comma.

First, review the materials you need for the job.
Finally, write a conclusion that makes your paper seem complete.

13h(6)
Expressions such as *I hope, I believe, she says*, and *I think* are separated from the rest of the sentence by commas when they are used as interrupters.

This is, *I believe*, the last time it will happen.
The money, *she says*, must last for the rest of the month.

Notice that when the expression is used at the beginning of the sentence, the rest of the sentence tells what is believed or said. In this case a comma should *not* be used.

> I believe this is the last time it will happen.
> She says the money must last for the rest of the month.

13i
Use commas to make your meaning clear.

You may have to think carefully about what you mean to say. The following sentences use the same words in the same order, but notice that the meaning of the sentence is reversed when commas are added.

> Women say the men are more suitable for that work.
> Women, say the men, are more suitable for that work.

In the first sentence women are speaking, and they say that men are better for a particular job. In the second sentence men are speaking, and the men say that the women are better for the job.

EXERCISE 5

Add commas and semicolons where they are needed in the following sentences.

1. Mr. Jenkins our neighbor won a new car last week.
2. There are however some good reasons for not smoking.
3. The boy who wrecked the car was not even scratched I believe.
4. We are Matt thinks part of a nationwide experiment.
5. We had three great days to enjoy our vacation at the beach as a result we all had terrible sunburns.
6. I say that we need a larger student recreation room.

7. Next decide which refreshments you will serve at the party.

8. Putting aside all doubts the people should move ahead with the plans.

9. George believes we will win the election therefore he has stopped trying to get votes.

Commas are used in the following ways. Read this list before doing Exercise 6.

1. Commas are used with coordinating conjunctions $\left\{\begin{array}{l} and \\ but \\ or \\ nor \\ for \end{array}\right\}$ to separate two main clauses.

2. Commas are used between dependent and main clauses when the dependent clause comes first.

3. Commas are used between the words or grouis of words in a series or list.

4. Commas are used between adjectives in place of *and*.

5. Commas are used to set off, or separate, the name of the person to whom you are speaking.

6. Commas are used to separate the names of speakers from their exact words.

7. Commas are used to separate the parts of names of places, dates, and addresses.

8. Commas are used to separate words or groups of words that may add information but are not essential to the meaning of the sentence.

EXERCISE 6

Add commas where they are needed in the following sentences.

1. Good drivers pay attention to the driving regulations and they are aware of other drivers on the road.

2. When Gail went to class yesterday she forgot to take some of her books with her.

3. The counter was stacked with dishes pots glasses cups and towels.

4. The old wrinkled man jumped up and threw the ball.
5. Here Martha is the recipe for the chocolate cake.
6. Mike said "The team will never win without Gill in the line."
7. May 21 1914 is an important date in that little town.
8. She lives in Norton Iowa at 2115 Graham Street.
9. Cross the bridge taking a right at the first stoplight.
10. Bob Jamison one of my classmates wrote the article.

13j
Do not use a comma to separate the subject from its verb.

	(subject)	(verb)

WRONG   Many people with dogs, never train them properly.
RIGHT   Many people with dogs never train them properly.

Be on your guard for this problem when your subject has more than one verb and when the second verb is not close to its subject.

(subject) (verb)   (verb)

WRONG   Biff never accepts life as it is, but wants life to conform to his dream.
RIGHT   Biff never accepts life as it is but wants life to conform to his dreams.

13k
Do not use a comma to separate the verb from its object

(verb)   (object)

WRONG   The two women *brought*, great *bunches* of flowers to the hospital every week.
RIGHT   The two women brought great bunches of flowers to the hospital every week.

Be on your guard for this problem when a verb has more than one object.

	(verb)	(object)	(object)
WRONG	Stanley divorced Catherine, and then Anne.		
RIGHT	Stanley divorced Catherine and then Anne.		

EXERCISE 7

Copy the following sentences. Omit any commas that are not needed.

1. King Henry VIII broke away from the Church, and made himself head of the Church of England.
2. All of the students with green sweaters, went to the platform.
3. Three of the boys found, boxes from the wreck.
4. The girl with red hair, was the best dancer at the party.
5. Sally's mother usually cooked, spaghetti with meatballs on Thursday.
6. Amanda is full of contradictions, and moves between the real world and her dream world.

131

Do not put commas around a *who* or *that* expression (relative clause) when it is essential to the meaning of the sentence.

When a clause beginning with *who* or *that* restricts or limits the person or thing it describes, you should not put commas around it. You omit these commas because you want to make clear what particular person or thing you are writing about.

WRONG	My aunt tells everyone, who will listen, about all her valuable antiques. [This is misleading because it suggests that everyone will listen when your aunt talks about her

antiques. She does not succeed in telling everyone—just
those people who will listen.]

RIGHT   My aunt tells everyone who will listen about all her valuable antiques.

13m

Do not use a comma before the first word or after the last word in a list or series.

WRONG   We planted, beets, peas, beans, and potatoes, in the garden.
RIGHT   We planted beets, peas, beans, and potatoes in the garden.

WRONG   Hard work, dedication, and many hours, will be needed
to complete that job.
RIGHT   Hard work, dedication, and many hours will be needed
to complete that job.

13n

Do not use a comma between adjectives if *and* cannot substitute for the comma.

WRONG   The team wore pale, green shirts and dark, green pants.
[The shirts were pale green, not pale and green; the pants
were dark green, not dark and green.]
RIGHT   The team wore pale green shirts and dark green pants.

WRONG   The noisy, jet plane ruined the music. [The jet plane was
noisy.]
RIGHT   The noisy jet plane ruined the music.

EXERCISE 8

Copy the following sentences. Omit any commas that are not needed.

1. Homer, and Kelly went to Pleasant Hill Community College for two
years.

2. Robert picked up the bat, and hit the ball over the high fence.
3. Some people may own five suits, and only one shirt.
4. Each desk held books, paper, and pencils.
5. The shiny, green van had a dark, blue stripe around the top.

13o
Do not use a comma when separating a dependent clause from a main clause if the dependent clause comes last in the sentence.

> **DEPENDENT CLAUSE FIRST** *If it rains on Tuesday and Wednesday,* we will go next week.
>
> **DEPENDENT CLAUSE LAST** We will go next week *if it rains on Tuesday and Wednesday.*

13p
Do not use a comma between the name of a state and the zip code.

> **WRONG** He lives at 809 Bernau Avenue, Greensboro, North Carolina, 27407.
>
> **RIGHT** He lives at 809 Bernau Avenue, Greensboro, North Carolina 27407.

13q
Do not use a comma unless there is a reason.

It is usually better to leave out needed commas than to add unnecessary commas. Read the following sentences and avoid similar mistakes.

> **WRONG** The music sounded, like thunder.
>
> **RIGHT** The music sounded like thunder.

WRONG	The resolution passed, by one vote.
RIGHT	The resolution passed by one vote.
WRONG	When traveling, by back roads, be sure to have a full gas tank.
RIGHT	When traveling by back roads, be sure to have a full gas tank.

You have studied the following rules about commas. Reread them before doing Exercise 9.

1. Do not use a comma to separate the subject from its verb.

2. Do not use a comma to separate the verb from its object.

3. Do not put commas around information essential to the meaning of the sentence.

4. Do not use a comma before the first word or after the last word in a series or list.

5. Do not use a comma between adjectives if *and* cannot substitute for the comma.

6. When separating a dependent clause from a main clause, the comma is not needed if the dependent clause is very short or if it comes last in the sentence.

7. Do not use a comma between the name of a state and the zip code.

8. Do not use a comma without having a reason.

EXERCISE 9

Add commas where they are needed in the following sentences. If any sentence is correct, write C next to it. Remove any unnecessary commas.

1. Garnet ran around the block twice but Jim only laughed and shook his head.

2. The boy with red hair can play a guitar sing and tap dance.

3. The newspaper reported three serious traffic accidents yesterday.

4. You will need pencil paper and eraser.

5. Graham had three dogs and two cats.

6. The marchers carried a large American flag.

7. The winter has been a cold snowy one.

8. If the delivery truck from Eason's comes before noon I will be there to pick up my materials.

9. The reporter was not there when the crowd came down the street.

10. Send the package to Mr. Harding in Jewett Illinois 62436.

11. I find that, when I play the piano, I can make up tunes to fit my many moods.

12. Start washing from the top of the car making sure you are loosening the dirt.

13. Clothes, such as fur coats and military uniforms often suggest a person's social position.

14. Where is the 7-Eleven that is closest to school?

EXERCISE 10

Add commas wherever needed in the following paragraph.

My room the sunniest of the four bedrooms is in the back of the house. In it I have pictures of apes a king-size bed a color TV set and my most prized possession my new stereo which cost over $4,000 and which includes two Bose 91 speakers a 200 watt-per-channel SONY receiver, an AIWA cassette deck a Pioneer computerized turntable and a graphic equalizer with built-in mixer. As you can certainly see I have all that is needed to make me a comfortable happy person until the bills start arriving.

CHAPTER FOURTEEN

The Semicolon

Use the semicolon between closely related main clauses and between groups of words that already contain commas.
Use the semicolon only when the parts to be joined are equal in importance.

14a

Use a semicolon between two main clauses that are closely related.

The semicolon is sometimes called a "weak period"; when it is used between two main clauses, it takes the place of a period at the end of the first sentence. Notice that the second sentence does not begin with a capital letter because it has been joined to the first sentence by the semicolon.

> John did not know what to do; he stood in the middle of the room and tried to decide how to move the boxes.

The above sentence is made up of two main clauses which have been joined by a semicolon. The sentences could be written separately:

John did not know what to do. He stood in the middle of the room and tried to decide how to move the boxes.

When both are closely related main clauses, the choice is up to you, the writer. Because you have a choice, you can vary the length of sentences and make your papers more interesting than they would be with only short, choppy sentences. Read the following examples.

Jim has never played football. He doesn't enjoy the game.
Jim has never played football; he doesn't enjoy the game.

The rain poured down. Mud ran into the street.
The rain poured down; mud ran into the street.

14b
Use connecting words like *also, however, still,* or *then* after a semicolon to introduce a main clause.

Some words or groups of words tell something about when or how the action of the sentence is taking place. These words are different from the coordinating conjunctions *and, but, or, so, yet, nor,* and *for,* which can be used with a comma to connect two finished sentences. (See also **13a**.) The connecting words have a semicolon in front of them and are usually followed by a comma. Some of these words are

also	however	nevertheless
as a result	in addition	on the other hand
besides	in fact	still
for example	instead	then
furthermore	meanwhile	therefore

The people were tired and hungry; *as a result,* no progress was made.
Love is a universal emotion; *still,* some people never know love.
Billie pushed all of the chairs and tables out of the room; *then* she started cleaning the dirty floor.

Words such as *also* and *however* can be used to introduce main clauses. When they are used as interrupters, however, they are usually set off from the rest of the sentence by commas.

USED AS CONNECTOR   It is my book; however, you are welcome to use it.

USED AS INTERRUPTER   Sally needs the book, *however,* by to-morrow.

14c
Use semicolons between groups of words that already contain commas.

This use of the semicolon helps the reader find the main divisions of the sentence and makes the ideas clear.

Mr. Howard bought a pot, knives, and bowls; two folding tables; and three kinds of bread from Graham's Bakery.

Some drivers seem to count every fence post; examine, discuss, and reject every side road; and enjoy delaying traffic.

14d
Do not carelessly use a semicolon instead of a comma.

14d(1)
Do not use a semicolon between a main clause and a dependent clause.

WRONG   When cold weather comes; many of the birds fly south. [The first part of the sentence is not complete. It should be separated from the complete portion by a comma.]

RIGHT   When cold weather comes, many of the birds fly south.

WRONG   While we watched with amazement; five men came running from the house.

RIGHT   While we watched with amazement, five men came running from the house.

RIGHT   Five men came running from the house while we watched with amazement. [No punctuation is needed between clauses since the main clause comes first.]

14d(2)

Do not use a semicolon between two main clauses separated by a coordinating conjunction. A comma is the correct mark to use. (See also 13a.)

WRONG   All of my friends like baseball; but I just can't get excited about the game.

RIGHT   All of my friends like baseball, *but* I just can't get excited about the game.

WRONG   Everyone talks about the need for good management in government; and no one does anything about it.

RIGHT   Everyone talks about the need for good management in government, *and* no one does anything about it.

14e

Do not confuse the semicolon and the colon.

The semicolon separates two main clauses, but the colon calls attention to what follows. (See also **17d**.)

SEMICOLON   Pick up your supplies tomorrow; be sure to have everything with you on Friday.

COLON   On Friday, bring the following supplies: a tack hammer, large tacks, a yard of burlap, and two yards of denim.

SEMICOLON   The provost talked about student government; the entire student body listened with interest.

COLON   The provost called for two things: more active participation in student government and involvement in community affairs.

14f

Do not use a semicolon unless you have a reason for it.

Some writers seem to use the semicolon for no particular reason. When you use a semicolon, make sure you are using it for one of the following purposes:

1. to divide two closely related main clauses.
2. to separate items that already contain commas.

EXERCISE 1

Use semicolons and commas correctly in the following sentences.

1. When Ruby found the lost dog she took it home with her.
2. All the books are here pick the ones you need.
3. Most people want good jobs however some people don't want to work.
4. Freedom isn't free it must be earned and guarded.
5. The car hit two trees a fence and Mr. Adam's bicycle.
6. Everyone went to the beach for a picnic as a result the package was not delivered.
7. After the mayor spoke there was a beautiful display of fireworks.
8. Ten families live on that block and they all have dogs.
9. Education is very important but not everyone should study the same things.
10. Our new neighbors were critical of small cars nevertheless they gladly accepted one as a gift.

EXERCISE 2

In some of the following sentences, the semicolon is incorrectly used. Correct any errors by omitting unnecessary semicolons and substituting commas when necessary. Write C next to any sentence in which the semicolon is correctly used.

■ **Example** The price of gas, the number of traffic accidents, and mechanical, car-related problems lead me to think that we would be better off⸖by returning to the horse and buggy for transportation.

1. You can talk to and love a horse; people would think you were crazy if you did this with an automobile.

2. When you feed your horse at home; you eliminate the need for gas stations and the long lines that usually are associated with them.

3. The horse can graze in your yard; and keep the grass trimmed.

4. The output of a horse is excellent fertilizer; while the output of cars is only pollution.

5. I believe the rate of collisions will be greatly reduced; because your mind will be working with that of the horse.

6. Let's face it; two heads are better than one; even if one of the two belongs to a horse.

7. Finally, horses will never have mechanical problems; and they respond to care in a personal way.

8. Cars come from assembly lines; horses come from other horses through a natural process that has enabled them to survive and be useful for many years.

CHAPTER FIFTEEN
The Apostrophe

The apostrophe (') is used to show possession or omission and to form some plural words.

The apostrophe is placed near the top of the written word in which it is used.

15a
The apostrophe shows that something belongs to or is related to something else.

The ideas of possession or relationship can be expressed in other ways, but the apostrophe makes it possible to write those ideas in fewer words.

WITH APOSTROPHE	WITHOUT APOSTROPHE
Jamie's book	the book that belongs to Jamie
everyone's hope	the hope of everyone
the cat's favorite food	the favorite food of the cat
a day's work	the work accomplished in a day
tomorrow's class	the class for tomorrow
a dollar's worth of gas	the amount of gas that is worth a dollar

Notice that the **'s** is not the same as an *-s* that is added to a noun to make it plural.

I saw the boy's car. [The car belongs to the boy.]
The boys saw the car. [Several boys saw the car.]

She slept in the girls' cabin.
She slept with the girls in their cabin.

For things which are not alive, the 's is frequently dropped or replaced by the words *of* or *in*.

the table leg   the leg of the table
the kitchen stove   the stove in the kitchen

There are certain ways to add the 's to words to show possession, as in the following examples.

15a(1)
If the name of a person or thing does not end in -s, add the 's.

Mary's dog was hit by a car.
Wind blew down the store's sign.

15a(2)
Use either 's or only ' after a word that ends in s.

If the extra *s* makes pronunciation difficult, the apostrophe by itself is acceptable.

Mr. Hopkins's car was stolen.
Mr. Hopkins' car was stolen.

15a(3)
If the noun is plural (meaning more than one), use this guide: write the plural form of the noun. If this plural form ends in -s, add an apostrophe. If it does not end in -s, add an apostrophe + s.

The children's feet made muddy tracks on the floor.
The men's hats were on the table.
[*Children* and *men* are plural words which do not end in *s*. Add 's.]

The little girls' toys were scattered over the yard.

The boys' jackets had disappeared.

[*Girls* and *boys* are plural words which do end in *-s*. Add ' only.]

EXERCISE 1

Copy the following sentences. Add apostrophes where they are needed.

1. The happiness on Carols face was enough of a reward for them.
2. My wifes family lives next door.
3. Our traffic controllers strike lasted several months.
4. Mrs. Hargis party was talked about for a week.
5. Albert Gans outburst shows a great sense of guilt.

15b

There are special rules for the use of the apostrophe with nouns and pronouns.

15b(1)

Use apostrophes with nouns to show possession; do *not* use apostrophes with pronouns to show possession.

Pronouns use apostrophes only in contractions. Unlike nouns, pronouns show possession without the aid of apostrophes.

Mary's book   BUT   *her* book

Do *not* use the apostrophe to show possession in *mine, yours, his, hers, its, ours, theirs,* or *whose.*

These special words already show ownership.

WRONG		RIGHT	
hi's	her's	his	hers
it's	our's	its	ours
your's	their's	yours	theirs
	who'se		whose

Here is John's sweater.
Here is *his* sweater.

That book belongs to Sally.
That book is *hers*.

15b(2)
**Pronouns that end in *one* or *body* are treated like nouns. They
should have 's added.**

EXERCISE 2

Copy the following sentences. Select the correct word to complete
each one.

1. Has _____ book been returned?
   (everybody's, everybodies)

2. It could have been _____
   mistake. (anybody's, anybodys)

3. The car lost _____ muffler
   when we hit a bump. (it's, its)

4. Do you know _____ painting
   won the prize? (who'se, whose)

5. She dropped _____ coat in
   the fish pond. (her's, her)

15c
**If something belongs to two or more people (joint
ownership), use 's with only the last of the names.**

> I went to Jane and Sally**'s** apartment. [Two people live in one
> apartment.]
> I went to Jane**'s** and Sally**'s** apartments. [Two people each have their
> own apartment.]
> The new coffee shop is named Mike and Ed**'s**. [Two people own the
> business.]

Words with hyphens have **'s** added to the last word only.

> Jack drove his brother-in-law**'s** car.
> The governor-elect**'s** speech was very boring.

EXERCISE 3

Add *'s* where needed in the following sentences.

1. The neighbor dog and our cat are always fighting.
2. Did you hear that John and Bill car was completely wrecked?
3. We saw Nita and Gina new stereos yesterday.
4. The man was wearing my father-in-law new hat.
5. He was quite impressed by the senator-elect article on tax reform.

15d
The apostrophe in contractions is used to show omission.

15d(1)
Use an apostrophe to show that a word has been shortened or that two words have been made into one by the omission of one or more letters.

This shortening is called a *contraction.*

CONTRACTED FORMS	LONG FORMS
o'clock	of the clock
we'll	we will
can't	cannot
don't	do not
class of '75	class of 1975
rock 'n' roll	rock and roll
they're	they are

Remember to spell contractions correctly by placing the apostrophe where the letter has been omitted.

isn't	NOT	is'nt
aren't	NOT	are'nt
wasn't	NOT	was'nt
weren't	NOT	were'nt
doesn't	NOT	does'nt
don't	NOT	do'nt
hasn't	NOT	has'nt
haven't	NOT	have'nt

15d(2)
Do not confuse *its* and *it's*.

Its is a possessive pronoun, which means that something belongs to *it*.

> Turn down that radio; *its* volume is too loud. [The volume of the radio is too loud.]

It's is a contraction meaning *it is*.

> Turn down that radio; it**'s** too loud. [The radio (it) is too loud.]

15d(3)
Do not use *'s* when you need only add *-s* to form the plural of a noun.

Only the special uses given in **15e** call for **'s** for plurals.

WRONG	Both front tire's were flat.
RIGHT	Both front tires were flat.

15d(4)

Know the meaning of some common contractions so that you do not confuse them in writing.

Sometimes students confuse certain contractions because they do not pronounce them distinctly. Here are the meanings of some frequently confused contractions.

I'm (I am)	I'll (I will)	I've (I have)	I'd (I had or I would)
you're (you are)	you'll (you will)	you've (you have)	you'd (you had or you would)
he's (he is or he has)	he'll (he will)		he'd (he had or he would)
she's (she is or she has)	she'll (she will)		she'd (she had or she would)
we're (we are)	we'll (we will)	we've (we have)	we'd (we had or we would)
they're (they are)	they'll (they will)	they've (they have)	they'd (they had or they would)

EXERCISE 4

Circle the correct contraction in each of the following sentences.

1. (She's, she'll) always on time.
2. (We've, we'll) finished writing.
3. (I'd, I'll) find my wallet sooner if you helped me.
4. (He'd, he'll) better wait for me.
5. (He's, he'd) very happy.
6. (You've, you're) heard all the excuses by now.
7. (They'll, they'd) come if they were able.
8. (I'm, I'd) going if I can.

EXERCISE 5

Add apostrophes where needed to show contractions in the following sentences.

1. Trudy said that they wouldnt be late.
2. My brother graduated in the class of 68.
3. The crowd lost its temper.
4. I dont know whats happening, but its something important.
5. Mary really liked that dress; its too bad that its sleeve is torn.
6. You cant imagine what a hurricane is like if youve never been through one.
7. Thats when you make your move.
8. Dont buy a dress you wouldn't wear in public.

15e
Use the apostrophe to form the plural of numbers, letters, and words referred to as words.

> The printer put *s*'**s** after all of the names, and half of the 5's are upside down.
> Put circles around the *and*'**s**.
> He spells his name with two *l*'**s**.
> Your paper would be better if you left out the *wow*'**s** and *oh*'**s**.
> The 1920'**s** were called the Jazz Years.

Note: Decades can also be written without the apostrophe.

> The 1920s were called the Jazz Years.

EXERCISE 6

Edit the following paragraph, correcting all errors in the use of the apostrophe.

> My ever-borrowing sister Edith came dashing up the stair's wearing a coat that was definitely not her's. She tossed Kevins' book on the table and gasped when she saw that it was seven o clock and that she was already late for a date with Francis brother. "Its late, but if he doesnt hurry, Ill make it," she said to herself. "Ive no clothes to wear; however, maybe I can borrow Jill's shirt, my mothers sweater, and my aunts bracelet. I cant believe theyll miss those things tonight."

CHAPTER SIXTEEN

Quotation Marks

> *Use quotation marks around the exact words*
> *of a writer or speaker and for some titles.*
> *Quotation marks may also be used to indicate*
> *words used as words.*

16a

When the exact words of a writer or speaker are repeated, or quoted, by another person, the words are enclosed in quotation marks.

The speaker may be named before, after, or in the middle of the quotation. The name of the speaker is not included in the quotation marks.

> Eloise said, "Jane spent all of her money at the grocery store."
> "Jane spent all of her money at the grocery store," Eloise said.
> "Jane spent all of her money," Eloise said, "at the grocery store."

Notice that each quotation begins with a capital letter and is separated from the name of the speaker by a comma. (See also **13f**.)

If the quotation is broken or separated within a sentence, the first word of the second part does not begin with a capital letter.

16a(1)
If the quotation has more than one sentence, the end quotation mark is placed at the end of the last sentence.

> "The family reunion was a wonderful event," Callie said. "We met cousins we had never heard of before. Everyone brought food, and we all had a good time."

Notice that the quotation marks are placed after the comma or period that ends a quoted section.

16a(2)
If more than one speaker is quoted, begin a new paragraph each time the speaker changes.

> "Help!" screamed Laura.
> "Can you hold on?" yelled George. "I'll be there in a minute."

Notice that a comma is not used between the quotation and the name of the speaker if an exclamation point or question mark is needed.

16a(3)
A quotation within a quotation is enclosed in single marks:

> "The correct quotation is 'A penny saved is a penny earned,'" he said.

See also Section **27b(3)**.

16a(4)
Do not enclose an indirect quotation in quotation marks.

You will probably use indirect quotations in most of your writing, so learn the difference between direct and indirect quotations. The quotation is indirect if the exact words of the speaker are not used, but such words as *for, that,* or *if* are used to tell what the speaker said.

DIRECT QUOTATION	Mr. Graves asked, "Did you count the tickets?"
INDIRECT QUOTATION	Mr. Graves asked *if* we had counted the tickets.
DIRECT QUOTATION	Edward said, "I will go tomorrow."
INDIRECT QUOTATION	Edward said *that* he would go tomorrow.

16a(5)
When other marks of punctuation are used with quoted material, all punctuation marks should be in the correct order.

Place periods and commas inside quotation marks except for the period or comma that follows identification of the speaker.

"If you wait," I said, "you'll miss the bus."

Place colons and semicolons outside the quotation marks unless they are part of the quotation.

Most of us recited "The Raven"; only three chose "Kubla Khan": Eddie, Julia, and Sam. [The colon and semicolon are not part of the quoted material.]

Read and summarize "Diets: Good and Fad" by Thursday. [The colon is part of the quoted material.]

Place question marks, exclamation points, and dashes inside the quotation marks if they apply to the quotation only and outside the quotation marks if they apply to the whole sentence.

> Jimmy asked, "Did you bring the bread and the pickles?" [Only the quotation is a question.]
>
> Did that sign say "Detour Ahead"? [The sentence is a question.]

EXERCISE 1

Add quotation marks where they are needed in the following sentences.

1. The professor said, Read the next chapter and answer the questions at the end.
2. I'm not sure I understand, said Henry. Will you repeat the directions?
3. Why doesn't he listen? grumbled Gerald.
4. What a beautiful day! sang Dana as she danced down the street.
5. Is your ticket marked Use only on Tuesday?
6. Jack said that all of the material would be ready soon.

16b

Use quotation marks to enclose the titles of short stories, songs, articles in magazines, parts of books, and short poems when they are referred to in other written material. (The titles of complete books or magazines and other long works are underlined or italicized [see 19a].)

> "Variation Under Domestication" is the first chapter of Darwin's *The Origin of Species.*
> The rock group played "Kansas City."
> Did you read "Truth in Accounting" in the last issue of *The Accounting Review?*

Notice that the names of the things referred to are *not* separated from the rest of the sentence by a comma. The sentence is punctuated just as though the quotation marks were not there. The quotation marks tell the reader that the words they enclose are the name of a song, title of a chapter of a book, or name of an article. Quotation marks are frequently used in this way in school writing.

16c

Do not use quotation marks around common nicknames, technical terms, or well-known expressions.

WRONG	I saw "Bill" yesterday.
RIGHT	I saw Bill yesterday.
WRONG	When "Lefty" ran in, all of his friends cheered.
RIGHT	When Lefty ran in, all of his friends cheered.
WRONG	Use a "vernier caliper" to obtain an accurate measurement.
RIGHT	Use a vernier caliper to obtain an accurate measurement.
WRONG	Anyone can learn to "tune" a motor.
RIGHT	Anyone can learn to tune a motor.

16d

Words used in a special sense may sometimes be enclosed in quotation marks, or they may be underlined. (See also 19a[4].)

The important thing to remember is that it is usually better *not* to underline words or enclose them in quotation marks unless there is no other way to express the idea.

WEAK	The word *love* makes some people interested and makes others yawn.
BETTER	The thought of love is interesting to some people, but others may yawn at the idea.

WEAK	That "mysterious atmosphere" is just propaganda.
BETTER	That mysterious atmosphere is just propaganda.

Notice that the same ideas can be expressed without the use of quotation marks or underlining. Good writers hold their readers' attention with well-chosen words and do not have to sprinkle a page with quotation marks.

16e
Do not put quotation marks around the title of your paper.

The title of your paper is original, and it should not be treated as quoted material unless you have taken a quotation to use as a title.
Here is an example of the title of a paper.

My First Job

I am sure that I will never forget my first job because the experience taught me . . .

EXERCISE 2

Proofread the following student paragraph, correcting all errors in the use of quotation marks.

"The Blues: My Favorite Music

People have sometimes asked me "what my favorite music is." I have had to reply honestly: "Blues Music." As a teenager, I grew up listening to the singing of Ma Rainey and Bessie Smith on records, and the songs St. Louis Blues and Beale Street Blues were very much a part of my teenage years. An article in Sunday's *New York Times* entitled Billie Holliday: the Blues Lady reminded me of the pleasure I took and still take in hearing the great blues singers. When I listen to some of the rock songs my children enjoy today, I can't help asking them, "Wouldn't you rather hear a spirited rendition of 'Gut Bucket Blues.'?"

CHAPTER SEVENTEEN

The Period and Other Marks

> *Use the period, the question mark, the*
> *exclamation point, the colon, the dash,*
> *parentheses, and brackets correctly*
> *in your writing.*

The period and the question mark are used more frequently than the other marks of punctuation, but all are important in your writing. The period, the question mark, and the exclamation point show the end of a complete sentence.

STATEMENT	The classroom is very crowded.
QUESTION	Is the classroom crowded?
EXCLAMATION	That classroom is too crowded!

The period also shows the end of most abbreviations. The colon, the dash, parentheses, and brackets are used within the sentence to call attention to a part of the sentence.

17a

Use a period to end a statement, a request, or an indirect question, and after most abbreviations. Use ellipsis marks to show the omission of a word or words from quoted material.

17a(1)

Use a period to end a statement or command.

Most of the sentences you write will be statements; in them, you are telling about something.

> The boy ran.
> The tall, thin boy ran home after school.
> The tall, thin boy in blue jeans and a green sweater ran rapidly down the street after school.
> Close the door, please.

All of the above sentences are statements or commands. It does not matter that two are short and two are longer. Each is a sentence because it tells what the subject (*boy*) did (*ran*) or commands that the subject (*you understood*) complete an action.

17a(2)

Use a period to end an indirect question.

Do not confuse an indirect question with a direct one. An indirect question is a type of statement. Even if the sentence states that someone asked a question, it is still a sentence and needs a period at the end.

> **WRONG**   Our neighbors wanted to know where the boxes came from?
> **RIGHT**   Our neighbors wanted to know where the boxes came from. [The sentence is *telling* what the neighbors wanted to know.]

WRONG	Mrs. Hildreth asked me to come to work the next day?
RIGHT	Mrs. Hildreth asked me to come to work the next day. [The sentence is *telling* what Mrs. Hildreth wanted me to do.]

17a(3)
Use a period after most abbreviations.

The period is used after abbreviations or short forms of words. The use of a person's initials instead of the name is an abbreviation.

In most of your writing, you should be careful to use complete words, but there are some titles, degrees, ranks, and other words that are usually abbreviated. Many of the abbreviations end with a period.

> I saw Mr. Bronson last week.
> Mrs. Saunders has a B.A. in history.
> Lt. Wilbur Carson, Jr., lives on South Hampsted Avenue. [The full words are *Lieutenant* and *Junior*.]

Do not abbreviate words such as *hour, inch,* or *foot.* Measurements of time or space may be abbreviated in some cases, but for your papers and themes, it is always best to use the complete words.

WRONG	I worked an hr. after lunch.
RIGHT	I worked an *hour* after lunch.
WRONG	Billy is over six ft. tall.
RIGHT	Billy is over six *feet* tall.
WRONG	Mercer lives on a st. near the college.
RIGHT	Mercer lives on a *street* near the college.

Abbreviations in common use include the following:

Mr.	A.M. OR a.m.
Mrs.	P.M. OR p.m.
Ms.	B.C.
Dr.	A.D.
C.O.D.	R.S.V.P. OR r.s.v.p.

Abbreviations of the names of large organizations, government agencies, and some technical terms are frequently used without periods.

NAACP	FBI
GOP	TV
YMCA	FM
NATO	AM
HEW	CB

17a(4)

Use ellipsis marks, which are three spaced periods (. . .), to show the omission of a word or words from quoted material.

If the ellipsis mark is at the end of a sentence, it is followed by another period, a question mark, or an exclamation point. Ellipsis marks are frequently needed in a library paper or other long formal paper.

> A large group heard his inspiring words: "The strength of the move-ment . . . is real and enduring."

Note: Do not use a period at the end of the title of a song, paper, book, magazine, or newspaper. (See **27.**)

TITLE USED IN A SENTENCE	The trio played "My Blue Heaven" while Sally danced.
TITLE BY ITSELF	An Unforgettable Day
TITLE USED IN A SENTENCE	*The Bridges at Toko-Ri* is an exciting book.
TITLE BY ITSELF	*American Opinion*

EXERCISE 1

Add periods where they are needed in the following sentences. Spell out any words which should not be abbreviated.

1. The rain finally stopped The st was flooded with water and littered with branches several ft long

2. Mr Wilson finished mowing the grass in twenty min

3. The TV was not working yesterday when Dr Adamson wanted to watch a special program on the CIA

4. Mrs George M Craig will speak Saturday at the club meeting on the advantages of owning a CB radio

5. Jamie wanted to know why we were not going on the trip I asked his father to explain the many reasons

6. Please hold on sudden stops are necessary.

17b
Use a question mark to end a question.

> Why is Ted leaving?
> Are you taking History 186?
> Did Marcie wear that old dress and coat to the party?
> When will people learn that they must help each other?

The above examples are questions. Each sentence asks for information, and each sentence uses asking words such as *when* or *why* or begins with part of the verb.

Remember that an indirect question does not end with a question mark. The indirect question is really a statement about what is being asked, and the correct end mark is a period.

17c
Use an exclamation point at the end of a sentence that shows strong feeling or surprise or one that gives a strong command.

Sometimes you may want a sentence to show strong feeling or surprise or to show that something is happening suddenly. You might yell or shout if you were saying the sentence instead of writing it. Such sentences end with exclamation points.

Help! The house is on fire!
I'll hate you as long as I live!
Hold on, Ginny!
We want a touchdown!
It was a wonderful surprise!

Exclaiming sentences are usually short. They can add strength and feeling to your writing, but they should not be used often. When you use an exclaiming sentence, be sure that the idea you are expressing is truly one of strong or sudden feeling.

EXERCISE 2

Edit the following student paragraph, correcting any errors in the use of periods or question marks.

A couple of years ago, my daughter Jean found a bottle that had washed up on the beach it contained a business card from a lemon pie manufacturer. Jean wrote him a letter telling him where she found the bottle and, as a "P.S.", asked if he knew how much she liked lemon pie? A couple of weeks later, Mr. Jackson, the president of the company, was at our door with a fresh pie I will bet that this is the first time a person has received a lemon pie in a bottle now, have you learned not to ignore messages that may be on the beach in bottles.

17d
Use the colon correctly.

17d(1)
Use a colon after a complete thought to call attention to something that follows.

A colon really tells your reader to pay attention to a list, word, quotation, or explanation that follows. It comes after a definite pause. The common pattern for the use of the colon in this manner involves the following:

1. statement or command
2. colon (:)
3. the item that follows

Here are some examples.

> I need only one thing to make my life complete: money.
> Keep the following rule in mind: "'Tis better to be silent and be thought a fool than to speak out and remove all doubt."
> Please bring the following supplies: paper, pencils, and erasers.

Caution: Remember *not* to use a colon when the list or item follows a verb or when that list or item merely completes the sentence.

> **WRONG**   Please bring: paper, pencils, and erasers. [*Paper, pencils, and erasers* are merely the objects of the verb *bring* and complete the sentence. No colon is needed.]
> **RIGHT**   Please bring paper, pencils, and erasers.

17d(2)

The colon is used after the beginning, or salutation, of a business letter. This is considered a formal beginning; a friendly letter uses a comma.

> Dear Sir:
> Dear Senator Townley:
> Dear Martin,

17d(3)

Use a colon to separate the figures that give hours and minutes, chapter and verse in the Bible, or volume and page of magazines.

> **WRONG**   I told Kevin I would be ready at 730, but at 645 the doorbell rang, and there he was.

RIGHT   I told Kevin I would be ready at 7:30, but at 6:45 the doorbell rang, and there he was.

WRONG   Exodus 203 is the first of the Ten Commandments.
RIGHT   Exodus 20:3 is the first of the Ten Commandments.

WRONG   See *Newsweek* 16232 for details.
RIGHT   See *Newsweek* 16:232 for details.

Caution: A colon is used more frequently in formal writing than in informal writing. Do not confuse the colon and the semicolon; the names and the marks may seem to be similar, but the semicolon joins two sentences and the colon calls attention to something that follows it. (See **14e.**)

17e
Use a dash to show a sudden or abrupt break in a sentence.

A dash may also set off a word or a group of words that summarizes the sentence. Do not confuse the dash with the hyphen (see **12b.**) In handwriting, the dash is a line as long as two or three hyphens. In typing, the dash is made with two hyphens.

> While I wait I enjoy my favorite dish—rice and gravy—with a glass of lemonade.
> Good grades, a diploma, a fine job—these are his immediate goals.
> Most men feel no thrill in killing—whether out of necessity or for sport.

EXERCISE 3

Decide whether a colon is needed in each of the sentences that follow. Then put it in the appropriate place. Write C next to any sentences that are already correctly punctuated.

1. There are five important ingredients in baked apples green apples, sugar, water, nutmeg, and cinnamon.

2. Mark has one driving ambition success.

3. The first bell rings at 815 in the morning.

4. The farmers were expected to remember the idea in Leviticus 2022.

5. There are three common types of billiards eight-ball, nine-ball, and rotation.

6. This procedure should include the gathering of necessary items such as clothes, food, and money.

7. A flood led Johnny Cash to write "Big Muddy" and "Five Feet High an' Risin'."

8. There is a goal that Trevor sets for himself the goal of creating something of his own.

9. Cars used to come in just one color black.

10. Sewing is complicated because you have to remember how to thread a needle, work the tension dial, and wind a bobbin.

17f
Use parentheses to enclose certain words, numbers, or letters.

Parentheses are always used in pairs. Use parentheses to enclose numbers or letters that go with items in a series.

> It is important to (1) use the correct materials, (2) follow the directions carefully, (3) observe all safety precautions, and (4) have proper storage for the finished product.

Use parentheses to enclose explanation or comment within a sentence. Periods and commas that are not part of the information enclosed in parentheses should be placed outside the parentheses.

> Although Frank had not expected to do well in college (he had started because he had nothing else to do), he found himself near the top of the dean's list.

17g

Use brackets to enclose a word or words of comment or explanation within quotation marks or parentheses.

The words in brackets are *not* part of the quotation.

> "It should be understood [the message continued] that the situation cannot be tolerated any longer."
> Write clearly and logically; do not use complex structures if they can be avoided. (They are usually [as here] difficult to follow.)

EXERCISE 4

Add any needed colons, dashes, parentheses, or brackets in the following paragraph.

> Complete sentences, correct punctuation, related ideas these things make a good paragraph. You can write good paragraphs if you follow these steps (a) plan what you are going to write about, b get your ideas in order, c write the paragraph, d proofread and correct (this is a very important and frequently overlooked step, e make a good final copy.

CHAPTER EIGHTEEN

Capitals

> **Learn when to use a capital letter
> and when not to use one.**

18a
Capitalize the first word of a sentence.

Show your reader exactly where each sentence begins by starting the first word of the sentence with a capital letter. If two short sentences have been joined to form a long sentence, only the first one begins with a capital.

> **M**y favorite sport is basketball.
> **W**hy do children rebel against their parents?
> **M**any new ideas have been developed; however, not all of them are valid.

18b
Capitalize proper names.

A proper name is the name of a specific, or particular, person, place, or thing.

people	man, woman, child	specific people	Tom H. Larson, Julia Cardin, Sally
places	city, state, nation	specific places	Baltimore, California, France
things	car, book, day, camera	specific things	Chevrolet, Bible, Tuesday, Kodak

18b(1)

Names of persons are capitalized. The initials of names stand for those names and are capital letters.

> Did John W. Trasmon tell Kelly about the new school?

Specific names of animals or pets are also proper names and begin with capital letters.

> One of Walt Disney's most popular creations was Dumbo, the little elephant with the big ears.

18b(2)

A title used before a name is capitalized.

> We all thought that Uncle Wilbur should go with us.
> They saw President Reagan leave the meeting.
> Did Professor Ritter call the office?
> My neighbors have met Captain Farley.

A title not followed by a name is not usually capitalized.

> A club president should be able to maintain order.
> Ask your professor about the old book.
> The captain of the men came forward.

18b(3)
I is capitalized.

When you use the word *I*, you are talking about a very specific person: yourself. *I* is used in place of your own name, and it is always a capital letter when used in this way.

> When **I** looked up, **I** saw people jumping from the windows.
> **I** thought **I** saw two people in the car.

EXERCISE 1

Write C (correct) or *I* (incorrect) next to each of the following words or expressions to show whether it contains any error in capitalization.

1. the Garbage Man _____
2. some Black cars _____
3. the Doctor _____
4. I think _____
5. brother-in-law _____
6. Tom t. Hall _____
7. every tuesday _____
8. my favorite Book _____

EXERCISE 2

Copy the following sentences. Add capitals where they are needed.

1. My sister josephine looks like something you would find in the comic page.
2. Her dentist is dr. t. l. osmondson.
3. the tall police officer talked to mr. johnson.

4. they saw sam and haley leave the yard together.
5. Did you hear professor Dixon's lecture on clean air?
6. when i walked to the store, i saw sally and Jill.
7. The program director introduced mrs. jason f. tomkies, sr.
8. when lieutenant halder opened the door, he saw five men waiting for him.
9. Did i miss all of the program?
10. the captain of the team is responsible for calling the plays.

18b(4)
The names of specific cities, states, countries, and continents are capitalized.

> We lived in **Des M**oines when I was a child.
> John has never driven in **C**alifornia.
> Her report is about **A**rgentina, but mine is about another country.

Notice that words such as *city*, *state*, *country*, and *continent* are not capitalized unless they are part of the name of a particular city, state, country, or continent.

> The **c**apital of a **s**tate may not be its largest **c**ity.

18b(5)
The names of specific avenues, streets, and routes are capitalized.

> Bill took the car to 714 **G**ayle **A**venue, and I walked to the next street.
> They live in the large yellow house on **B**ridge **S**treet.
> Did you locate U.S. **R**oute 66 on the map?

Notice that words such as *avenue, street,* or *route* are not capitalized unless they are part of the name of a particular avenue, street, or route.

> All the **r**outes in the town have **a**venues or **s**treets leading into them.

18b(6)
The names of specific mountains, parks, bodies of water, planets, and buildings are capitalized.

> They visited **M**ount **R**ushmore and **Y**ellowstone **N**ational **P**ark while they were on vacation.
>
> Charles A. Lindbergh was the first person to fly alone across the **A**tlantic **O**cean.
>
> Life on other planets, especially **M**ars, has long been a favorite theme of writers.
>
> Many people visit the **E**mpire **S**tate **B**uilding each year while they are in New York City.

Notice that words such as *mountain, lake,* or *park* are not capitalized unless they are part of the name of a particular mountain, lake, or park.

> The picnic can be held at the **l**ake in the new **p**ark.

EXERCISE 3

In the following sentences, capitalize the names of any specific places.

1. The people of south america live between the atlantic ocean and the pacific ocean.
2. The city of natal in brazil is an important port.
3. The amazon river flows from the andes mountains into the atlantic ocean.
4. There are many rivers and cities in brazil, which is a very large country.

18b(7)

The names of months, days of the week, and holidays are capitalized.

> My favorite month is **N**ovember.
> In the United States, **M**ay and **J**une are warm months.
> The class will meet for three hours each **M**onday for the next five weeks.
> There will be a parade on **V**eterans **D**ay.

Notice that words such as *month, day, week,* or *holiday* are not capitalized unless they are part of the name of a particular month, day, week, or holiday.

> There are **m**onthly meetings scheduled every **d**ay for the next two **w**eeks.

18b(8)

The names of departments and branches of government, political parties, companies, and organizations are capitalized.

> The **J**ustice **D**epartment occupies several large buildings and has many employees.
> A rally was planned by the **R**epublican party.
> The **M**etropolitan **I**nsurance **C**ompany has an office on Main Street.
> The large building on the corner belongs to **M**eglo **C**orporation.
> The **C**hesapeake **H**istorical **S**ociety meets every month.

18b(9)

The names of historical events and documents are capitalized.

> The **B**attle of **W**aterloo was an important event in French history.
> The **R**evolutionary **W**ar marks the beginning of our nation.
> The **T**reaty of **V**ersailles was signed in France.

18b(10)

Words that refer to God, religious denominations, and sacred books are capitalized.

Words referring to God or the Deity	our **M**aker **A**llah the **T**rinity the **M**essiah **J**esus the **L**ord the **A**lmighty
Religious denominations	**C**atholic **J**ewish **B**uddhist **M**oslem **P**rotestant
Sacred books or writings	the **B**ible the **K**oran the **O**ld **T**estament the **S**criptures the **V**edas

18b(11)

Words that come from names that are capitalized are themselves capitalized.

San Francisco	a **S**an **F**ranciscan
England	an **E**nglish course
Rotary Club	the **R**otarians

See **19b(5)** for information on the abbreviation of capitalized words.

Use the following reference list as a guide.

CAPITALIZED (SPECIFIC)	NOT CAPITALIZED (GENERAL)
Valley **H**igh **S**chool	my high school
the **C**onservative party	a political party
the **E**xchange Club	a club for civic leaders

Chase Bank Building	the bank building
the Medal of Honor	a medal for bravery
an All-Star game	a basketball game
the Richmond Coliseum	a sports arena
the Churchland Raiders	a football team
History 312	a course in history
Emporia College	a college
the Spanish people	people of another country
the Middle Ages	an era in history
Pepsi-Cola	a cola drink
New York State	the state on the map
the Orient	an oriental country
the Blue Ridge Mountains	some mountains in Virginia
Veterans Day	a day to honor veterans
the Southern Railway System	a railway network
Cousin Jimmy	a cousin
Golden Gate Bridge	a long bridge
Christmas in December	a day in winter
Springdale Acres	a housing development
the South	the southern part of the United States

EXERCISE 4

Add capital letters where they are needed in the following sentences.

1. Beginning spanish will be offered on monday and wednesday at 9:00.

2. We went to the football game on thanksgiving day.

3. Susan met her friends at the large department store on center avenue and vine street.

4. winter came early that year, and october was cold and rainy.

5. john belongs to the golden gate toastmasters club.

6. This country gained a large area of land by means of the louisiana purchase.

7. i went to kemper high school for two years.

8. The women of greensville methodist church cook and serve delicious meals every thursday evening.

9. We will study the talmud and the koran next year.

10. our basketball team lost the game to maytown high last saturday.

18c
Use correct capitalization in titles.

Capitalize the first, last, and important words in the titles of books, plays, songs, poems, movies, TV programs, records, and tapes. Capitalize the second part of important hyphenated words. Do not capitalize short prepositions (*to, for,* and so on), short coordinating conjunctions (*and, but, or,* and so on), or the words *a, an,* and *the.*

> The class will discuss **A**nimal **F**arm next week.
> Study the first two chapters in **H**istory of the **B**order **S**tates.
> The group sang "**T**he **S**tar-**S**pangled **B**anner."
> Her first published poem was called "**L**eaves of **A**utumn."

Notice that little words like *the, a, an,* and *of* are not capitalized unless one of these words begins or ends the title.

> The article was called "**A** Talent I Know **Of**."
> She sang "**D**o You Know **of a** Beautiful Home?" while the group assembled.

18d
Capitalize *I* and *O* when they are used as words.

> All of the books which **I** wanted were very expensive.
> Tell me, **O** reader, how to solve this problem.

The word *O* is always spelled with a single capital letter. The word *oh* begins with a capital letter only when it is the first word of a sentence, title, or quoted material. Review **18b(3)** for additional information on the word *I.*

18e
Capitalize the first word of quoted sentences.

> Tom said, "**T**he game is over, and we lost."

"**W**hen the bell rings," said Miss Johnson, "everyone may leave quietly."
The man exclaimed, "**I** do not know who you are. **W**hat right have
you to question me? **T**ell me your name, and then I may talk to
you."

EXERCISE 5

Correct any errors in capitalization in the following sentences.

1. As Head Usher I arrived at the Church early.
2. Our Grandmother puts the star on the tree every christmas.
3. Get on College drive and continue until you get to Gary Player road.
4. It is not necessary to take a Child Development course to be a good babysitter.
5. I can still hear Adele's mother saying, "take care of yourselves" as we left her house.
6. When I was in the San Francisco bay area in august, I was surprised to see a store called Harry's holistic Auto Repair Shop.
7. Willie Nelson made outlaw music famous with songs such as "Blue Eyes Crying In The Rain" and "Red-headed Stranger."
8. If you expect to major in foreign languages, you need to take an introductory language course.
9. I wish i had seen judy garland in the *wizard of oz*.
10. It is hard for my Mother to get up early enough to watch *the today show*.

18f
Do not use more capitals than you need.

18f(1)
Do not capitalize the name of a school subject unless it is the name of a specific course or a language.

My favorite **s**cience course is **B**iology 309.
Sue made low grades in **G**erman and **h**istory, but she made an honor grade in **c**hemistry.

18f(2)

Do not capitalize the names of seasons or directions.

> The flowers were beautiful in the spring.
> Every winter I have trouble with my car.
> Turn west after you pass the school and the shopping center.

18f(3)

Do not capitalize the names of trees, fruits, vegetables, birds, or flowers.

> Huge oak trees were planted on each side of the street.
> The cherry trees make spring in Washington a beautiful sight.
> The girls brought peaches, pears, and grapes.
> Six crows sat on the fence and selected the corn that they would have for dinner.
> The robins and the cardinals started to build nests.
> All of the roses were in bloom.

18f(4)

Do not capitalize the names of games or sports unless the name is a trademark.

> Tables were arranged for checkers, Scrabble, Monopoly, bridge, and dominoes.
> The tennis game was not very lively.
> Our football team went to see the Redskins in the playoff.
> The great American sport is said to be baseball, but the spectators far outnumber the players.

Notice that the names of specific teams are capitalized.

18f(5)

Do not capitalize the name of a disease unless it is named for a person, and then do not capitalize the word *disease*.

> The school was closed because many of the students had the measles.

A young child may be very ill with **p**neumonia.
I didn't realize how serious **H**odgkin's **d**isease could be.

18f(6)

Do not capitalize the names of musical instruments.

I wear ear plugs when my sister practices on her **v**iolin.
Eddie enjoys playing the **d**rums in the school combo.
The large **B**aldwin **p**iano stood in the middle of the stage.

Notice that the names of the companies that manufacture the instruments are capitalized.

EXERCISE 6

Rewrite each of the following words or expressions, using capitals where needed.

1. tuberculosis
2. a les paul guitar
3. the dallas cowboys
4. major league baseball
5. a chemistry exam
6. a summer shower
7. a mocking bird's nest
8. drafting 211
9. a harley davidson motorcycle
10. a california redwood tree

CHAPTER NINETEEN

Underlining, Abbreviations, and Numbers

> *Use underlining, abbreviations, and numbers correctly.*

It is important to know how to use the standard forms for underlining, abbreviations, and numbers because even if you do not use them in your writing, you will be reading them in material which other people have written.

19a

Underline the titles of books and some other published materials; titles of works of art; TV series; record albums; names of ships, trains, and other special vehicles; and some words when you refer to them in your papers.

Some words or groups of words are underlined in handwritten or typewritten papers. If the material is printed, the underlined words are shown in italic type.

HANDWRITTEN *She read an article in the Review of the News.*

| TYPEWRITTEN | She read an article in the <u>Review of the News</u>. |
| PRINTED | She read an article in the *Review of the News*. |

19a(1)

Underline the titles of works that are published separately, such as books, periodicals, newspapers, bulletins, motion pictures, plays, and long musical compositions.

In the examples below, complete published works are underlined.

<u>The Flight of the Phoenix</u> is the story of a desperate struggle for life.
Did you see the <u>Reader's Digest</u> this month?
Shakespeare's <u>Romeo and Juliet</u> was given a modern musical setting in <u>West Side Story</u>.
Handel's <u>Messiah</u> is usually performed at Christmastime.
Our library carries <u>The New York Times</u> on microfilm.

Do not underline articles, poems, songs, stories, or chapters from books because they are only parts of published works. Use quotation marks instead.

"Mr. Flood's Party" is a poem in <u>Literature: Structure, Sound, and Sense</u>.

Study the examples and notice the following points:

1. The words *a, an,* and *the* are underlined or italicized when they begin the title of a book; frequently they are not underlined when they begin the title of a periodical or newspaper.

2. The name of an author is not underlined or italicized.

A few references are not underlined.

1. Do not underline references to the Bible or its divisions.

2. Do not underline references to legal documents.

3. Do not underline the titles of your papers, because a title is not italicized when it stands at the head or beginning of a book or other separate publication.

4. Do not underline the titles of short stories, songs, short poems, articles from periodicals, and subdivisions of books; these titles are usually enclosed in quotation marks. (See **16b.**)

19a(2)
Underline the names of works of art.

> The <u>Mona Lisa</u> is Leonardo da Vinci's most famous painting mainly because of the subject's mysterious smile.

19a(3)
Underline titles of TV series and record albums.

> Did you see <u>Hill Street Blues</u> this week?
> "Body and Soul" is my favorite composition from the album <u>The Hawk in Hi Fi</u>.

19a(4)
Underline the names of ships, trains, and other vehicles that have names.

Do not underline the names of companies that operate the vehicles.

> My father often recalled with pleasure his trip to Europe aboard the Cunard Line's <u>Queen Elizabeth</u>.
> The <u>George Washington</u> was a luxury train operated by the Chesapeake and Ohio Railway Company.
> We watched the launching of the spaceship <u>Columbia</u>.
> The <u>Enola Gay</u> was the B-29 that dropped the first atomic bomb.

19a(5)

Underline words, letters, and numbers used as illustrations or spoken of as such. (See also 16d.)

The words right and write sound alike.

The word fear may mean many different things.

Plurals of most names of things are formed by adding -s to the singular word.

The last 7 in the list should be a 1.

19a(6)

Do not use underlining for emphasis or stress if it can be avoided.

Use stronger or more specific words in place of those words you may tend to underline.

WEAK	The noise was awful. [Underlining is used for emphasis.]
BETTER	The noise hurt our ears and shook the walls. [Underlining is not needed.]

EXERCISE 1

In the following sentences, underline the words which should be underlined in your writing.

1. After reading Wuthering Heights, Martha imagined she was wandering over the moors and ended up walking into a street sign.
2. Broiled snails were served for lunch on Air Force I.
3. "Why go to see Albee's play Zoo Story," my father asked, "when we have our own little zoo right here in this apartment?"
4. All class members are expected to read five articles from Modern Science or Chemistry Review.
5. Picasso's Guernica is a famous mural showing the horrors of war.
6. Wells's War of the Worlds is still an exciting book.

7. Read the editorial in the Wednesday Sun Times.
8. Is the number in the third line a 6 or an 8?
9. Sir Francis Drake had a sailing ship called The Golden Hind.
10. Place a dot over every i and cross each t.

19b

Abbreviations are shortened versions of names or titles and are often used where there is not much space.

Some abbreviations are accepted in all kinds of writing, but most of the time it is better to spell out the words.

19b(1)
Use the abbreviations *Mr., Mrs., Ms., Dr.,* and *St.* (for *Saint*) before proper names.

> *Mrs.* James Timmons and *Dr.* Stanley Wood were in charge of the meeting.
> It rained on *St.* Swithin's Day last year.

Spell out *doctor* and *saint* when they are not followed by proper names.

> Did you see the *doctor* before he left?
> She has some very beautiful pictures of *saints*.

19b(2)
Some abbreviations—such as *Prof., Rep., Hon., Gen.,* and *Capt.*—may be used before full names or before initials and last names. They should not be used before last names alone.

> **WRONG**   Sen. Harmon spoke to the group.
> **RIGHT**   *Sen.* James Harmon spoke to the group.
> OR
> *Senator* Harmon spoke to the group.

WRONG	She invited Rev. Wilson to have dinner with them.
RIGHT	She invited *Rev.* K. R. Wilson to have dinner with them.

OR

She invited *Reverend* Wilson to have dinner with them.

WRONG	I saw Capt. Allison in the library.
RIGHT	I saw *Capt.* C. W. Allison in the library.

OR

I saw *Captain* Allison in the library.

19b(3)

It is customary to abbreviate titles and degrees if they appear after proper names.

Jr.	M.A.
Sr.	M.D.
D.D.	C.P.A.
Ph.D.	

R. H. Bryant, *Jr.*, lives on the next street.

19b(4)

It is customary to abbreviate words used with dates and numbers.

A.D.	P.M. OR p.m.
B.C.	no. OR No.
A.M. OR a.m.	$

At 9:30 *A.M.* the TV sets went on sale for *$376.59.*

19b(5)

It is customary to abbreviate the names of many organizations, expressions, and government agencies usually referred to by their initials.

Remember to use capital letters for each word that is capitalized in the full name or expression.

North Atlantic Treaty Organization   NATO
GOP   FBI   NASA   HEW   FHA   USA
The *AMA* published a report on the new medicine.

19b(6)
Use *D.C.* to designate the District of Columbia.

Washington, D.C.
Mr. Kermit Wells, Jr., lives in Washington, *D.C.*

19b(7)
Spell out the names of states and countries, months and days of the week, units of measurement, names of courses of study, and first names.

Karen lives in *California,* but she spends several months each year in *Mexico.*
The workshops are scheduled for the third and fourth *Wednesdays* in *April.*
Please bring me five *pounds* of sugar and a *quart* of salad oil.
George [NOT Geo.] Caton is taking *biology, history,* and *Spanish* this quarter.

19b(8)
Spell out words such as *Avenue, Street,* and *River* when they are part of proper names.

Oakhill *Avenue* is the prettiest street in town.

19b(9)
Do not use & (for *and*), *Inc., Co.,* or *Bros.* unless such an abbreviation is part of an official name or title.

Harcourt Brace Jovanovich, *Inc.,* is a large publishing company.
The House *&* Grounds *Company* builds and repairs houses.

19c

Spell out most numbers that can be expressed in one or two words. Use a hyphen with compound numbers.

There are *seven thousand* students at my college, but only *fifty-five* are taking physics.

Use numerals for large numbers that need more than two words to express.

The building cost *$14,700,000.*

19c(1)

Use numerals for numbers in a series or in statistics.

The lot is *250* feet long and *365* feet deep.

19c(2)

Use numerals for addresses and ZIP codes.

Jim lives at *702* Farley Court, Perkins, Oklahoma *74059.*

19c(3)

Use numerals for decimals and percentages and for money used with the dollar sign.

Interest on the loan was figured at *7* percent.
Marian wrote a check for *$350.*

19c(4)

Use numerals for pages and divisions of books.

Read pages *8* and *9* in Chapter *1.*

19c(5)

Use numerals for identification numbers, such as television stations, serial numbers, and telephone numbers.

He watched Channel *10* every evening at 6:00.

19c(6)

Use numerals for dates and specific times of day.

The package arrived on April *21, 1975.* [Not April 21st, 1975.]
OR
The package arrived *21* April *1975.*
Tomorrow the sun will rise at *5:53* A.M.

Note: Spell out a number at the beginning of a sentence, or rewrite the sentence.

WRONG	*7:30* is the time for the dinner.
RIGHT	*Seven-thirty* is the time for the dinner.
	OR
	The dinner will begin at *7:30.*
WRONG	*117* boys are in the class.
RIGHT	There are *117* boys in the class.

19c(7)

Use a hyphen between compound numbers and fractions.

Compound numbers from twenty-one to ninety-nine are separated by hyphens.

twenty-two
eighty-seven

EXERCISE 2

In the following sentences, underline the correct word in parentheses. Review the information on abbreviations and numbers if you are not certain which item is correct.

1. I saw (Wm., William) Swanson yesterday afternoon at the (doctor's, dr.'s) office.
2. Did you hear (Sen., Senator) Barnes last night on Channel (Three, 3) at (ten P.M., 10 P.M.)?
3. Maria works for (Prof., Professor) Harrison, who lives on Maple (Ave., Avenue).
4. Pollsters often say, "As (Me., Maine) goes, so goes the nation."
5. Classes will be held in Room (3190, three thousand one hundred and ninety) on the (3rd, third) (Tues., Tuesday) of each month.
6. He poured (one half, one-half) cup of sugar over (2, two) pounds of fruit and hoped for the best.
7. Why is it that now that (Mr, Mr.) Johnson has his (PHD, Ph.D.), he doesn't seem to have much better sense than he had before?
8. Review Chapter (6, six) and list (5, five) physical properties of oxygen mentioned in your (chem., chemistry) text.
9. (HEW, Health, Education, and Welfare) and (OEO, Office of Economic Opportunity) have offices on the (7th, seventh) floor.
10. (10, Ten) men from this campus are attending the conference on aging in Washington, (D.C., District of Columbia).

PART FOUR
WORDS

CHAPTER TWENTY

Learning to Use the Dictionary

Learn to use a dictionary to help you find the best words to express your ideas and to help you spell the words you use.

20a
Learn to find the words you want to use.

To find a word in a dictionary, all you have to know is the alphabet, because the dictionary is simply a long alphabetical list of words. A word with the information about it is called an *entry*.

The guide words printed at the top of each page of a dictionary help you find the word you are looking for.

Here are the guide words found at the top

Beaker is the first entry at the top of the left-hand column of the page.

beaker   beat

Beat is the last entry at the bottom of the right-hand column of the page.

All the entries that come alphabetically between *beaker* and *beat* can be found on this page.

Do not be surprised if your dictionary entries are not exactly the same as the examples given in this section. Not all dictionaries are exactly the same, but these examples should give you a general idea of the way most dictionaries are organized and the kind of information they give.

EXERCISE 1

In each numbered item below, the words on the left represent the guide words that would appear on a dictionary page. The words on the right represent entries that might appear on that page. Choose the entries from the right that you would find on a dictionary page having the guide words given on the left.

GUIDE WORDS	ENTRIES
1. prude . . . psychology	prune, psychopathic, probe, pseudo
2. empty . . . enchantment	empire, enamel, en-, endeavor
3. calmly . . . cameo	calm, calf, camel, calorie
4. resistor . . . response	resole, resort, respiration, respond

20b
Learn the kinds of information given in a dictionary.

Now that you see how words are arranged in a dictionary, you need to know some of the things you can learn about a word from a dictionary.

You can learn more from a dictionary than just how to spell and define a word.

EXERCISE 2

Using the following dictionary entries, answer the questions below them.

As·to·ri·a (as·tô′·rē·ə *or* as·tō′·rē·ə), *n.*: city in NW Oregon that was established as a fur-trading post by John Jacob Astor in 1811. Population 11,000.

brain·y (brān'·ē), *adj.*, **brain·i·er, brain·i·est.** *Informal:* intelligent; clever— **brain i ness,** *n.*

C.O., 1. Commanding Officer. 2. *Informal:* conscientious objector.

Dic·ta·phone (dik'·tə·fōn), *n.*, *Trademark:* instrument which records and reproduces words that are spoken into it.

Ed·wards (ed'·wərdz), *n.* 1. Jonathan, 1703–1758. American clergyman, theologian, and metaphysician. 2. his son, Jonathan, 1745–1801. American clergyman.

1. Does the abbreviation C.O. always have the same meaning?
2. Is the Dictaphone a new type of telephone?
3. Was Jonathan Edwards's son a minister?
4. Would you say someone was brainy if you were writing a formal letter of recommendation for him?
5. Had the city of Astoria been established when the first Jonathan Edwards was born?

20b(1)
Use a dictionary to learn how to divide and pronounce a word.

Two things you can learn about a word from the dictionary are how to divide the word when you write it and how to pronounce it when you say it.

ko·a·la (kō·ä'·lə)

The dictionary uses dots (·) to show you where you can divide the word. The heavy stress mark (') shows you which part of the word should be said with greatest emphasis.

Do not include the dots or the stress marks when you write a word in a sentence. If you need to divide a word at the end of a line as you are writing, use a hyphen, as shown in the next sentence.

When we went to Australia last summer, we saw a ko-ala in a eucalyptus tree.

In a dictionary entry, do not confuse the dot (·) with the hyphen (-)

ko·a·la   self-as·sured

EXERCISE 3

Use your dictionary to find the following words. Write the words, using a hyphen to show where you would divide them at the end of a line.

■ **Example**   insinuate _____ *insin – uate* _____

1. illustrate _____

2. primarily _____

3. sensational _____

4. determination _____

5. warranty _____

6. authority _____

In most dictionaries, the key to the sound symbols used to show you how to pronounce each word is found at the bottom of the page on which the word appears.

ko·a·la (kō·ä′·lə)

hat, āge, cāre, fär; let, bē, term; it, īce; hot, gō, ôrder; oil, out; cup, pùt, rüle, ūse; ch, child; ng, long; th, thin; th, then; zh, measure: ə represents a in *about*, e in *taken*, i in *April*, o in *lemon*, u in *circus*.

This key to the sound symbols used in the entry above tells you that the o in *koala* sounds like the o in *go*, the a sounds like the a in *far*, and the last a (ə) sounds like the a in *about*.

EXERCISE 4

Use the dictionary key below to figure out the following sentences. Write the sentences correctly.

---

hat, āge, cāre, fär; let, bē, term; it, īce; hot, gō, ôrder; oil, out; cup, pút, rüle, ūse; *ch*, child; *ng*, long; *th*, thin; *th*, then; *zh*, measure: ə represents *a* in *about*, *e* in *taken*, *i* in *April*, *o* in *lemon*, *u* in *circus*.

■ **Example**   Ū kan′ot trust ə smīl′ing kat.
You cannot trust a smiling cat.

1. Serf′ing duz′nt māk Travis tīrd.
2. Stud′ē ing duz māk Travis tīrd.
3. Rēd′ing gúd búks iz härd werk fôr Travis.
4. Hiz fā′vər it rēd′ing iz thə sen′tər fōld in *Fun Tīm Mag′əzēn*.

20b(2)
Use a dictionary to learn how and when to use a word.

You already know that you can find out what a word means by looking it up in a dictionary. You can also find out how and when to use, or not to use, certain words by looking them up in a dictionary.

Here are the five most common labels used in dictionaries to indicate how and when to use, or not to use, certain words. If there is no label given, the word is considered Standard or Formal.

INFORMAL   The word or meaning is used in everyday speech or writing but not in formal speech or writing.

brain·storm (brān′·stôrm), *n.*, *Informal*: a sudden, inspired idea.

SLANG   The word or meaning is used in very informal speaking situations only.

jerk (jerk), *n.*, *Slang*: an unsophisticated or stupid person.

DIALECT   The word or meaning is used only in the informal speech of a particular region or group.

pone (pōn), *n.*, *Dialect. Southern U.S.*: 1. bread made of corn meal. 2. loaf or cake of the bread.

SUBSTANDARD   The word or meaning is not acceptable in general standard English speech or writing.

bust (bust), *v.* 1. *Substandard*: burst.

ARCHAIC or OBSOLETE   The word or meaning is very rare except in old books or in books written in the style of an earlier period.

per·chance (pər′·chans *or* pər·chans′), *adv.*, *Archaic*: perhaps.

EXERCISE 5

Use your dictionary to find any labels explaining when and how to use, or not to use, the following words. Write the word, the label(s) your dictionary gives it, and its meaning.

1. blow
2. ain't
3. br'er
4. gobbledygook
5. alarum
6. hassle
7. broke

EXERCISE 6

Use your dictionary to find the following information about each of the words listed below. Copy each word and write the information beside it.

a. What the word means
b. How to divide the word (dots)
c. How to pronounce the word (sound symbols)
d. How and when to use, or not to use, the word (*Informal, Slang,* and other labels)

1. solder (as a verb)
2. pandemonium
3. than
4. crib
5. bootlicker
6. library
7. pass
8. loony

20c
Use a dictionary to spell words correctly.

Dictionaries often have sections that explain the general rules for spelling, adding prefixes and suffixes, and forming plurals of words. Locate the spelling aids in your dictionary and learn to use them.

20c(1)
Use a dictionary to confirm the spelling of a word.

If you are not certain about verb forms, endings of words, or irregularities of spelling, confirm or correct the spelling by using a dictionary. Especially in a paperback dictionary, you may need to look for a word at the end of a dictionary entry. For example, if you looked for *informality* as a separate entry, you would not find it because it is part of the entry for *informal.*

> **in·for·mal** (in·fôr′·ml), *adj.* 1. not formal; not in the regular or prescribed manner. 2. done without ceremony. 3. used in everyday

common talk, but not used in formal talking or writing. —
in·for·mal·i·ty, *n.* —in·for·mal·ly, *adv.*

A dictionary will help you to spell verb forms correctly because the
main forms of the verb are given if there is any irregularity in spelling. The forms are usually near the beginning of an entry.

> **run** (run), *v.*, **ran, run, running,** 1. move the legs quickly; go faster
> than walking.

Some dictionaries may give this type of information at the end of
the entry.

> 2. go hurriedly; hasten. 3. flee.　—**ran, run, running.**

See Chapter **7** for additional help in spelling verb forms.

20c(2)
Use a dictionary to correct misspelled words.

When a paper is returned to you, there may be the symbol *sp* or the
number *12* (referring to the spelling chapter of this book) written
by or over a word; this indicates that the word is not spelled correctly. When the problem in spelling is at the beginning of the
word, you may have trouble locating the word in a dictionary if you
do not know the beginning letters. Here are some useful hints to
help you locate words that you have misspelled.

1. The letter *c* may sound like *s* or *k*. If you cannot locate a word in the
   s or *k* section of the dictionary, you may have to look in the *c* section.

   capsize　*c* sounds like *k*
   certain　*c* sounds like *s*
2. The sound of *ch*, as in *church*, may be spelled *tch, te, ti,* or *tu*. Although
   the alternate spellings of the sound may not be the first letters, they
   may still keep you from locating the word easily.

hatch	the *ch* sound is spelled *tch*
righteous	the *ch* sound is spelled *te*
question	the *ch* sound is spelled *ti*
future	the *ch* sound is spelled *tu*

3. The letters *ch* may have the sound of *k*, as in *chemistry*.

4. The sound of *f* may be spelled *ph*, as in *photograph*.

5. The sounds of *g* and *j* are easily confused if the *g* has a soft sound. The words *generally*, *gentle*, *ginger*, and *gymnast* all sound as though they begin with *j*.

6. The letters *in* and *en* may sound alike at the beginning of a word. The beginnings of words like *enchant*, *encircle*, or *endure* all sound very similar to the beginnings of *indent*, *incubate*, or *indirect*. Learn to look for such words in both the *in* and *en* sections of the dictionary.

7. Words that sound as though they begin with *n* may have a silent letter before the *n*.

   pneumonia sounds like "newmonia"
   knife sounds like "nife"
   gnaw snounds like "naw"
   knot sounds the same as *not*, but the meaning is different
   know sounds the same as *no*, but the meaning is different

8. The sound of *r* may be spelled *rh* as in *rhyme* or *rhythm*.

9. The sound of *sh*, as in *she*, may be spelled many different ways.

sure	the *sh* sound is spelled *su*
ocean	the *sh* sound is spelled *ce*
machine	the *sh* sound is spelled *ch*
mention	the *sh* sound is spelled *ti*
issue	the *sh* sound is spelled *ss*
special	the *sh* sound is spelled *ci*

10. Some words that begin with a *w* may sound as though they begin with a different letter because the *w* is silent. There may be another word that sounds the same, so be sure that you are using the word you mean to use.

    wring sounds the same as *ring*
    write sounds the same as *right*
    wrap sounds the same as *rap*

The *wr* beginning for a word is quite common, so remember to look in the *wr* section of the dictionary if you cannot find the word in the *r* section. Additional examples of such words are *wreck, wrestle, wrong,* and *wrought.*

20c(3)
A word may be marked "misspelled" because you used the wrong word.

By leaving off the ending letters, you may spell a different word. For example, *fine* is a describing word that means "not coarse," or a verb that means "to impose a punishment by requiring payment of a sum." The word *fine* is a word in the dictionary, but if you meant "locate," then you should have spelled the word *find.* Do not stop with the spelling of the word: look at the definition and be sure that you are using the word you mean to use.

Do not forget the *h* in words such as *where* and *while.* If you use *were* for *where* and *wile* for *while,* you are using words that are different in both meaning and pronunciation.

See Chapter 21 for additional help in deciding on the correct word.

EXERCISE 7

Use your dictionary to spell the following words correctly.

1. Use *f* or *ph* to spell these words that begin with an *f* sound.

    _____ anatic   _____ antom   _____ orum   _____ ysical

2. Use *c, k,* or *ch* to spell these words that begin with a *k* sound.

    _____ aracteristic   _____ ibitzer   _____ onsecrate

3. Use *j* or *g* to spell these words that begin with a *j* sound.

    _____ ypsy   _____ ealousy   _____ ocular   _____ esture

4. Use *n, kn, pn,* or *gn* to spell these words that begin with an *n* sound.

_____ eumatic   _____ atural   _____ uckle   _____ arled

5. Use *r, wr,* or *rh* to spell these words that begin with an *r* sound.

_____ eumatism _____ umble _____ eckage _____ inkle _____ inocerous _____ ong

CHAPTER TWENTY-ONE
Using the Right Word

Use words correctly.

The words you choose help give your reader a good or a bad reaction to what you write. It is important to use the words you mean to use and to use the best words you can think of or find in a dictionary.

21a
Use the words you mean to use.

You can ruin a perfectly good sentence by using the wrong word. If you are in doubt about a word, consult a good dictionary. If you can possibly help it, do not use a word that does not exist or that does not say what you think it says. It is better to use a word that sounds too simple to you than to use a word that is incorrect.

> **WRONG**   Some foreign cars are considered better investments than American cars. [*Considerated* does not exist.]
>
> **RIGHT**   Some foreign cars are *considered* better investments than American cars.

INACCURATE	Customers will sit down at the counter and indulge in the tempting food.
ACCURATE	Customers will sit down at the counter and *eat* the tempting food.
INACCURATE	We hope that gas rationing will not be reinforced.
ACCURATE	We hope that gas rationing will not be *reinstated*.
INACCURATE	They chalked their sticks frequently as the game prolonged.
ACCURATE	They chalked their sticks frequently as the game *continued*.

21b
Use clear or specific words.

Sometimes a word will be used correctly, but it will not be the best word you could have used. The best word is the one that gives the reader the clearest picture of what you mean to say. Which of the words below give you the clearest picture of what the writer is saying—those in the left-hand column or those in the right-hand column?

a fat man	a man weighing over three hundred pounds, with a short neck, three chins, and a body shaped like a barrel
an old car	a 1958 Buick sedan
a happy woman	a woman who feels as if she has just found a million dollars
a broken record	a record that was smashed to bits

Of course, the words on the right are much more vivid and give the reader a clearer picture of what the writer is describing than those on the left. It really will improve your papers if you choose words that give your readers a clear, not a vague, picture of what you want to tell them.

VAGUE	I like Amanda because she has a nice personality.
CLEAR	I like Amanda because she laughs at my jokes and doesn't get angry—even when I tell her I'm going to be late picking her up.
VAGUE	My room is very cheerful.
CLEAR	My room has plenty of sunlight; a warm red rug; big, soft yellow chairs; and a welcome sign hanging on the door.
VAGUE	People buy all kinds of ridiculous things for their pets. What's more, there is now a variety of clothing and accessories to choose for them.
CLEAR	A few of the many products for pets include gold jewelry, evening gowns, top hats and tails, and pajamas. If your pet is a little flabby, you can get it a jog-a-dog machine for $575. Also available are clip-on diapers, wigs, false eyelashes, eyeglasses, mascara, and nail polish in a dozen colors.

EXERCISE 1

Rewrite the following paragraph, putting in clear or specific words and details to illustrate the italicized vague words.

Daydreaming used to be called "woolgathering." Usually people daydream about *agreeable things*. In a daydream you can revisit *the past* or place yourself in *the future*. Daydreaming makes possible *the impossible*. It allows you to rid yourself of *unhappy feelings*. It is creative and essential for natural growth. In our daydreams all that we want to happen does happen. Daydreaming offers us a release from *the cares of society*.

21c
Use appropriate words.

When you write a theme, you should use appropriate language. That means that you should keep in mind that a theme is designed to present ideas clearly and correctly to a reader. There are certain kinds of language that are not appropriate for good formal writing.

21c(1)
Avoid slang and informal language.

There are some words that you might feel free to use when talking with friends but that are not acceptable in formal writing. Try to avoid words or expressions like the following:

a swell guy	kick the bucket
a cool chick	get your act together
a real jerk	make someone mad

EXERCISE 2

The student who wrote the following paragraph needs to be more careful in his choice of words. Rewrite the paragraph, putting it into acceptable formal English.

> Last week I got a call from a neat chick who wanted to visit my beachfront cottage. She told me she was flat out exhausted from work and would love to lay out and catch some rays. When she asked if it would be cool to crash at my pad for a day or two, I had to admit that that sounded like a fun thing for her to do and decided to invite some other kids who are into sunworshiping. After we all got our acts together, we met where the gang usually hangs out. We were all as laid back as could be.

21c(2)
Avoid clichés and trite expressions.

Trite expressions have been used so many times that they do not contribute anything clear or distinct to your paper. If anything, they annoy your reader and keep you from expressing yourself effectively. Here are some common clichés:

last but not least	light as a feather
beating around the bush	better safe than sorry

> pretty as a picture
> a sight for sore eyes
> out of this world
> the bitter end
> put your best foot forward

> hit the jackpot
> better late than never
> drop in the bucket
> right as rain
> under the weather

EXERCISE 3

The following sentences contain clichés or trite expressions. Rewrite the sentences, eliminating all worn-out words, clauses, or phrases.

1. You can thank your lucky stars that you didn't burn the candle at both ends last night.
2. The little woman has become thin as a rail since she has gone on her miracle diet.
3. I have to say in no uncertain terms that getting ahead in life is easier said than done.
4. To add insult to injury, my blind date turned out to be as ugly as sin.
5. I fell head over heels in love with a man who was clumsy as an ox and old as the hills.
6. My sister turned green with envy when I got a new sports car, and I'm afraid she gave me a hard time about it.
7. Last but not least, strike while the iron is hot.

21c(3)
Avoid overusing regional expressions.

Some expressions are often used in a particular region, but they can interfere with communication when they are used in formal writing. Here are some examples:

> He *might should* have come.
> I am going to *leave out of* here soon.
> *You'uns* can wait for us here.

21c(4)
Avoid jargon.

Jargon is language associated with certain fields such as business, psychology, education, or government. Usually people use jargon because they think it is the "in" or accepted language of their profession, but many times the person who uses jargon could say the same thing more clearly by avoiding this language.

JARGON	Try to implement the plan.
SIMPLER EXPRESSION	Try to *make* the plan work.
JARGON	Harriet has a poor self-image.
SIMPLER EXPRESSION	Harriet has a poor *opinion of herself.*
JARGON	When you speak to the issue of teenage unemployment, you should get some feedback from community leaders.
SIMPLER EXPRESSION	When you *consider the issue* of teenage unemployment, you syould *see how community leaders feel about it.*
JARGON	Before you begin, determine your goals and objectives and set your priorities.
SIMPLER EXPRESSION	Before you begin, *decide what you want to do and when you want to do it.*

EXERCISE 4

The following sentences contain slang, informal expressions, regional expressions, clichés, and jargon. Rewrite them, putting them in clear, correct formal English.

1. My family is all the time getting together for reunions and parties.
2. Jack was screaming and hollering at the kids.
3. Everyone is scared of Uncle Oscar.
4. We don't have time to mess with that problem.
5. The way people drive their cars often tears them up.

6. Somewhere Fred fell by the wayside.
7. Mrs. Allen wants to put her best foot forward.
8. Ms. Johnson wasn't verbally oriented.
9. Cut off the lights before leaving the room.
10. We need more input before we can know how this change will impact on the decisions we make.
11. That old dude is really loaded.

21d
Learn how to use these problem words.

Here is a list of some confusing words that have caused students problems in writing. Be sure that you know how these words are used.

a	is used before a consonant sound.
an	is used before a vowel sound.
	a beer, *a* cork, *a* habit.
	an alligator, *an* elevator, *an* hour.
accept	means to "receive."
except	means "not included."
	I *accept* your apology.
	Everyone *except* my St. Bernard was invited to the cookout.
affect	means "to influence."
effect	usually means "result."
	President Nixon's resignation speech *affected* me deeply.
	Who knows what the *effect* of a nuclear war would be?
a lot	is not spelled *alot*.
already	means "before now" or "by this time."
all ready	means "completely prepared."
	The crowd is *already* assembled.
	We are *all ready* to go.

always	means "all the time."
all ways	means "every manner."
	Judy is not *always* prepared for class.
	I try to be helpful in *all ways*.
amount	means "a sum or total of things."
number	means "persons or things that can be counted individually."
	You can buy those items for a small *amount* of money.
	Let me know the *number* of oysters you need.
as, as though, as if	introduce clauses.
like	introduces prepositional phrases.
	He acts *as though* he is angry.
	He is *as* strong as an ox. [*Is* is understood.]
	He looks *like* you.
at	See **to, at.**
between	refers to two persons or things.
among	refers to more than two persons or things.
	A woman shouldn't have to choose *between* marriage and a career.
	The will divides his money *among* several heirs.
borrow	means "to get, with the intention of returning."
lend	means "to let someone have something you expect to get back."
	I *borrowed* some money from my brother.
	Lisa didn't want to *lend* me any of her clothes.
bought	means "purchased."
brought	means "caused to come here."
	Liz *bought* a ticket for the Sweepstakes.
	I *brought* along my knitting.
bring	means "to cause to come here."
take	means "to cause to go there."
	Bring that photograph album to me.
	Take that ugly vase into the other room.
effect	See **affect, effect.**
except	See **accept, except.**

Using the Right Word **283**

fewer   means "not as many." It is a plural word and refers to things that can be counted.

less   means "not as much." It is a singular word referring to a quantity.

I have *fewer* problems than I had ten years ago.

I have *less* money than I had ten years ago.

foot   is singular.

feet   is plural.

The stool is less than a *foot* tall.

I am five *feet* tall.

When the measurement comes before the person or thing it describes, however, use the word *foot*.

This is a ten-*foot* ladder.

from   Do not use *off* or *off of* when you mean *from*.

off   The meanings are often similar, but *off* usually means "from the top of."

WRONG   Jim copied *off* my paper.

RIGHT   Jim copied *from* my paper.

hole   See **whole, hole, hold.**

idea   means "thought."

ideal   means "model of perfection."

That is a good *idea*.

Your paper lacks a central *idea*.

He has high *ideals*.

in   means "located within."

into   means "toward the inside" of a place.

We were all gathered *in* my aunt's room.

Joe just walked *into* my aunt's room.

its   means "belonging to it."

it's   means "it is" or "it has."

Virtue is *its* own reward.

It's a small price to pay for being beautiful.

learn   means "to gain knowledge."

teach   means "to pass on knowledge."

I *learned* how to surface-dive from my brother.

Let me *teach* you how to stay awake in class.

leave	means "to go away from."
let	means "to allow to."
	I am *leaving* my past life behind.
	I will *let* him have my answer soon.
lend	See **borrow, lend.**
less	See **fewer, less.**
mind	means "intelligence" or "pay attention to."
mine	means "belonging to me."
	Exercise your *mind* as well as your body.
	Mind your parents.
	This umbrella is *mine*.
like	See **as, as though, as if, like.**
loose	means "not tight" or "unfastened."
lose	means "to allow to get away" or "to misplace."
	Susie seems to have a *loose* tooth.
	It's sad to *lose* an old friend.
number	See **amount, number.**
off	See **from, off.**
passed	means "went by."
past	means "former times" or "belonging to former times."
	The parade *passed* through the town.
	It is often sad to remember the *past*.
principal	is an adjective or noun meaning "first or most important."
principle	is a noun meaning "essential rule."
	He is the *principal* of my school.
	Act according to a high *principle*.
take	See **bring, take.**
teach	See **learn, teach.**
than	is used in a comparison.
then	can mean "at that time."
	George is faster *than* lightning.
	Wait awhile; Lou will *then* be free to help you.
that	See **who, which, that.**
their	means "belonging to them."

there	means "in that place" and sometimes introduces the subject of a sentence.
they're	means "they are."
	Let them have *their* way.
	There are many reasons for avoiding those rock concerts.
	They're here! *They're* here!
to	means "toward" or "in the direction of." It also appears before the verb in expressions like *to want* and *to have*.
too	means "also" or "more than enough."
two	means "one plus one."
	We all hate *to* go *to* the dentist.
	I am *too* angry to speak.
	I tried *two* or three times to teach Lisa.
to	means "toward" or "in the direction of."
at	means "near" or "in the location of."
	WRONG They arrived to our house.
	RIGHT They arrived *at* our house.
	OR
	They came *to* our house.
who	refers to persons.
which	refers to things.
that	can refer to persons or things.
	Betsy Ross is the woman *who* made the first American flag.
	Which of these stories did you prefer?
	This is the wrench *that* I need for the job.
who's	means "who is" or "who has."
whose	means "belonging to what person."
	Who's at the door?
	Whose jellybeans are these?
whole	means "entire."
hole	means "opening."
hold	means "to keep."
	I can't believe I ate the *whole* pie!
	Every doughnut has its *hole*.
	I won't believe I have the money until I *hold* it in my hand.

your	means "belonging to you."
you're	means "you are."
	Take *your* seat.
	I think that *you're* mistaken.

EXERCISE 5

Write *to*, *too*, or *two* in each of the blanks in the following sentences.

1. Americans drive cars that burn _____ much gasoline.

2. I was _____ tired _____ understand what I was doing.

3. The nail was _____ inches _____ long.

4. Mark has dedicated his life _____ his family.

5. I was _____ proud _____ admit that I wasn't ready to be on my own.

6. _____ much freedom makes people lazy.

7. Tom was _____ afraid _____ stay home alone.

EXERCISE 6

Write *a* or *an* in each of the blanks in the following sentences.

1. That elephant had _____ unbelievably long trunk.

2. Compare Providence to _____ uncrowded city, and you'll see in _____ instant what I mean.

3. My boyfriend is twenty-seven; I never thought I could fall in love with _____ older man.

4. It only took them _____ hour to find _____ place to eat.

5. Eve wanted to get _____ job in _____ office.

6. You can hang _____ clothesline in the yard.

7. Leo is _____ good quarterback.

EXERCISE 7

Write *their, there,* or *they're* in each of the blanks in the following sentences.

1. _____ own land was rich farmland.

2. _____ going to be late if they don't hurry.

3. I'll never learn all _____ is to learn about that subject.

4. George had never been _____ before.

5. _____ are many stresses that can bring on a heart attack.

EXERCISE 8

Underline the correct word in parentheses in the following sentences.

1. I walked (in, into) the kitchen and saw my brother frying bacon.

2. When the firefighters arrived (at, to) our house, they wanted to know where the fire was.

3. My uncle is (in, into) his workshop.

4. If you can get (to, at) the store by 10:30, you probably won't find it crowded.

5. It looks as though the crowd is already (at, to) the ball park.

EXERCISE 9

In the following sentences, if any italicized word is incorrectly used, change it to *who* or *which.*

1. He is the only man *that* I have ever loved.

2. Pick up the pliers, *which* are on the workbench.

3. The attendant *which* parked your car doesn't seem to be around right now.

4. Kris Kristofferson, *who* has written some great country tunes, was once a Rhodes scholar.

EXERCISE 10

Underline the correct word in parentheses in the following sentences.

1. (Who's, Whose) clothing did Elaine borrow this week?
2. It's easy to tell (whose, who's) put too much squash on his plate.
3. Guess (who's, whose) coming to dinner!
4. I wonder (who's, whose) been nibbling at this cake.
5. Just as we started to relax, the sergeant called out, ("Whose, "Who's) gear is this piled on the floor?"

EXERCISE 11

Underline the correct word in parentheses in the following sentences.

1. My father is afraid to (learn, teach) any of us to drive.
2. Talk to your teenage daughter (like, as though) she is an adult.
3. People who have the blues (alot, a lot) have other emotional problems.
4. What is the central (idea, ideal) of your theme?
5. Since you have (brought, bought) gas for less money than that, you must know that it is possible to do it.
6. Before zip codes were put into (affect, effect), clerks had to look up all the names of small towns.
7. Lucy is willing to (accept, except) the job even though it has (fewer, less) benefits than her old one.
8. If you misplace (your, you're) wallet, (your, you're) in trouble.
9. We began to (loose, lose) sight of the ground as we (past, passed) through the clouds.
10. (Let, Leave) us make up our minds once and for all.
11. I wanted to (lend, borrow) a chain saw (from, off, of) my uncle, but he was afraid to (lend, borrow) it to me.
12. (Bring, Take) those books to the library before you have to pay a fine.
13. Mr. Emerson asked the salesclerk to (whole, hole, hold) that camera for him until payday.

14. On Friday nights my friend Jim is always trying to (lend, borrow) me ten dollars or so until I can get a job.

15. (Its, It's) a good day for staying at home by the fire.

16. The answers to the difficult questions are (always, all ways) hidden (in, into) the back of the manual.

17. (There's, Theirs) no point in rushing; (your, you're) (already, all ready) late.

18. John is a handsome six-(foot, feet)-tall man.

19. The election comes down to a choice (among, between) two very good candidates.

20. It takes (fewer, less) people than you might think to make a good basketball team.

CHAPTER TWENTY-TWO
Too Few Words

> ***Do not leave out necessary words.***

Many times readers can understand what a writer means to say even if the writer leaves out an occasional word in a sentence, but it is not a good idea to omit words. Most people omit words in their writing because they are careless, because they have developed the habit of leaving out certain words in writing, or because they often omit these words in speech and this habit has been transferred to their writing.

22a
Do not develop the careless habit of leaving out short words like *the, and, he, she, it, his, her, of,* or *that.*

> **WRONG**   As I got to swamp, I knew I had to go in.
> **RIGHT**   As I got *the* swamp, I knew I had to go in.
>
> **WRONG**   It was my letter convinced my sister to come and see what was going on.

RIGHT   It was my letter *that* convinced my sister to come and see what was going on.

WRONG   He dribbles well also assists in points made by other players.
RIGHT   He dribbles well *and* also assists in points made by other players.

In particular, if you are giving directions, do not carelessly omit the words *it* and *the*. You may see such omissions in cookbooks and technical manuals, which try to save space, but you should include these words in your papers.

WRONG   Take from bowl second half of dough and roll the same way you rolled the first piece.
RIGHT   Take from *the* bowl *the* second half of *the* dough and roll *it* the same way you rolled the first piece.
WRONG   Pull out locking rod and remove cylinder. Push rod with wire tip through barrel.
RIGHT   Pull out *the* locking rod and remove *the* cylinder. Push *the* rod with *the* wire tip through *the* barrel.

Remember to include *of* in expressions like *kind of, type of,* and *sort of.*

WRONG   He is the type person you don't want to mess around with.
RIGHT   He is the type *of* person you don't want to mess around with.

22b

Sometimes when you say a sentence quickly, you leave out the verbs *is, are, was,* or *were.* Do not make this mistake in writing.

WRONG   This a description of my brother.
RIGHT   This *is* a description of my brother.

22c
When you compare two people or two things, do not leave out any words that would make your comparison clear.

> WRONG Use our product. You'll feel cleaner than your soap. [You can't compare a person and a soap.]
>
> RIGHT Use our product. You'll feel cleaner than *you would using* your soap.

22d
When you use *so* in a comparison, be sure the comparison is complete.

> WRONG I was so tired.
>
> RIGHT I was so tired *that I fell asleep immediately.*

EXERCISE 1

Insert any words that are needed to complete the meaning of the following sentences.

■ Example Be sure that your air conditioner properly grounded.
  Be sure that your air conditioner *is* properly grounded.

1. Nosy neighbors can tell you what happening in your neighborhood.
2. The first thing came into my mind was that Bob hadn't come over my house for a long time.
3. Disney World offers many games and rides for family.
4. Even with his great size wouldn't hurt the smallest animal.
5. It was end of summer.
6. During the traffic jams, some people got out their cars.
7. My sister and her husband been late for our family reunion every year.
8. It was the weather made us decide to stay home instead of going to the beach.

9. John is the type man you wouldn't trust with much of your money.
10. I like Al Green's singing better than Lou Rawls.

EXERCISE 2

Edit the following paragraph, inserting any words or expressions that the student left out.

My baby brother can ruin any date. When a date comes my house, my brother always pulling and kicking him. Once my date takes seat, here comes my baby brother, jumping up his lap and trying to attract his attention. Even though I try to pull him away, in a few minutes there he is again, pulling at my date's clothing. Finally, tired of whole thing, he leaves early. I then try to talk to my brother, but, as usual, he not listening.

CHAPTER TWENTY-THREE
Too Many Words

> *Leave out any words that repeat something you have already said or that serve no purpose in your sentence.*

23a
Do not use the same word too often in a single sentence or short paragraph.

Sometimes it is difficult to think of a word that has the same meaning as the one you have just used. Finding a new word is usually worth the effort, though, if you can thus avoid repeating yourself needlessly. Usually a little thought will suggest a better way to say something.

REPETITIOUS	Mr. Barnes was chosen coach of the Tigers because he was well-qualified for coaching the team. [There is no need to repeat the idea that Mr. Barnes is a coach.]
BETTER	Mr. Barnes was chosen coach of the Tigers because he was well-qualified *for the job.*

REPETITIOUS	The section to be plated has to be roughed in order to be plated. [There is no need to repeat that the section is to be plated.]
BETTER	The section to be plated has to be roughed *first*.

23b
Do not use a synonym (a word that has the same meaning as a word you have already used) unless it serves a definite purpose.

23b(1)
Do not bore your reader by repeating an idea that does not have to be repeated.

REPETITIOUS	Moving your fingers on the frets or neck of the guitar will give you the desired sounds you want. [*Desired sounds* and *sounds you want* mean the same thing. Only one of the expressions is needed.]
BETTER	Moving your fingers on the frets or neck of the guitar will give you the desired sounds.
REPETITIOUS	Replace the jack back in the trunk. [*Replace* means "to put back." Omit the word *back*.]
BETTER	Replace the jack in the trunk.
REPETITIOUS	My brother is neither fat nor thin, which helps him play football because of the way he is built. [*The way he is built* is unnecessary because the sentence says that he is *neither fat nor thin*.]
BETTER	My brother is neither fat nor thin, a fact which helps him play football.

23b(2)
Avoid using expressions that are themselves repetitious.

REPETITIOUS	ink pen	return back
BETTER	pen	return

REPETITIOUS	school teacher	continue on
BETTER	teacher	continue
REPETITIOUS	the modern world of today	repeat again
BETTER	the modern world	repeat
REPETITIOUS	in my opinion, I think	true facts
BETTER	I think	facts

23b(3)

Do not repeat the subject by using *he, she, it,* or *they* right after the subject you have just named.

REPETITIOUS	The coach, he is just there to help the quarterback decide what plays to run.
BETTER	The coach is just there to help the quarterback decide what plays to run.

23b(4)

Avoid using *at* in a *where is something* expression.

It is incorrect because *at* repeats the idea of location expressed in the word *where.*

WRONG	Where is the library at?
RIGHT	Where is the library?

EXERCISE 1

Rewrite the following sentences, eliminating any unnecessary words.

1. The reason I am happy is because today is my birthday.
2. When I practiced my speech, some of the contents of my speech were twisted, which caused distortion in the development of my speech.
3. Through the years bikes have been improved and made better.

4. Many violent films are rated R because of their violence.

5. Rembrandt, he was the greatest art painter of all time.

6. Do not hold or depress the tongue down.

7. The rope has no use, no purpose, and no reason for being.

8. In my opinion, I feel television will play an important role in our modern society.

9. Champ can catch a ball in his mouth and return it back to you.

10. Where is the registrar's office at?

23c
Train yourself to say things plainly.

Many beginning writers (and unfortunately some experienced ones) think that in order to have an effective style they have to use words that "sound good." Others think it is better to lead up to a point instead of making it directly. Actually, in most types of writing, the best style is the simplest one. Decide that after you have written something, you will take time to delete unnecessary words and to reword sentences to make your work shorter and clearer. Ask yourself whether every word or group of words is really necessary to the meaning of a sentence.

Here are some sentences that are wordy (contain unnecessary words). How could they be simplified?

> **WORDY** My sister dressed to assume the appearance of Goldilocks. [*To assume the appearance of* is a pretentious way of saying *as.*]
>
> **BETTER** My sister dressed as Goldilocks.
>
> **WORDY** College prepares you for the field you may be entering, or if you aren't planning to work, it still helps you talk about things in a conversation that is interesting to you and other people. [This could have been said in far fewer words.]

BETTER   College prepares you for an occupation and makes you a
good conversationalist.

Avoid groups of words that add length but not clarity to your sentences.

WORDY   our modern world in which we live
It tends to seem to this observer that
To me, I think
at this point in time
BETTER   our world
I believe that
I think
now

EXERCISE 2

Eliminate wordiness in the following sentences. Rewrite any sentences where it is necessary.

1. Put the jack in a position where it will lift the car in a way so that you can change the tire.
2. To me, I believe that the jet plane has changed the entire course of existence in this modern world in which we now live.
3. I was wondering what it was possible for me to do about the problem I was having deciding whether to go back to school or to look for some kind of job.
4. The snow began to reach a higher level on the ground on which it lay.
5. When I was in high school, I never studied enough to accumulate the knowledge of the many and varied important things I needed to know.
6. Quite a few people have a limited amount of time to engage in shopping. Most of those individuals find that a large part of this time is spent searching for desired yet hard-to-locate bargains in the many stores that line the streets of our major cities.
7. Mismanagement of money causes it to be used up sooner than is desirable resulting in a loss of ability to buy more items until more money is accumulated.

23d
Avoid long introductions and the repetition of words and ideas you have used elsewhere.

Be certain that everything you write has a definite purpose. This passage shows that the writer was groping for ways to fill space.

> One of the most difficult adjustments any individual has to make is learning how to get along with others. People have individual differences in appearance, personality, and personal habits. Knowing that people are all different in the above-mentioned ways and aspects makes a person feel confused about how to adjust to others. There are several essential behavior patterns that all people have in common. It is each person's job to look for these patterns in order to understand and adjust to others.

As you can see, the writer never gets anywhere in this passage. Once the point is made that certain patterns of behavior exist in all individuals, the writer says nothing further.

EXERCISE 3

Eliminate all unnecessary repetition in the following passages by writing the essential ideas in one or two sentences.

1. The team is an eleven-man unit. This means that every man works as a part of the team and that they all work together toward the same objective. If every man does his job in the right situation, the play will be successful.

2. Many people find commercials on TV very vexing because they interrupt the programs. Some programs have commercial breaks eight to ten times every half hour. A viewer watching pay TV is not distracted by continual advertising urging him to buy a special cleaner or hear about the heartbreak of hemorrhoids. Quite a few people have a limited time to watch TV. A large part of this time is spent watching commercials. If they had pay TV, they could watch more programs without the wasted time of commercials.

PART FIVE

MOVING TOWARD THE COMPLETE PAPER

CHAPTER TWENTY-FOUR
Improving Sentences

> *Improve your sentences by giving them variety, point, and clarity.*

24a

Vary the length of your sentences. Avoid a series of short, choppy sentences.

If your papers are now fairly free of really serious mistakes like fragments and verb errors, you probably feel very much relieved. But there are still some things you must concern yourself with if you want to keep your reader's attention and interest. Sooner or later, all writers must give some thought to the length and variety of their sentences if they want their readers to enjoy what they have written.

Read the following paragraph:

> There is a chapel in North Carolina. I love to visit it. It is situated among tall pine trees. The trees are covered with Spanish moss. It looks like a storybook cottage. It is a red brick building trimmed in white. The patterns of the stained glass windows seem to glow with a life of their own even on the cloudiest days. The most impressive of these windows depicts Christ kneeling in prayer. The chapel always makes me feel that I have been transported to a serene,

almost holy place. This is a place where even the most troubled person would find peace.

As you read that description of the chapel, you probably noticed that you got a good idea of what the place looked like. There were many specific details, yet the paragraph seemed monotonous. Did you notice that all the sentences were about the same length? Using the same information, the writer could have written a better paragraph by varying the length of the sentences and combining some of them:

> There is a chapel in North Carolina that I love to visit. Situated among tall pine trees and covered with Spanish moss, it looks like a storybook cottage. It is a red brick building trimmed in white. The patterns of the stained glass windows seem to glow with a life of their own, even on the cloudiest days. The most impressive of these windows depicts Christ kneeling in prayer. Whenever I see that chapel, I always feel that I have been transported to a serene, almost holy place, somewhere that even the most troubled person would find peace.

EXERCISE 1

Vary the length of the sentences in the following paragraph. Combine sentences when possible to avoid choppiness.

> My dog is named Bunny. She hates to go to the vet. She sometimes has a problem that requires a vet. Preparations are made to carry her there. She gets nervous. Bunny will hide under the bed. To get her from under the bed, I have to give her a cookie. She paces from the back seat to the front seat of the car on the way to the vet. She usually cries and moans just like a child. She is not the bravest dog in the world.

24b

Give your sentence a point. Use coordination and subordination correctly.

24b(1)

Avoid strung-together *and* and *but* sentences. Use coordination only when you are joining two equal ideas.

If you write:

> My second year in high school I was in chorus, and I sang first soprano, and I was in mixed chorus, and I was in regional chorus also.

your sentence does not really have a point. You are not saying anything in particular about your singing career but are just listing singing activities during a particular year. If you mean to make a list, it would be better to write:

> During my second year in high school, I sang first soprano in mixed and regional chorus.

Do not be an *and* sentence writer. It is true that some clauses may be joined by coordinating conjunctions like *and* and *but* when you are listing or contrasting ideas.

LISTING	I thought you would be here, *and* I was right.
CONTRASTING	I thought you would be here, *but* I was wrong.

If you have no reason for using *and* or *but*, however, you may find yourself writing strung-together sentences that suggest to the reader that you have not really sorted out your ideas.

In the following example, the writer overused *but* to join sentences. It is difficult for the reader to see what the point of the sentence is.

> My little brother wanted to see *Lady Chatterley's Lover*, but my mother wouldn't let him because of its R rating, but I don't think she knew what was in it.

Is the point that the writer's brother wanted to see *Lady Chatterley's*

Lover, that his mother would not let him or that his mother did not know much about the movie?

> Because of *Lady Chatterley's Lover's* R rating, my mother kept my brother from seeing the movie, without really knowing what was in it.

You can now tell that the writer is emphasizing the fact that his mother would not let his brother see the movie.

24b(2)

Use subordination. Make it clear when the thing talked about in one sentence *causes* the thing talked about in the next sentence. Use the word *because* or *since,* and join the sentences.

When one thing happens because another thing happened, make that idea clearer by using the word *because* or *since* and joining the two sentences. Notice that if the sentence begins with *because* or *since,* you have to put a comma where the sentences are joined. (See **13b** for more information.)

Compare the following ways of joining sentences. You can say:

> His bus was not on time. He was late for work.

You can join these ideas with *and:*

> His bus was not on time, *and* he was late for work.

These sentences do not make it very clear that one event caused the other. You can show the connection between the sentences better by writing:

> *Because* his bus was not on time, he was late for work.
>
> OR
>
> He was late for work *because* his bus was not on time.

24b(3)

Sometimes when you write two short sentences, you want to suggest that one thing happens after, before, or at the same time as another thing. You will make this point more clearly if you use the word *when, before, after,* or *while* and join the sentences.

UNCONNECTED	My dog missed his footing on the boat dock. He plunged head first into the muddy water.
BETTER	*After* my dog missed his footing on the boat dock, he plunged head first into the muddy water.
UNCONNECTED	We ate peanut butter sandwiches and chocolate chip cookies. We talked about our plans for the rest of the summer.
BETTER	We talked about our plans for the rest of the summer *while* we ate peanut butter sandwiches and chocolate chip cookies.

Notice that when the word *when, before, after,* or *while* introduces the sentence, you have to put a comma where the sentences are joined.

24b(4)

Use words like *if, unless,* and *although* and join two short sentences to help give your sentence a point.

If you want to say that you wish you were a millionaire, it is not as clear to say

I am quite happy. I wish I had a million dollars.

as it is to say

Although I am quite happy, I wish I had a million dollars.
OR
I wish I had a million dollars *although* I am quite happy.

Notice that you have to use a comma where the sentences are joined only when words like *if* and *although* introduce the sentence.

EXERCISE 2

Give each sentence a point by using words such as *because, when,* and *although.*

■ **Example**   I overslept this morning, and I missed breakfast, and my whole day went wrong.
Because I overslept this morning and missed breakfast, my whole day went wrong.

1. I left the house this morning, and my car wouldn't start, and there was no gas in the tank.
2. I decided to go to driving school, and I knew I couldn't afford it, but I went anyway.
3. All the TV shows went off, and we all listened to the radio, and finally everybody got sleepy, and we all went to bed.

EXERCISE 3

Improve each of the following pairs of sentences. Begin each pair with an introductory word—such as *because, since, when, after, before, while, if, although,* or *unless*—and join the two sentences.

■ **Example**   I got to know Michael. I started to like him.
After I got to know Michael, I started to like him.

1. Robert introduced me to his sister. He told me we both had the same name.
2. You are so angry with me. I am afraid to ask a favor of you.
3. The game started. We had already taken our seats.
4. I got my car started. I was on my way to work.
5. Fred likes it here. He would rather be at the beach.
6. Beth will let me know when you get here. I can meet you at the station.

7. Gus read your letter. He didn't know you were planning to visit us.

8. Rabbits sure do dig up a garden. They make nice pets for children.

9. I heard your uncle George lost his job last week. I started worrying about my own job.

10. Hank's wife left him for another man. He just hasn't been the same.

24c
When you are describing a person or thing, one well-developed sentence is usually better than two short sentences.

WEAK	My father's old felt hat looks as though it has been through the wars. It is sitting on the mantel.
BETTER	My father's old felt hat, *which looks as though it has been through the wars,* is sitting on the mantel.
WEAK	Joe Louis was undoubtedly the greatest heavyweight fighter of all time. He died practically penniless.
BETTER	Joe Louis, *who was undoubtedly the greatest heavyweight fighter of all time,* died practically penniless.
WEAK	*Jaws* was the biggest moneymaker in years. It kept thousands of frightened teenagers away from the Atlantic coast beaches.
BETTER	*Jaws, the biggest moneymaker in years,* kept thousands of frightened teenagers away from the Atlantic coast beaches.
WEAK	Joe Namath was a famous quarterback. Now he is an actor of sorts.
BETTER	Joe Namath, *a famous quarterback,* is now an actor of sorts.

EXERCISE 4

Combine each of the following pairs of sentences, following the pattern given in the example.

■ **Example**   Carl Simpson left a cigarette on the car seat.
　　　　　　　He found a burning hulk when he returned.

Carl Simpson, *who left a cigarette on the car seat,* found a burning hulk when he returned.

1. Uncle Jack watches all the horror movies on TV. He sometimes can't sleep at night thinking about them.
2. My dog Fred never bit a soul. He has a sign on his outdoor kennel which reads "Beware of Dog."
3. Marilyn's mother-in-law was never sick a day in her life. She is always worried about her health.
4. My mother thinks she is an expert on politics. She was positive that Ronald Reagan would never be elected President.

EXERCISE 5

Combine each of the following pairs of sentences, using the italicized pattern given.

■ Example   My sister is the biggest baby in the world. She cried when she stubbed her toe on the screen door.
My sister, *the biggest baby in the world,* cried when she stubbed her toe on the screen door.

1. Robert Redford is my favorite actor. He sends goosebumps down my spine.
2. Their only son is a real problem for the family. He wrecked both their cars last year.
3. Carl Yastremski is well over forty. He may be the best hitter in baseball.
4. The new boy in school was named Jim McDonald. He seemed to have more money than the rest of us.

EXERCISE 6

Combine each of the following pairs of sentences, using one of the patterns given.

■ Example   My house is a real white elephant. It will not bring much money on the market.

My house, *a real white elephant,* will not bring much money on the market.

OR

My house, *which is a real white elephant,* will not bring much money on the market.

1. My sister's hope chest is a standing joke in our family. It will probably never leave our house.
2. The garbage can is full to overflowing. It should have been emptied two days ago.
3. Our car is an antique according to my father. It sure runs like an antique.
4. Brighton Beach is a recreation area. It is not very far from downtown Manhattan.

24d

Make your writing more interesting by varying the beginnings of your sentences.

The following paragraph shows the need for such variety.

My friend is not very athletic, but she is interested in sports. Her favorite sports are basketball, tennis, and baseball. She doesn't dislike any kind of game. She wishes she had more natural ability.

One of the reasons this paragraph is dull is that all the sentences start with the subject, which is followed immediately by the verb.

SUBJECT	VERB
My friend	is
Her favorite sports	are
She	doesn't dislike
She	wishes

Here are some ways that sentences can be varied:

1. Put words like *when, if, although, because, as soon as,* or *in spite of* before one of the short sentences, and join the sentences.

Although her favorite sports are basketball, tennis, and baseball, she doesn't dislike any kind of game.

2. Begin the sentence with a word or phrase that adds something to the sentence. Introductory words or phrases like *as a matter of fact, in addition, without a doubt, at that time, suddenly, unbelievably, in the morning,* and *after dinner* give variety to sentences.

   She doesn't dislike any kind of game. As a matter of fact, she wishes she had more natural ability.

3. Occasionally, use a question, a command, or a statement of surprise for variety.

   As a matter of fact, she wishes she had more natural ability. What an admirable person she is!

The writer of the following paragraph varied her sentences by using some of the methods listed above. Can you spot these variations?

Do you recognize the all-day bargain hunter when you meet him in a store? He is the person who arrives at the store before the employees and stays until closing time. This shopper is usually a coupon and ad collector who has clippings from magazines and every newspaper in town. As soon as the store opens, he runs to a table of merchandise and rummages through it, searching for the best buys. Watch out for him because he won't let anyone get in his way when he is bargain hunting. As a matter of fact, this shopper could be given a gold medal for endurance and determination.

EXERCISE 7

Write a sentence using each of the following beginnings.

1. Unexpectedly,
2. Unless you get a letter tomorrow,
3. At the same time,
4. After a long bath,
5. In the past,
6. In the first place,

7. As soon as possible,

8. In spite of your objections,

9. Next to the door,

10. For this reason,

Remember, to improve your sentences,

1. avoid too many short, choppy sentences.

2. avoid too many sentences joined by *and* or *but*.

3. use *because* or *since* and join short sentences when you want to say that one thing caused another.

4. use *when*, *after*, *before*, or *while* and join short sentences when you want to tell when something happened in relation to another thing.

5. use words like *if* and *although* and join two short sentences to express the relationship between one idea and another.

6. when describing persons or things, try to combine two short sentences into one clear sentence.

7. vary the beginnings of your sentences. Use introductory words, questions, commands and statements of surprise.

EXERCISE 8

The following paragraphs contain short, choppy sentences. Rewrite them, varying the length and beginnings of the sentences.

1. Most rare electric guitars were produced in the 1950s. Most guitarists prefer Gibson or Fender brands built during that time. These instruments are scarce and expensive. The Fender "telecaster" model is still very popular today. Today's production model looks exactly like the 1955 version. There is no comparison in the craftsmanship. The mid-fifties Gibson brand Les Paul model is probably the most popular of all old guitars. The Les Pauls produced today are considered the finest on the market.

2. Every summer I work as a grocery clerk. There is one problem that always upsets me. Sometimes parents send their children to the store for something. I usually find out that they do not have enough money

after I have rung up the groceries. Then I have to void the ticket. It takes several minutes. Then my line has backed up. I have to work even harder to get everyone through the line. I am usually very tired after a day of problems like this one.

3. I once lived in a beautiful valley in West Virginia. It was surrounded by the rugged mountains of the Appalachian region. My little white house was situated at the base of one small mountain. It was in the middle of the prettiest, sweetest-smelling bottomland in the world. Cooper's Creek, with its cool, delicious spring waters, flowed the length of my heaven. My little mountain was covered with several acres of apple trees. I shared it gladly with my neighbor's old cow. Fried apples using apples fresh from the tree and fresh fish from the little pond nearby were on my daily menu. Cooper's Creek is gone now. It is the victim of society's need to be able to move swiftly from one point to another without reflecting on what it sees. The joys of a simple life I once knew remain planted in my mind.

CHAPTER TWENTY-FIVE
The Paragraph

Learn to write clearly developed paragraphs.

A paragraph is a group of sentences about one idea or topic. Physically, a paragraph is easy to see on a page because its first word is indented from the left margin.

A paragraph looks like this:

```
    Sentence 1
_____ . Sentence 2
                        . Sentence 3
_____ . Sentence 4
Sentence 5              . Sentence 6
        . Sentence 7                    .
```

The length of your paragraph will change with the type of topic you are writing about. That is, some topics are more difficult than others and take more words to develop. The average length of your paragraphs will probably be five to eight sentences or about 75 to 150 words.

Most paragraphs will be about as long as the following one.

My Brother

My brother keeps himself physically fit. He runs four laps around a mile-long track twice in the morning and evening. In his spare time, he works out in the neighborhood gym, doing calisthenics and yoga, lifting weights, and sprinting. He always keeps two closets full of health foods and drinks. In the morning, he gets up at 6:00 and does one hundred sit-ups before he goes to work. If he keeps this up, he will either make the U.S. Olympic team or kill himself at an early age.

25a

Before beginning to write your paragraph, pick a topic or think about the topic you have been assigned.

Be careful not to confuse a topic with a topic sentence.

TOPICS	TOPIC SENTENCES
My brother's physical condition	My brother keeps himself physically fit.
Patience	Patience can be thought of as the ability to tolerate difficulties while hoping for better things.
Touring a movie theater	I read a newspaper article about the intricate brass and woodwork in some of the old movie theaters in the area and decided to take a look for myself.
Underwater explorations	Underwater explorations are far more important than most people believe.

After you have your topic, jot down as many ideas as you can think of about it. You will use these ideas in writing your topic sentence now and in writing your paragraph later.

25b
You should usually begin your paragraph with a topic sentence.

The topic sentence tells the reader what you are going to write about in the rest of your paragraph. It makes a statement that needs to be developed with examples and details.

Be sure that what you write is a topic sentence, not just a topic. These are topics, not topic sentences:

My friend Lo Van	Lo Van
Lo Van's activities	Lo Van, my busiest friend

It is better to state directly the topic of the paragraph than to tell what you mean to say.

WEAK	In this paper I will tell about my friend Lo Van.
WEAK	This paper will describe my friend Lo Van.
WEAK	In this paragraph I will show that Lo Van is the busiest person I know.
BETTER	My friend Lo Van is the busiest person I have ever met.

My Friend Lo Van

TOPIC
SENTENCE → My friend Lo Van is the busiest person I have ever met. Every morning he attends an English class at the community center. After class Lo Van works at a neighborhood market, and in the evening he is a waiter in his uncle's restaurant. Lo Van is even busy on Sunday mornings delivering newspapers. I am sure that at night his mind is hard at work dreaming of the next day's activities.

The topic sentence underlined above tells the reader that the rest of this paragraph will be about Lo Van and the reasons that make him the busiest person the writer has ever met.

EXERCISE 1

Eliminate any of the following that are topics but not sentences. Then put a check by any *good* topic sentences you find in the list.

1. My best friend
2. This paragraph will attempt to define fear.
3. An attack on the "blue laws"
4. Mercy killing is a very humane practice as long as it is not abused.
5. The recent court decision suggests that the present insanity plea in criminal cases should be reexamined.
6. How to travel five miles without owning a car
7. The reaction to disaster in almost any part of the world is basically the same.
8. In this paragraph I will show that many of the conditions of life at sea have changed tremendously during the last two hundred years.
9. The role of the two-year college in higher education
10. My favorite sport is golf.

25c
Decide on the purpose of your paragraph.

Once you have written your topic sentence, you have really decided on the purpose of your paragraph. The topic sentence will tell you whether you intend to describe, to narrate, to instruct, to compare and contrast, to classify, to define, to analyze or explain, or to argue or persuade. These are the most common reasons for writing a paragraph. Below are some topic sentences that should suggest what the writer's purpose is.

1. *to describe*

   My bedroom is the messiest room in my house.
   My best friend, Sarah, always wears the latest styles.

2. *to narrate*

   Last Monday I forgot everything I was supposed to do.

3. *to instruct*

   If you want to make a foul shot almost every time, there are three easy steps to remember.

4. *to compare or contrast*

   A baseball and a basketball are different in appearance and in purpose.

5. *to classify*

   Shotguns can be classified as single-barreled or double-barreled.

6. *to define*

   Daydreaming is a practice that temporarily removes the dreamer from the real world.

7. *to analyze or explain*

   My neighborhood could be improved by the addition of several streetlights.

8. *to argue or persuade*

   A disadvantage of the work-release program is that it gives a known criminal the opportunity to commit another crime.

After you have used your topic sentence to help you decide on the purpose of your paper, you are ready to develop your paragraph, using an appropriate method.

25d
Select an appropriate method to develop your paragraph.

There are many methods you can use to develop or give order to a paragraph. Once you have decided on your purpose, select a method that is suitable. Here are some of the common ways to arrange the contents of your paragraph.

25d(1)
Use space order.

The space order method is frequently used in a description of a person or a place. Space order begins at one point and moves logically toward another—from one side to another or from top to bottom. You might describe a room, for example, by starting at one end and moving around the room in a certain order. Here is a description of a person. Can you see the order it follows?

> The immaculate, neatly pressed uniform fitted well on Officer Dooley's small, but solid, almost rock-like frame. His cap, smartly squared on top of his head, covered his close-cropped red hair yet added an intangible flair to the fresh, rosy-cheeked Irish face that looked back at him from the mirror. With a glance downward, he picked up the holster he had placed on the bench beside him and buckled it on with that peculiar movement of ease and carefulness that he had acquired over the years. He then took a look at his gleaming black shoes and, seeing his face reflected in the glossy shine, could not suppress a momentary flush of pride in his crisp, tidy appearance as he prepared for another day of serving and protecting the people of Boston.

25d(2)
Use time order.

The time order method is used when you want to tell about a series of events or relate the steps to follow in a series of instructions. It is used in a narrative paragraph when you want to tell what happened from the first to the last event. In giving directions, you will want to recite the steps in order. Here is a paragraph describing how to hit a sacrifice bunt in baseball, using three steps.

> The most often used bunt or short-distance hit in baseball is the sacrifice bunt. This bunt has three basic steps. The first is the shift of the feet. The left foot is moved back, and the right foot is moved up toward the pitcher so the feet are in a line perpendicular to home plate. The second step is the shift of the hands. One hand is kept down on the handle near the knob of the bat, and the other is slipped up the handle until the label of the bat is felt under the

thumb. The third and most important part of the sacrifice bunt is getting the ball onto the ground, because a pop-up is an easy out. The bottom of the bat is held down at a 45-degree angle to the ground, and as the ball comes in, the batter guides it down to the ground.

25d(3)
Move from the general to the particular.

Many paragraphs begin with a general statement or observation which you then develop by giving specific details in the rest of the paragraph. The paragraph "My Brother" on p. 316 uses this method. Many good descriptions, comparisons, classification paragraphs, and paragraphs of instructions start with a general statement which is then illustrated by particular details, examples, or a list of steps. In a paragraph classifying German shepherds, for example, you might begin with a general statement about the three important uses for trained German shepherds. In the rest of the paragraph, you could describe those uses—for guarding businesses and homes, for police work, and for aiding the blind. The example below begins with a general statement about the technique of blowing bubbles. It then illustrates that technique by listing the steps.

> Blowing a really impressive bubble from a wad of gum requires the proper technique. Hold the gum flat against the back of your closed front teeth. Use your tongue to spread it so that it covers the entire front fourth of your mouth. While starting to exhale slowly, begin pushing the gum between your teeth and lips. Continue to blow steadily, using your lips to round the bubble as it emerges. Not only do your lips form the bubble's shape, but they become the base of the bubble itself. This enables you to keep the size of the bubble under control. After all, you can only form a bubble as big as the wad just before it comes loose from your mouth. Be sure to keep away from drafts, for your bubble is extremely susceptible to breezes at this point.

25d(4)
Move from the particular to the general.

Sometimes you will want to lead up to the main point that you make in the last sentence of your paragraph. You use this method because you want your reader to reach the same conclusion you have reached. In the paragraph below, the writer is trying to convince us that it is our notions of what is feminine that control the kind of anger we expect a woman to express.

> Women have been denied the forthright expression of even healthy and realistic anger. They may show anger in defense of a child but must never take up their own cause. To express anger—especially openly, directly, or loudly—makes a woman unfeminine and unattractive. When a woman is called aggressive, this accusation may repel other women, frighten men, and send the woman herself into despair. Women are the nurturers, the soothers, the peacemakers, and the steadiers of rocked boats. All our definitions of femininity have perpetuated the myth that the truly feminine woman is devoid of anger.

Of course, some paragraphs illustrate a combination of methods. The paragraph on the sacrifice bunt (page 320), for example, uses time order, but it also moves from the general to the particular. The important thing is to organize your paragraph to make it clear and effective.

EXERCISE 2

Suggest a method that you could use to develop each of the following topic sentences.

1. My mother is the most generous person I know.
2. On May 11, 1983, I was involved in a serious automobile accident.
3. In order to throw a football successfully, you must master certain skills and follow several basic steps.

4. My hometown has changed so much since I moved away that I hardly knew the place when I went back for a visit last month.

5. The best definition of laziness is an illustration of what the word means in action.

25e
Use details and examples that develop your topic sentence.

In writing the paragraph, be careful to develop the topic sentence, not just the title. All the sentences in the paragraph should give details about the topic sentence and should give your reader a better understanding of the subject you are writing about than the topic sentence alone does.

The following paragraph is not developed. Some of the sentences do not give details about the topic sentence.

My Cousin Kay

UNDEVELOPED TOPIC SENTENCE → My cousin Kay is very jealous when she is around me. When Kay comes to town to visit our relatives, she doesn't even speak to me. Kay has short black hair and small brown eyes. When I am around her, Kay is always talking to me. She doesn't want to have anything to do with me. Kay has a big mouth and a small nose. She talks about me behind my back. Kay has small hands and is about five feet tall. I hope she finds peace with herself.

To develop this paragraph, all the sentences should tell about Kay's jealousy. Instead, some of the sentences tell how Kay looks, and others tell how she acts. The paragraph is about the title, "My Cousin Kay," but it is not about the topic sentence.

The following paragraph is better. All the sentences give details about the topic sentence.

My Cousin Kay

BETTER ——————→ My cousin Kay is very rude when she is around me.
TOPIC
SENTENCE
When Kay comes to town to visit our relatives, she doesn't speak a word to me. When I am around her, Kay ignores me completely, although when I'm not around her, her big loud mouth is always talking about me behind my back. She probably acts like this because she dislikes me, and she doesn't want to have anything to do with me. Kay is not an easy person to get along with because she is rude and immature.

The sentences in this paragraph all tell about Kay's rudeness to the writer.

EXERCISE 3

Read the following paragraph and write down any sentences that do not develop the topic sentence.

The Worst Day in My Life

TOPIC ——————→ Working in an emergency room at a hospital gives
SENTENCE
a person many opportunities to experience bad days, but my worst day came recently after a heavy rain and sleet storm. On the other hand, just last week I had three pleasant days in a row. On that day our emergency room was overrun by drivers who were unused to the slick streets, little old ladies who had slipped on the ice, police officers who were hauling in the previously mentioned drivers, and a physician (only one) who was bleary-eyed and sneezing. The hospital staff physicians are poorly paid and don't seem to care about the patients. With a few more days like that one, I will be a good candidate for geriatric nursing. I hope I can get off early on Friday.

EXERCISE 4

Choose one of the topic sentences from Exercise 2 and list at least five details, examples, or steps that would develop it.

25f
When you develop your paragraph, use transitional words so that the reader moves smoothly from one detail to the next.

After deciding on your organizational method and details, use transitional words to develop your paragraph. For example, in a paragraph comparing and contrasting two people or ideas, you might use words like *in the same way, likewise, but, however,* or *yet.* If you are moving from the general to the particular, you might introduce your details or examples with words like *for example* or *for instance.* Transitional words are particularly important in a paragraph that uses time order so that the reader can move easily from what happens first to what happens last.

The details in the following paragraph are arranged from first to last.

How to Groom Your Cat

TOPIC
SENTENCE ——————→ To groom your cat properly, you must follow a definite procedure very carefully. *First,* plan the procedure *before* your cat knows you intend to groom it. *This procedure* should include gathering the necessary tools—such as comb, brush, and baby powder—and getting your cat's attention, maybe by playing with its favorite toy. *After* you've gathered the tools and lured your cat to a likely spot, the kitchen table, *for example,* you're ready to begin. *Now,* holding your cat firmly at the shoulders with one hand, begin brushing its coat with your other hand. *When* you come to a tangle that won't come out with the brush, use the comb to get rid of it. *Once* you have removed all the tangles, sprinkle a little baby powder into your cat's fur and brush through it again to make its coat look fluffy and

clean. *Now* your cat shold be ready to win a blue ribbon at any cat show.

The italicized transitional words in the paragraph above,

$$\left\{ \begin{array}{lll} \textit{first} & \textit{after} & \textit{when} \\ \textit{before} & \textit{for example} & \textit{once} \\ \textit{this procedure} & \textit{now} & \textit{now} \end{array} \right\}$$

join details and help the reader move smoothly from one detail to another.

The way you choose to arrange the details should be the way that develops your topic sentence best. Whatever way you choose, it should be clear to the reader and easy to follow.

25g
Make the last sentence complete your paragraph.

The following paragraph tells how to write a paragraph.

TITLE ──────────────▶ Writing a Paragraph

TOPIC SENTENCE ──────▶ To write a paragraph, you must follow certain basic steps. Writing a paragraph is a process you can

BRIDGE TO DEVELOPMENT ─ learn if you are willing to think and plan before beginning to write, and to follow your plan when you start

FIRST STEP ──────▶ to write. *First*, you must pick a topic, or think about

SECOND STEP ─────▶ the topic you have been given. *Next*, you must jot down as many ideas as you can think of about your

THIRD STEP ──────▶ topic. *Then*, you should look back over your list and pick out the main points you will use in writing your

FOURTH STEP ─────▶ topic sentence. *Now*, write your topic sentence. *After*

FIFTH STEP ──────▶ you've written your topic sentence, you're ready to develop your paragraph using the main points included

SIXTH STEP ──────▶ in your topic sentence. To develop your paragraph, *then*, write a series of sentences which explain your

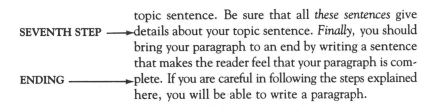

topic sentence. Be sure that all *these sentences* give

SEVENTH STEP ──▶details about your topic sentence. *Finally,* you should bring your paragraph to an end by writing a sentence that makes the reader feel that your paragraph is com-

ENDING ──────▶plete. If you are careful in following the steps explained here, you will be able to write a paragraph.

Now you know that a paragraph has certain basic characteristics.

1. The topic sentence is a statement of the topic, or subject, of the paragraph.
2. The writer uses a method to give order to the paragraph.
3. Details in a series of sentences develop the topic sentence.
4. The ending is the last sentence of the paragraph. It should make the reader feel that the paragraph is complete.

EXERCISE 5

Read the following paragraph. The topic sentence, developing details, and last sentence are scrambled so that the paragraph does not make sense. Rewrite the paragraph, rearranging the sentences so that the paragraph makes sense. Underline the topic sentence.

The Community Recreation Center

From the lobby I wandered into the gym, where the paint was peeling off the walls in places and cigarette butts were scattered over the floor. The exterior of the building needed a new coat of paint, and the front door creaked on rusty hinges as I opened it. The neglect and abuse that the center had suffered made me want to leave as soon as possible, and as I walked back outside, I felt cold and sad. When I recently returned to the community recreation center I had enjoyed as a child, I was sadly surprised to see the playground full of weeds and trash. Inside, the lobby was dark and dirty; there was writing on the walls and a trash can was overflowing with paper cups and candy wrappers.

PART SIX
THE COMPLETE PAPER

CHAPTER TWENTY-SIX

The Full-Length Paper

Learn to write a good full-length paper of more than one paragraph.

You have just read about how to write a clearly developed paragraph, a group of sentences about one subject. Now you can think about the full-length paper, a group of paragraphs about one subject.

A full-length paper looks like this:

Paragraph 1
_____
_____
_____
_____

Paragraph 2
_____
_____
_____
_____

Paragraph 3
_____
_____

_____

_____

_____

_____

Paragraph 4 _____

_____

_____

_____

As you can see, there are several paragraphs in a full-length paper and you must indent each paragraph.

The length of your paper will change with the type of topic you are writing about since some topics are more difficult than others and take more words to develop. The average length of your papers will probably be three to five paragraphs or about 300 to 500 words.

Your papers should be about this long:

Who Will Make the Squad?

I figured that because I was a sophomore I had a better than 50 percent chance of making the junior varsity basketball squad. Later, I learned that I had actually less than a 50 percent chance because the coach preferred to carry more freshmen than sophomores. He liked to let the first-year students gain as much on-the-court experience as possible to strengthen future teams. While playing basketball in high school, I learned just how much high expectations and hours of practice would help me in making the squad.

These thoughts had to be placed second in my mind behind the desire to represent my school on the court. Practice was hard. It was all I could do to keep up with everybody else while running sprints. Fundamental drills were basically easy because I was able to hustle while running the drills. Through hustling I had hoped to catch the coach's eye. Hustling also had its price. Every night after practice I was bushed.

The first cut, which was to eliminate thirty of the sixty participants, rolled around after a week of practice. I was definitely pleased but not surprised to find my name on the list to report to practice that night. This was my first big break. It meant that I was halfway home.

That night at practice, I pushed myself harder than ever before with a desire that grew by the minute. With only one cut to go, tension mounted. The last night of practice was really hectic. Everyone played harder than he had ever played before. At the conclusion of the practice, everyone wondered if he would return the next night.

The next morning, the cut list went up. Everyone gathered around to see who made the team. Finally, I was able to wedge my way through the crowd to see the all-important list. Dejection ran through my blood when I saw nothing of my name. Bitterness was my reaction toward the coach. But soon I learned to live with my disappointment. I realized that the world just wasn't quite ready for another Larry Bird.

26a
Choose a usable topic.

Before beginning to write your paper, pick a topic or think about the one you have been assigned. If you have to pick a topic of your own, keep these things in mind:

1. The topic should be something you are interested in or know something about. Do not pick a topic that you think your instructor would like but that you know nothing about.

2. The topic should be something you can develop in the time and space you have to write your paper.

TOO BROAD	The family
BETTER	The disappearing American family

Many of your papers will be written in class without advance preparation. When this happens, you must pick a topic that requires no research and that is limited enough to be developed clearly and completely in about 300 words, during a fifty- to sixty-minute class period.

EXERCISE 1

List any of the following topics that you think could be developed in about 300 words during a fifty- to sixty-minute class period.

1. Sports
2. Basketball
3. How the Carlton Raiders won the state championship in 1976
4. Hurricanes
5. Hurricane patterns along the Gulf Coast of the United States
6. The destruction of Biloxi, Mississippi, by hurricane Camille
7. How to train your cat
8. Plans for the Los Angeles Olympics
9. Governmental scandal during the last decade
10. My biggest problem in college

26b

Use brainstorming to make a working outline and to write a thesis statement for a simple, in-class paper.

Some of your papers will be fairly short (about 300 words) and may be written in class. For these themes, brainstorming may help you get some ideas, develop a rough plan or working outline, and form a thesis or controlling idea.

26b(1)
Begin by brainstorming.

One method you may find helpful in starting a full-length paper is to brainstorm. Brainstorming is an unrestricted flow from your mind of ideas that are waiting to be developed. When you brainstorm, make a list of all the ideas that occur to you on the topic you have chosen. Do not worry about whether the ideas are good or bad, and do not put them in any particular order. Just think about your topic for five to ten minutes and write down whatever occurs to you.

26b(2)
Make a rough or working outline for your paper.

After you have finished brainstorming, read over the list you have made, keeping your topic in mind as you read. Cross out any ideas that are not directly related to your subject. Then organize the remaining ideas so that they will make sense to your reader. Below is a list of ideas for the topic "Types of People at a Shopping Mall," which the student narrowed from the broad subject "Shopping." After brainstorming, she crossed out everything that did not relate to her topic: the kinds of people at a shopping mall.

1. veteran shoppers
2. shopping ~~is fun~~ but hectic
3. parking ~~at shopping~~ malls
4. in-and-out shoppers
5. the ~~Christmas~~ shopping rush
6. seasonal shoppers
7. nonshoppers
8. spouses and relatives of shoppers
9. people who just look
10. the ~~rudeness of~~ salesclerks
11. ~~noisy malls~~
12. ~~coupon clipping~~

Then she arranged the remaining points into the rough outline shown below. Points 7, 8, and 9 seemed repetitious since spouses and relatives of shoppers and people who just look could be considered nonshoppers. For this reason, she made them types of nonshoppers in her outline.

Types of People at a Shopping Mall

1. Veteran shoppers
2. In-and-out shoppers
3. Seasonal shoppers
4. Nonshoppers
   a. Spouses and relatives of shoppers
   b. Just lookers

26b(3)
Write a good thesis statement.

After you have made your rough or working outline, use it to write your thesis statement. The thesis statement of a full-length paper is like the topic sentence of a paragraph: it is a kind of summary of the rest of your paper. Once you have a good working outline, it should be easy to write your thesis statement since this statement just tells the reader what the paper will be about. After the student made her rough outline showing the types of people that are at a shopping mall, her thesis statement seemed obvious:

> Thesis statement: There are four main types of people at a shopping mall.

Make sure that your thesis statement is a complete sentence, not just a topic, and that it summarizes the points you intend to make in your paper.

WEAK	How to get rid of a man. [This is a topic, not a thesis statement.]
WEAK	This paper will explain how to get rid of a man. [This tells about the purpose of the paper. It does not state directly what the paper is about.]
WEAK	In this paper I will explain to the reader the steps to follow in order to get rid of a man.

	[This tells about the intention of the writer. It does not state directly what the paper is about.]
THESIS STATEMENT	Getting rid of a man is easy enough to do if you are constantly complaining, criticizing his friends, and making him aware of his short-comings. [This sentence states directly how to get rid of a man, which is the subject of the rest of the paper.]

The thesis statement usually appears in the first paragraph of a full-length paper.

EXERCISE 2

Choose a broad subject from the list below, and limit it to a topic that you could use to write a paper of about 300 words during a fifty- to sixty-minute class period. Then brainstorm to create a list of ideas related to the subject and construct a working or rough outline from those ideas. Finally, write a thesis statement that states directly what your paper will be about.

1. A true experience
2. Home computers
3. Family traditions
4. Sports
5. Spectators

EXERCISE 3

Below is a list of ideas that you might use to write an in-class paper on the advantages of attending a two-year college. Eliminate any ideas from the list that you could not use to develop your topic. Write a working outline, including a thesis statement.

1. Low tuition
2. Specialized research facilities

3. Quality instruction
4. Small classes
5. Good football teams
6. Convenient location
7. Good preparatory programs
8. Wide variety of doctoral programs
9. Community services
10. Hot lunches

26b(4)
Use the working outline and thesis statement to write your paper.

The following is the in-class paper "Types of People at a Shopping Mall." The thesis statement and the four parts of the rough outline are underlined and labeled.

Types of People at a Shopping Mall

THESIS
STATEMENT

POINT 1

POINT 2

Since the introduction of the suburbs, shopping malls, which sprang up in response to the needs of those suburbs, have become an extension and a reflection of the people they serve. There are four categories of people frequently seen shopping at these malls.

The first group is known as veteran shoppers. These people usually have a certain gleam in their eyes. This gleam comes from knowing exactly where everything is in the mall and having a mental price list for every item in each store. They know the best times to shop, the good parking spots, and the name of every experienced sales-clerk. They are on a first-name basis with all the store managers, and their checks are accepted without a credit check. Be warned! If you desire to join this exclusive group, you must be willing to make shopping a way of life. It will take three or four trips a week for many years to become a veteran shopper.

The next group of shoppers consists of very fast movers, so you have to keep your eyes peeled to spot them.

These in-and-out shoppers go to the mall knowing exactly what they want and plan on shopping in the shortest time possible. There is no time for browsing when you accompany an in-and-out shopper.

POINT 3 ———▶   The third main group in a mall is the seasonal shoppers. These people show up only during the main holidays like Christmas or Easter. You can pick them out by the harried expressions on their faces. Around Christmas an air of forced gaiety is added, and you can imagine them saying to themselves: "I'm going to have a good time Christmas shopping, even if it kills me." The seasonal shoppers usually select Friday night or Saturday to shop. The fact that all seasonal shoppers have this same idea explains why they always complain about the crowded malls.

POINT 4 ———▶   There is a small group of people, known as nonshoppers, who are also present during business hours. Some of these people are the spouses or relatives of the serious shoppers. They are there because nothing was on television, or they were the ones who had to drive. They sit patiently on the benches and watch all the people scurry to and fro. Still other types of nonshoppers are just there to browse and pass the time. They love the excitement of the mall and enjoy window shopping.

Shopping malls are an American institution. Different people with diverse tastes can come to one shopping area and find all their needs answered. Shopping malls are great places to engage in the sport of people watching.

26c

Use a detailed, formal outline to write a full-length paper when your topic requires it.

For a longer paper, particularly one on a complex subject, begin with these steps.

1. Brainstorm: write down, in any order, all the ideas you can think of on your limited topic.

2. Choose the three or four ideas you want to develop in your paper.
3. Form a thesis statement based on the ideas you have chosen. [See **26b(3)** on the thesis statement.]
4. Arrange the ideas so that they develop the thesis statement.

At this point you will probably find that you need a more formal outline than the rough or working outline you used for a short, in-class paper. A formal outline shows in detail how you plan to develop your paper. It usually includes an introduction and a conclusion. In other words, it does much of your work for you before you ever begin to write. If you use a detailed outline, you will not have to plan as you go; instead, you can concentrate on saying things clearly and effectively.

26c(1)
Learn to construct a sentence outline.

Below is a detailed sentence outline for a longer paper. In addition to the main headings shown by Roman numerals (I, II, III), the outline uses subheadings indicated by capital letters (A, B, C) and some supporting points or details (1, 2, 3) for those subheadings. This is a skeleton of a detailed outline. Use as many main headings, subheadings, and supporting points as necessary for your subject.

Thesis statement
Introduction
I. Main heading
    A. Subheading
    B. Subheading
        1. Supporting point
        2. Supporting point
II. Main heading
III. Main heading
    A. Subheading
    B. Subheading
Conclusion

The following is a sentence outline for a long, out-of-class paper called "Life at Sea—Yesterday and Today." The student used the above skeleton to make his outline.

Life at Sea—Yesterday and Today

Thesis statement: Even today life at sea is a challenge, but a comparison of daily living conditions two hundred years ago and today shows that many conditions of life at sea have changed tremendously.

Introduction: From the viewpoint of a sailor of two hundred years ago, going to sea was like being jailed, with the added risk of drowning.

I.   Food is just one aspect of sea life which has changed over the years.
    A.   Only food that could be stored was used in earlier times.
    B.   There are fewer limitations on food today.
II.   Living conditions are another aspect of life at sea which has changed.
    A.   Room for berthing was not considered then.
    B.   Berthing is a major consideration today.
III.   Besides these changes in living conditions, there have been major changes in working conditions at sea.
    A.   Working hours were very long.
        1.   The daily routine allowed little sleep.
        2.   The watches were long.
    B.   Working conditions are better today.
        1.   Sailors work eight-hour days.
        2.   Watches are not as long.
IV.   Finally, there have been changes in the forms of discipline used at sea.
    A.   Punishment seemed unfair and harsh.
    B.   Today discpline is fairer.

Conclusion: In spite of the difficulties, life at sea has always been an irresistible challenge.

26c(2)
Learn to make a good topic outline.

Some writers prefer using a topic outline instead of a sentence outline. A topic outline consists of headings or topics, usually written as words or phrases. Here is a topic outline for the paper "Life at Sea—Yesterday and Today."

Thesis Statement: Even today life at sea is a challenge, but a comparison of daily living two hundred years ago and today shows that many conditions of life at sea have changed tremendously.

Introduction: From the viewpoint of the sailor of two hundred years ago, going to sea was like being jailed, with the added risk of drowning.

   I. Food rations at sea
      A. Kinds of food then
      B. Kinds of food today
  II. Living conditions at sea
      A. Room for berthing not considered then
      B. Berthing major consideration today
 III. Working conditions at sea
      A. Working conditions then
         1. Daily routine
         2. Watches
      B. Working conditions today
         1. Daily routine
         2. Watches
 IV. Discipline at sea
      A. Harshness of earlier punishment
      B. Fairness of discipline today

Conclusion: In spite of the difficulties, life at sea has always been an irresistible challenge.

When you use the topic outline, remember that unless you make your headings clear and arrange them logically, they will not help you much when you are ready to write your paper. The purpose of an outline is to furnish you with a skeleton of your paper, but you need to be able to tell what the parts of that skeleton are. For example, you can see that the following topic outline is very confusing.

I. Changes in food
    A. Size of ships
    B. Become worm-infested
    C. Better today
II. Living conditions
III. Working conditions
    A. No sleep
    B. Strange hours
    C. Eight-hour days
IV. Discipline
    A. Harsh punishment
    B. Is easier and fairer today

The writer caused several problems by not making his headings consistent. For example, the first main heading (I) shows that the writer is talking about changes in food, but II, III, and IV do not mention *changes* in other aspects of life at sea.

In addition, it is not always clear what a heading means. In III, when were the "Strange hours," and what does that heading mean? When did the "Eight-hour days" occur—then or now? Do you see other confusing headings in this outline?

When you use the topic outline, be sure your categories are parallel in form. This means that if you use a noun or noun phrase in one heading, you should use nouns in your other headings; if you use a verb, you should use other verbs; if you use an adjective, you should use other adjectives. In the confusing topic outline shown above, the subheadings of IV are not parallel in form.

CONFUSING   IV. Discipline
          A. Harsh punishment [noun phrase]
          B. Is easier and fairer today [verb phrase]
BETTER   IV. Discipline
          A. Harshness of earlier punishment [noun phrase]
          B. Fairness of discipline today [noun phrase]

26c(3)

Use either a topic or a sentence outline; do not combine the two.

If you decide to use a topic outline, do not include sentences as headings.

> WRONG   II. Changes in living conditions
> A. No berthing two hundred years ago   [topic]
> B. Conditions are better today.   [sentence]
> RIGHT   II. Changes in living conditions
> A. Room for berthing not considered then   [topic]
> B. Berthing major consideration today   [topic]

26c(4)

Whether you use a sentence or a topic outline, check headings carefully for clarity and correctness of form.

Make certain that your subheadings are really parts of the headings under which they appear.

> INACCURATE   II. Living conditions are different now.
> A. Room for berthing was not considered then.
> B. The desertion rate is much lower today. [Subheading B is not clearly related to living conditions aboard ship.]
> ACCURATE   II. Living conditions are different now.
> A. Room for berthing was not considered then.
> B. Berthing is a major consideration today.

Make certain that each heading is different from the others.

> OVERLAPPING   IV. There have been changes in the forms of discipline used at sea.
> A. Punishment was unfair and hard.

B. A minor offense would require several lashes.

NO OVERLAPPING IV. There have been changes in the forms of discipline used at sea.

A. Punishment was unfair and hard.
B. Today's discipline is fairer.

Make certain that each heading that you have divided has at least two subheadings. If you have a I, you need a II; if you have an A, you need a B; if you have a 1, you need a 2.

WRONG III. Working conditions are better today.

A. Men work eight-hour days.

RIGHT III. Working conditions are better today.

A. Men work eight-hour days.
B. Watches are not as long.

See **26c(6)** for the complete paper, "Life at Sea—Yesterday and Today," that was written from the outlines in **26c.**

26c(5)
Be prepared to make outlines for different kinds of papers.

Here are some sample outlines for different kinds of papers that students often write in a composition course. They may give you some ideas that will help you organize these papers.

The Process Paper

A process paper lists the steps followed in performing a job or activity. This outline lists the three steps for replacing a power transistor.

Thesis statement: To replace a power transistor there are three major steps: remove the old transistor, apply the silicon lubricant to the vacated area, and insert the new transistor.

Introduction: When a power transistor is overtaxed or otherwise defective, it may become inoperative. Therefore, anyone working with electronic equipment should know the procedure for replacing defective power transistors.

I. Remove the old transistor from the board.
    A. Remove the anchoring nut.
    B. Melt adjacent points of solder.
II. Apply lubricant to the vacant area on the board.
III. Insert the new transistor in the board.
    A. Place transistor pegs into available holes.
    B. Replace the anchoring nut.
    C. Resolder points adjacent to the nut.

Conclusion: Several items must be emphasized for a safe and successful job: first, the soldering iron must be handled carefully, and, secondly, the heat-dispersing agent must be applied.

The Comparison Paper

A comparison shows the similarities or differences between two persons, processes, ideas, and so on. This outline suggests that the writer will stress the differences between water skiing and snow skiing.

Water Skiing Versus Snow Skiing

Introduction: You may consider water skiing and snow skiing to be similar sports.
Thesis statement: Even though water skiing and snow skiing are somewhat similar, they have several distinct differences.

I. One difference is the means by which skiers are powered along different surfaces.
    A. Water-skiers are pulled across the water by a speeding motorboat.
    B. Snow-skiers depend on their own energy, strength, and ability to ski the steep snow-covered slopes.
II. Another difference is the kinds of equipment and clothing that skiers must wear.
    A. Water-skiers use skis, a towrope, and a ski belt and wear bathing suits.

B. Snow-skiers use skis, ski poles, and boots and wear warm clothing.
III. The amount of physical exertion that each type of skier uses is another difference.
 A. Water-skiers must use many leg, arm, and back muscles.
 B. Snow-skiers use mainly leg and ankle muscles.

Conclusion: Although water skiing and snow skiing do differ in some respects, many people enjoy the thrill and excitement of both sports.

The Classification Paper

A classification paper divides one idea or category into more than one part based on some particular principle. In this outline the writer describes three kinds of sleepers.

Three Kinds of Sleepers

Introduction: Having been raised as the youngest of four daughters sharing beds in a small home, I quickly developed an uncanny knack for recognizing each of my sisters by her unique sleeping habits.

Thesis statement: Through the years, I shared a bed with three kinds of sleepers: the "octopus," the "bed hog," and the "dead man."

I. The "octopus" was my oldest sister Irma.
II. My second sister, Jean, was an unrelenting "bed hog."
III. When Kathy fell asleep, she did not move for the remainder of the night; she was the "dead man."

Conclusion: Although I lived with my sisters for many years and felt as though I knew them well, I quickly came to realize that deep within each of them there lurked a monster that reared its ugly head only at bedtime.

The Analysis Paper

In an analysis paper the writer discusses the causes or effects of something. In the following simple plan, the author lists three effects of the women's liberation movement.

Some Effects of the Women's Liberation Movement

Thesis statement: The current women's liberation movement has had many effects on society.

I.   More and more women are entering traditionally male-dominated fields.
II.   Medical care has been affected by the women's liberation movement.
III.   The media depict women in nontraditional roles.

Conclusion: There have been many changes in society because of the women's liberation movement, but the most important have been the changes in the consciousness of both men and women.

The Persuasion Paper

In a paper of argument or persuasion, a writer states convincing reasons for supporting a particular position. The following outline states four reasons that income taxes should be used instead of real-estate taxes as a source of revenue. The conclusion of this paper is actually its thesis statement since it follows logically from these four reasons.

Fair Taxation: An Improved Method

Thesis statement: Real-estate taxes should be eliminated in favor of income taxes.
Introduction: Could your home be taken from you?

I.   Real-estate taxes are not proportional to a person's ability to pay since they are levied on only a small percent of a wealthy person's assets while an average person is taxed on about 100 percent.
II.   Real-estate taxes are a form of double taxation.
   A.   Income is taxed once by the income-tax system.
   B.   The same income, if invested in a house, is then taxed not only again but annually.
III.   Elimination of the real-estate-tax system would save the costs of its operation.

IV. Funds to operate local governments could be efficiently obtained from the state income tax.

Conclusion: Real-estate taxes should be eliminated in favor of income taxes.

EXERCISE 4

A. From the list below, choose a topic that you consider appropriate for a process or classification paper. Then construct a detailed topic outline on that subject.

B. From the list below, choose a topic that you consider appropriate for a paper of comparison, analysis, or persuasion. Then construct a detailed sentence outline on that subject.

1. Should TV Programs Be Censored?
2. Some Needed Reforms in the Auto Industry
3. How to Stop Smoking
4. Three Types of Restaurants
5. Some Suggested Reforms in the Food Stamp Program
6. How to Plan a Party
7. A Comparison of Football and Soccer
8. Three Kinds of Gifts No One Wants
9. My Neighborhood: Then and Now
10. Should the Sale of Firearms Be Regulated?

26c(6)

Write the paper, making use of the detailed outline you have made.

Now that you have your thesis statement and your detailed outline for the ideas you will use to develop it, you are ready to begin writing your paper. If you have written a sentence outline, you may use the actual sentences from your outline as the topic sentences of the paragraphs in the paper.

Compare the sentence outline of "Life at Sea—Yesterday and Today" on p. 340 with the paper that was written from it.

Life at Sea—Yesterday and Today

INTRODUCTION

THESIS ──────► STATEMENT

From the viewpoint of a sailor of two hundred years ago, going to sea was like being jailed, with the added risk of drowning. Even today life at sea is a challenge, but a comparison of daily living conditions two hundred years ago and today shows that many conditions of life at sea have changed tremendously.

TOPIC ──────► SENTENCE OF FIRST PARAGRAPH

Food is just one aspect of sea life which has changed over the years. Two hundred years ago when a ship went to sea, a typical sailor would not expect to see land again for some time. Ships were small, men were crowded together, and there was limited storage space, so the only foods that could be taken were those that stored easily and would not spoil readily. The normal fare was salted meat in barrels, hard sea biscuits that usually became worm-infested long before the cruise was over, and water that became so green and slimy in a short time that a sailor drank it only when necessary. A rare captain might provide some cheese or raisins, but since the cost of outfitting the ship came out of his pocket, extra rations were rare. Today when ships go to sea, sailors can look forward to an unlimited variety of foods and beverages. Meals are planned for quality, quantity, and proper nutrition. Usually little is spared to satisfy the crew, and although they may occasionally gripe, they may never in their lives receive better meals.

TOPIC ──────► SENTENCE OF SECOND PARAGRAPH

Living conditions are another aspect of life at sea which has changed. It has only been in recent years that berthing of sailors aboard ship has even been considered. In early days a man slept wherever he could find a soft plank. In many cases, on warships, men were required to sleep near their battle stations. Men were not allowed to live ashore because of the high desertion rate, but they were allowed to have their wives aboard ship while in port. Many a lad was sired alongside a ship's cannon, giving rise to the old saying, "son of a gun." Today, living conditions are a major morale factor, and sailors enjoy spacious bunks, adequate locker space, and additional recreation areas. In some cases, the crew are lucky enough to have wardrooms to live in.

TOPIC ——————→ SENTENCE OF THIRD PARAGRAPH

Besides these changes in living conditions, there have been major changes in working conditions at sea. In the days of sail it was considered too risky to allow idle hands. In consequence, a work day would last from sunrise to sunset. Men were divided into port and starboard watches. This routine allowed a man four hours' sleep out of his first thirty-two hours and eight hours' sleep out of his second thirty-two hours. Imagine living this routine for months at sea! This does not even consider the fact that all hands were required for such evolutions as changing sail. Nowadays, a sailor may work a normal eight-hour day with adequate time for recreation and relaxation. On merchant vessels there is often overtime pay for extra hours. Unhappily, the Navy has not reached this point yet.

TOPIC ——————→ SENTENCE OF FOURTH PARAGRAPH

Finally, there have been changes in the forms of discipline used at sea. Life at sea creates its own unique community, which requires rules that a landlubber may not comprehend. In the Navy of two hundred years ago, the slightest infraction usually called for harsh punishment. The usual form of punishment was flogging with a "cat" (the tackle used to hoist the anchor). A routine minor offense would require twelve lashes, and the number would increase with the severity of the offense. The worst punishment was usually a deceptive disguise for sure death—a dozen through the fleet. In this punishment a man was given a dozen lashes, but he was tied in a boat and rowed to each ship in port where crews were called out to witness punishment. Multiply these twelve lashes by fifty ships in port! Discipline is still a problem, and sailors still must face the mast, but gone are the whippings and the cruelty of bygone days. Sailors nowadays are fined, reduced in position, or jailed for serious offenses, but they have all the rights of every citizen and can appeal any cases. Justice at sea is very similar to justice in any of our courts.

CONCLUSION

It is easy to see that life was much more difficult for the sailor of two hundred years ago than it is now. In spite of the difficulties, life at sea has always been an irresistible challenge.

26d
In a full-length paper, develop each paragraph clearly and adequately.

Whether your topic is simple or complex, improve your papers by using appropriate details, by putting each new idea into a separate paragraph, and by developing ideas fully.

26d(1)
Choose appropriate details to develop the paragraphs of your paper.

The kinds of details you select to use in your paper will depend on the type of paper you plan to write. Here are some suggestions for details to include.

In a paper describing a person, use details that describe the person's

> physical characteristics—hair, eyes, nose, size, age.
> personality or character—happy or sad, generous or selfish, kind or cruel.
> actions—things that people do to show what they are like.

In a paper describing a place, use details that describe the place's

> size.
> residents.
> points of interest.
> condition.
> history.
> type (suburban, rural, urban).

good qualities.
defects.

In a paper describing an experience or event, use details that tell

the time and place of the experience or event.
the type of experience or event.
the people involved, if any.
what actually happened.
the outcome.

In a paper explaining how to do something, use details that tell

the materials, ingredients, talents, skills needed.
the steps that must be followed.
the reason(s) for any special step(s).
any cautions that must be observed.
the value of the finished product.

In a paper defining something, use details that give

the origin of the word or thing.
information concerning its discovery and development.
synonyms for the word.
a physical description.
a description of how it works.
an explanation of its uses.
comparisons and contrasts of the word or thing with others.
different types.
examples and illustrations.

26d(2)
Begin a new paragraph in your paper when you introduce a new point in your plan.

Here is a full-length paper that is not divided into paragraphs.

A Temporary Home

It had been a long, exhausting trip, and we had arrived late. Without really thinking or caring what the place was like, I went to bed. My wife cried herself to sleep, and I just lay in bed thinking about what a mistake I had made. We had left our home, uprooted the children, and come halfway around the world to a tiny island called Guam. It was the sun that woke me in the morning. It hung in a sky that seemed to be a reflection of the clear blue ocean below. It shone so brightly that it hurt my eyes, and already the heat from it was heavy and oppressive. I dragged myself to the window to have a look at my new surroundings. The calm of the sea below was destroyed by huge waves that suddenly appeared from nowhere, crashed with a thunder upon the reef, and then were gone as mysteriously as they had come. I turned my attention to the land. There were palm trees that swayed in the gentle breeze of the trade winds. On my right were mountains that would have been considered hills on any continent. Covering the mountains were more palm trees and the impenetrable jungle. That was what my eyes saw my first morning on Guam. Everything was so different, so new, and we knew we had to live with it for two years. But as time went by we adjusted to our new home. In fact, when the two years were over, we found a crowd of friends coming to see us off, waving and crying and yelling for us to write. My wife cried the night we left, and I sat alone thinking about what a mistake I was making.

This paper is easier to follow when it is divided into paragraphs every time a new point is introduced.

A Temporary Home

It had been a long, exhausting trip, and we had arrived late. Without really thinking or caring what the place was like, I went to bed. My wife cried herself to sleep, and I just lay in bed thinking about what a mistake I had made. We had left our home, uprooted the children, and come halfway around the world to a tiny island called Guam.

It was the sun that woke me in the morning. It hung in a sky that seemed to be a reflection of the clear blue ocean below. It shone so brightly that it hurt my eyes, and already the heat from it was heavy and oppressive. I dragged myself to the window to have a look at my new surroundings. The calm of the sea below was destroyed by huge waves that suddenly appeared from nowhere, crashed with a thunder upon the reef, and then were gone as mysteriously as they had come. I turned my attention to the land. There were palm trees that swayed in the gentle breeze of the trade winds. On my right were mountains that would have been considered hills on any continent. Covering the mountains were more palm trees and the impenetrable jungle.

That was what my eyes saw my first morning on Guam. Everything was so different, so new, and we knew we had to live with it for two years. But as time went by we adjusted to our new home. In fact, when the two years were over, we found a crowd of friends coming to see us off, waving and crying and yelling for us to write. My wife cried the night we left, and I sat alone thinking about what a mistake I was making.

26d(3)
Do not separate your paper into incomplete paragraphs.

Avoid putting each sentence into a separate paragraph or writing paragraphs that are too short to do their part in developing the thesis statement of your whole paper.

This full-length paper is divided into incomplete paragraphs.

Why Refrigerators Should Be Cleaned Once a Year

Many changes have lightened a homemaker's tasks over the past several years, but one inescapable chore remains.

It is my position that all refrigerators should have an annual cleaning.

One of the reasons for this radical stand is the inner space factor. Remember this around the holiday season.

There will be no room for the special culinary delights synonymous with the season if there are forty Tupperware containers jammed into the fridge.

There is yet another problem posed by the overstuffed refrigerator. A new supply of liquid refreshment will be without a cool home if the half-full jars of pickles are not thrown to the great god of garbage.

Another reason for cleaning the refrigerator is known as family pressure. Eventually, your spouse will get tired of trying to find the leftover pork chop when there are twenty tinfoil-wrapped objects, and none of them is labeled for content.

The children become quite unreasonable when told the chocolate syrup is "somewhere in the back" when they cannot find the middle, much less the back. The final blow comes when your mother comes over and tries to help by getting her own milk for her coffee. The despairing cry of "How can you find anything in here?" is a sure-fire method of making you feel guilty.

There is a third reason for attempting to clean out the refrigerator. It is the threat from everyone to call the Health Department.

You are reminded that it is illegal to grow mold and fungus without a medical laboratory license. A mumbled mention of being a "threat to public health" makes you realize that a thorough cleaning may be necessary.

Finally, bowing to the inevitable, you break out the Arm and Hammer baking soda and get the job done.

"That," you can say, "is it—until next year."

In the following, the same paper is divided into complete paragraphs. The writer begins a new paragraph only when a new point is introduced.

Why Refrigerators Should Be Cleaned Once a Year

THESIS ——→ STATEMENT   Many changes have lightened a homemaker's tasks over the past several years, but one inescapable chore remains. It is my position that all refrigerators should have an annual cleaning.

FIRST REASON   One of the reasons for this radical stand is the inner space factor. Remember this around the holiday season. There will be no room for the special culinary delights synonymous with the season if there are forty Tupperware containers jammed into the fridge. There is yet another problem posed by the overstuffed refrigerator. A new supply of liquid refreshment will be without a cool home if

FIRST
REASON
(continued)

the half-full jars of pickles are not thrown to the great god of garbage.

Another reason for cleaning the refrigerator is known as family pressure. Eventually, your spouse will get tired of trying to find the leftover pork chop when there are twenty tinfoil-wrapped objects, and none of them is labeled for content. The children become quite unreasonable when

SECOND
REASON

told the chocolate syrup is "somewhere in the back" when they cannot find the middle, much less the back. The final blow comes when your mother comes over and tries to help by getting her own milk for her coffee. The despairing cry of "How can you find anything in here?" is a sure-fire method of making you feel guilty.

There is a third reason for attempting to clean out the refrigerator. It is the threat from everyone to call the

THIRD
REASON

Health Department. You are reminded that it is illegal to grow mold and fungus without a medical laboratory license. A mumbled mention of being a "threat to public health" makes you realize that a thorough cleaning may be necessary.

CONCLUSION

Finally, bowing to the inevitable, you break out the Arm and Hammer baking soda and get the job done. "That," you can say, "is it—until next year."

EXERCISE 5

Organize the following paper into complete paragraphs by putting all sentences about one point together. Avoid one-sentence paragraphs.

An Electric Coffeepot

Before you make that next pot of coffee in your electric pot, take a minute to familiarize yourself with the assembly parts that work together to brew that delicious cup of coffee.

An electric coffeepot has four assemblies made up of two or more parts. These assemblies are the cover, the body, the basket, and the base.

The cover assembly consists of a cover knob (usually made of plastic), a round metal cover, and a spreader held together by an assembly screw.

The spreader has many small holes in it. This assembly fits into a lip of the body assembly to retain the liquid and heat in the body.

The body assembly has a metal body with a groove (or lip) at the top for the cover assembly.

At the bottom of the body on the inside is a pump well.

A plastic handle and spout are attached to the outside of the body with screws. The spout is hollow and fits over a hole in the body.

The body holds approximately ten cups of liquid.

The basket assembly consists of two parts: the basket and the pump.

The basket is perforated with many holes to allow water to drip through.

It fits onto a long, slender round tube called the pump.

The basket assembly rests in the pump well of the body.

The base assembly is the heart of the pot. The base, made of plastic, houses the parts that heat the liquid in the body.

Inside the base are a pilot light, a thermostat, and a control wheel mounted on a metal bracket. These parts are connected to a heating element and a terminal pin set by wires. The terminal pin set protrudes through the base so that an electrical cord can be attached.

The bottom of the base has a little window to allow the pilot light to become visible when it lights. The base assembly is connected to the body assembly by a screw.

You can see, then, that an electric coffeepot is a complex mechanism composed of four different assemblies that work together to give you a simple cup of coffee.

Now that you are more familiar with the construction of your coffeepot, go ahead and make that pot of coffee.

26e
Write an effective introduction to your paper.

In a paragraph-length paper, the introduction is usually the first or topic sentence. One sentence is all you can really afford in a paragraph essay. When you write a full-length paper, however, your introductory paragraph will probably have three or four sentences which prepare the reader for what will appear in the rest of the paper. Often it will contain a few sentences to arouse your reader's interest and the thesis statement of the paper. For example, the introductory paragraph for the paper "Fair Taxation: An Improved Method" (outlined on p. 347) uses sentences 1–3 to make the reader think about the disadvantages of real-estate taxes and then states the thesis statement in the last sentence.

> Could your home be taken from you? Real-estate taxes could do this very thing if you are on a low, fixed income. People retiring on Social Security are finding that they must give up their homes because of skyrocketing real-estate taxes. This problem could be eliminated if real-estate taxes were eliminated in favor of income taxes.

26f
Add a conclusion to your paper.

You should bring your paper to an end by writing a sentence or two that make your reader feel the paper is complete. Often an ending returns to the idea stated in the topic sentence of the whole paper.

Do not change your topic in the conclusion. Use the conclusion to finish what you were saying in the whole paper. This is a poor conclusion for a paper defending mercy killing:

WEAK   Many doctors have been involved in malpractice suits in recent years.

The writer changed the subject by writing a sentence about malpractice suits. A better conclusion finishes what the writer was saying in the paper:

BETTER   Is euthanasia really an inhumane practice? Many feel that it is more humane to let people die than to prolong their lives when they are not really living.

You should include the following things when you write a full-length paper.

1. The *thesis statement*, which states directly what the whole paper is about.
2. The *outline*, which organizes your ideas about the thesis statement so that your paper will make sense.
3. *Paragraphs*, which give details developing the thesis statement of the whole paper.
4. An effective *introduction* and a *conclusion*, which makes your reader feel that your paper is complete.

EXERCISE 6

Read the following full-length paper. The paragraphs are scrambled so that the paper does not make sense. Number the paragraphs so that the whole paper makes sense. Underline the thesis statement.

How to Feed a Baby

The first thing you need, of course, is a baby. Next you need a good highchair that has a strap to tie the baby down. If you do not have a strap, you may substitute a dish towel, belt, or anything similar that is handy. An absolute must is a bib because without it you will find yourself bathing the baby and changing his clothes after feeding time is over. Have the food ready before you put the baby into the highchair. Babies do not like to wait in highchairs.

The last step is to remove the baby from the highchair and change his diaper. A diaper always needs changing after he eats, and that job must be done right away. Experience is the best teacher, but if you follow these simple steps, you will be much better off when you are given the task of feeding the baby.

The feeding should be progressing very well now, but the baby may stop eating at any time. If this happens, it is probably due to one of three reasons: (1) the baby may have decided he does not like the food; (2) he may just want to be coaxed; (3) he may be sleepy. You can deal with reasons 1 and 2. Just pretend the spoonful of food is a choo-choo about to go into a tunnel, and, complete with sound effects, shove the food into the baby's mouth. Or you may feign gratitude and tell the baby how good he is to eat all the food. If reason 3 is the cause of the baby's refusal to eat more, just forget the remainder of the food and go to the next step.

Now you are ready to begin. Place the baby in the highchair, and strap him down to prevent him from getting out or falling out. Take a small amount of food on a spoon and allow him to swallow it. Do not push. Let him take his time. Babies do not like to be forced and once angered are slow to forgive and forget.

Feeding babies is a skill every father should master. I have only become an expert by diligently studying under three children who have taught me, or should I say *forced* me to learn, almost every trick.

When the baby has eaten all he intends to, remove the bib and spoon. They will quickly become toys and cause more mess if you do not. Then clean the excess food off the baby. Food will probably be in his hair and all over his face and hands. This is still better than it would have been without the bib.

26g
Proofread your paper carefully.

The final step in the writing process is always to edit your paper carefully. See Section **28c** for specific suggestions on effective proofreading.

CHAPTER TWENTY-SEVEN
The Library Paper

Learn how to prepare a library paper.

You may first need to know what a library paper is and why it goes by such a name. The library paper is usually prepared from materials found in a library. The paper may also be called a *research paper* because it has taken research to locate the information. A library paper is not an original story or article; it is made up of numerous pieces of information that are put together to prove a point or develop an idea. But the paper should be original in the way in which the materials are selected and used. You must carefully record the location, or source, of the information because you are using facts from someone else. This record, or documentation, is in the form of notes in parentheses within the body of the text and a list of the works cited at the end of the paper, both of which are fully explained in this section. (For information on documentation in the form of endnotes or footnotes and bibliography, see **27f.**)

A library paper may be longer than other papers you have written, but you may have more time to write it. If you plan your work carefully, follow the steps presented in this section, and use accepted writing skills, you will write a well-prepared paper. You may find that getting started is difficult, so choosing a subject will be the first step to be discussed in detail.

27a
Choose a suitable subject for a library paper.

Your paper will be more interesting to you and will be easier to write if you choose a subject that you like or know something about. For example, if you are writing a paper for an English course, you will probably have to work with a specific topic. But you may not have a clear idea about that specific subject until you do some looking (or research) and reading. Where should you begin? Your first ideas may come from the textbook you are using in the course. If the instructor has not assigned subjects for the papers, you will be free to find out more about any subject that interests you. Choosing a broad, general topic will give you a starting point. Next, you will learn to narrow your topic through research.

27a(1)
Use the card catalog.

The library card catalog is the first place to look for information on your topic. The catalog lists all of the books in the library. Information about the books is usually on cards filed in drawers, although the catalog may also be in large books or on microfiche or other film. Each book is listed separately by subject, title, and author, and the subject cards are usually in a different section of the card catalog from the author and title cards. Since you are trying to decide on a subject for your paper, you will be interested in the subject section of the card catalog. If you, like the student whose paper appears on pages 384–94, choose a general topic like cartoons or caricature, you may find a subject card that looks like this:

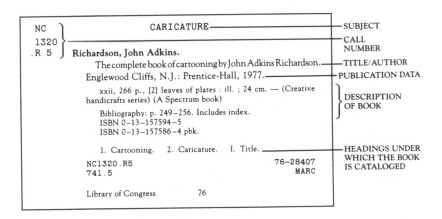

If there does not seem to be any material on the subject you are interested in, you may have to consult a subject-heading listing or guide (such as the Library of Congress Guide) or a *see* card in the card catalog. The listing or cards will give other ways in which a subject may be listed; they will frequently list specific headings under the broad topics or headings.

Subject-Heading Guide

Cartooning   (*Indirect*)
    Caricature
    Caricatures and cartoons
    Wit and humor, political
  Vocational guidance
    Cartoonists

Cartoonists *(Indirect)*
    Cartooning—Vocational guidance
    Caricaturists
    Artists
    Caricatures and cartoons
    Wit and humor, Pictorial
  Correspondence, reminiscences, etc.

A "See" Card

Cartoons
  See Caricatures and cartoons
Cartoons, Editorial
  See Editorial cartoons

You are now ready to look through some of the available books in order to narrow the broad topic to an interesting subject that could be covered in a paper of the assigned length. The student whose paper appears on pages 384–94 narrowed his broad topic of cartoons to political cartoons.

27a(2)
Use indexes to magazines.

Books are only one of the sources of information available in a library. The *Reader's Guide to Periodical Literature* is a listing of articles in popular magazines, and it can serve as a valuable source of ideas for possible subjects for a paper. This group of books, usually one for each year, is located in the reference section of the library. Each article is listed in the *Reader's Guide* under subject, title, and author. Articles may be listed under several subject headings. The library you are using may not have all of the periodicals listed. If you are considering a political cartoonist, for example, as the subject for a research paper, the *Reader's Guide* will let you know what articles appeared on political cartoonists in any one year and will also give the name and date of the magazine and the page numbers of the article. An entry in the *Reader's Guide** looks like this:

TRUDEAU, Garry
> Meet Ms. Caucus: excerpts from Joanie, cartoons for children; with introd by N. Ephron, il Ramparts 13:45–8 N '74

This entry tells that an article concerning Garry Trudeau appeared in *Ramparts* in November 1974. It was written by N. Ephron and was four pages long. Any abbreviations and symbols used in the entries are explained in the front of the *Reader's Guide*. Many libraries also have specialized guides or indexes (such as the *Art Index*) that are concerned only with a narrow field of interest. You should also find the annual PMLA (Publication of the Modern Language Association) index helpful if you are writing a paper on literature.

The topic of political cartoonists is still a broad one. Suppose that you, like the student whose paper appears on pages **384–94**, decide to write a library paper on Garry Trudeau, an American political cartoonist. Now that you have chosen a specific subject, you can begin gathering the information that will go into the paper.

EXERCISE 1

Find one book listing in the library card catalog and one article listing in the *Reader's Guide to Periodical Literature* for each of the following subjects. For each book, give the title, author, and date of publication. For each article, give the name of the magazine, date of issue, title of the article, and number of pages in the article.

1. Folk music
2. Automobile racing
3. Careers in business
4. Caring for house plants
5. Soybeans

Reader's Guide to Periodical Literature. Copyright © 1970, 1971, by The H. W. Wilson Company. Material reproduced by permission of the publisher.

27b
Take notes that will help you write your paper.

Now that you have decided on a subject, it is time to read what has been said about that subject. It is important to keep an open mind when you start to take notes. You may think you know where your research will lead you, but after you have read some books and articles on your subject, you may change your mind. For example, the student who wrote "The Growth and Development of 'Doonesbury'" (pages **384–94**) originally intended to write a paper on political cartoonists. When he started taking notes, he found much more material on the subject than he had expected, so he restricted his paper to the development of one cartoon. Once you have chosen a topic, you have made a good beginning; but it is only a beginning. Let your paper take final shape in your mind only after you have looked through the available material.

27b(1)
Gather your sources and prepare to take notes on them.

You have already consulted the *Reader's Guide* and the card catalog to help you decide on a topic. Now start gathering sources that may help you write your paper. It is a good idea to make a list of the possible books and articles on your subject. You will not be able to find all of the books and magazines you need in your library, but locate as many as you can in the card catalog. Your library may have a special card catalog for periodicals. On your list, put the call number of each possible source next to the name of that source. Then look at the sources available.

Be sure to consult the table of contents and the index of each book you use to be sure you have not missed any information on your subject. Also remember that the text, the endnotes or footnotes and the bibliography of a book or an article are often good places to look for the names of other sources. (See **27e** if you are not sure about endnotes or footnotes and bibliography.)

27b(2)
Prepare bibliography cards.

You should make a bibliography card for every book or article you plan to use in any way in your paper. Since you will not be certain, when you begin your research, whether a book or article will really be of importance, it is a good idea to make a card for each work that seems to have some information on your subject. These cards form your working bibliography and from them you will make your list of works cited. On the bibliography card, list the call number, author, title, place of publication, publishing company, and date of publication of the book. For an article in a magazine or newspaper, list the title and the author of the article, the magazine or newspaper, the volume number, date, inclusive pages, and call number (if your library uses call numbers for periodicals).

There are different forms for edited works, translated works, special collections, and so on (see pages **377–80** for other information that may be necessary for a correct bibliography). Remember that even though you do not have to concern yourself about bibliographical form when you are just beginning your research, you can save yourself time when you are writing your paper if you note all the necessary bibliographical information at the beginning.

```
                                    PN 6728
                                    D 65
                                    T 724

  Trudeau, Garry P. The Doonesbury
  Chronicles. New York: Holt, Rinehart
  and Winston, 1978.
```

BIBLIOGRAPHY CARD FOR A BOOK

> Parachini, Alan. "Social Protest Hits the
> Comic Pages." Columbia Journalism
> Review, November-December, 1974, 4-7.

BIBLIOGRAPHY CARD FOR AN ARTICLE

27b(3)
Prepare note cards.

Make at least one note card, in addition to a bibliography card, for every book or article that you consult and wish to mention in your paper. The number of note cards you use for each book depends on how valuable the book is as a source for your topic. On each card, write the name of the author or the title of the book or article and the pages from which you are taking the information.

There are three basic types of notes you can take:

1. You can jot down a few words or a sentence on a note card to help you remember what was in the book or article. This type of note-taking is best if the book or article does not have much information directly on your particular topic. You may read a book for background information or may wish to list a book in your notes as a useful general source on your subject. You will probably not have many cards of this sort since it is a good idea to limit your references mainly to works that you have quoted or have referred to directly in your paper. Here is an example of this type of card:

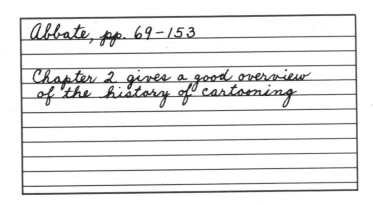

Abbate, pp. 69–153

Chapter 2 gives a good overview
of the history of cartooning

2. You may want to use a direct quotation from the author of a book or article, perhaps because you feel that the way he or she has said something is important. When you quote directly, be very accurate. Reproduce all marks of punctuation that appear in the material that you are quoting. If you leave out part of a passage, use ellipsis marks (. . .) to show that you have done so. If a complete sentence comes before the omitted part, put a period in front of the ellipsis marks.

For example, the following is a quotation from the essay "Life at Sea," which was discussed in Section **26c**. On the left is a passage that originally appeared in the essay. On the right is a student's note quoting parts of that passage.

ORIGINAL MATERIAL	STUDENT'S QUOTE
It has only been in recent years that berthing of men aboard ship has even been considered. In early days a man slept wherever he could find a soft plank. In many cases, on warships, men were required to sleep near their battle stations. Men were not allowed to live ashore because of the high desertion rate, but they were allowed to have wives aboard ship while in port.	It has only been in recent years that berthing of men aboard ship has even been considered.... In many cases, on warships, men were required to sleep near their battle stations. Men were not allowed to live ashore..., but they were allowed to have wives aboard ship while in port.

Be sure to record on your note card the correct page number for each quotation. Make up a new note card for each quotation. Your note card may look like this.

Parachini, p. 4

Parachini felt that "Doonesbury" was
Trudeaus' "vehicle to inveigh against
social and political wrongdoing and to
cuff wrongdoers."

3. You may want to restate what the author has said, putting the ideas
into your own words. You will probably use this type of note most often
since the material you read will be too long to be included whole. If
you are taking notes on a really useful article, you may even choose to
summarize the entire source on note cards. Your summaries may vary
in length. If you are recording the general idea of the source, your
summary may be one or two sentences. If you are summarizing an
important book or article, your summary may take up several note
cards. If you are summarizing several passages, write only one passage
on each note card, and include a page reference for each passage. Both
of the cards below summarize the essay "Life at Sea" (Section **26c**).
The first card gives a one-sentence summary; the next card gives a
longer summary.

Life at Sea
By comparing food, living conditions,
working conditions, and discipline, one can
see that the life of a sailor is much easier
today than it was 200 years ago.

> ### Life at Sea
>
> The life of a sailor is much different today than it was 200 years ago. Because of the smaller ships and crowded conditions, few kinds of food could be stored. Now meals are well planned and varied. Sleeping conditions were crowded and uncomfortable, but now living accommodations are comfortable. Work days are shorter, and recreation time is provided. The formerly severe discipline is fairer. No matter what the conditions, however, men will always be attracted by the sea.

No matter how long your summary is, you should:

1. Keep the same proportions as the passage you are summarizing. If the author wrote one paragraph on the causes of a disease and two paragraphs on the symptoms of that disease, you might write one sentence on the causes and two sentences on the symptoms of the disease.
2. Use your own words, unless you are quoting.

Sometimes you will not want to summarize the entire source but only use some important passages. It is important to put those passages in your own words whenever you are not quoting. Then you will be able to tell which passages are direct quotations when you look over your notes. Remember that at any time you use three or more words of an author in the same order that the author used them without enclosing the words in quotation marks, you are plagiarizing, or pretending that you have written the material yourself. Most people who plagiarize do not realize that they are doing so. Plagiarism can be easily avoided by careful note-taking.

EXERCISE 2

Make two bibliography cards on your topic, being sure to include all the information mentioned on page **367**.

EXERCISE 3

Read the student paper "Why Refrigerators Should Be Cleaned Once a Year" (page 355). Make the following four note cards on that paper:

1. A few words to help you remember what was in the paper
2. A quotation from the paper
3. A one-sentence summary of the paper
4. A summary one-third as long as the paper

EXERCISE 4

Read the student paper "Who Will Make the Squad?" (page 331). Which of the following summaries is likely to lead students to plagiarize, or to pretend that they have written the paper?

SUMMARY A

In "Who Will Make the Squad?" the student tells us that in spite of all his expectations and practice, he never made the basketball squad. "The world must not have been quite ready for another Larry Bird."

SUMMARY B

In "Who Will Make the Squad?" the student counted on making the junior varsity basketball squad. He was able to hustle while running the drills. The last night he played harder than he had ever played before. But he had to realize that the world wasn't quite ready for another Larry Bird.

27c
Organize your material and make your outline.

Now that you have taken all your notes, it is time to decide how to put your paper together. Spread all your note cards on a large table and see what you have. The student who wrote "The Growth and Development of 'Doonesbury' " (pages **384–94**), found that his cards could be put into several piles corresponding to what became the main headings of the paper: original strip, rise to syndication, problems due to satirical content, and success of the strip. When he started taking notes, the student knew that he wanted to write about "Doonesbury," but he did not know what precise statement he could make until after he completed his research. Now that you have finished your research, it is time for you to decide what precise statement you want to make. That precise statement is the thesis statement of your paper.

After you decide on your thesis statement, think about how to organize your material. Make several piles of note cards; each pile should contain only those cards that show a point that supports your thesis. You will find that some of the cards will have to be discarded because they have little or nothing to do with the main point. On a sheet of paper, list the points that lead to or support your theses, and arrange them in logical order in the form of an outline. (If you have forgotten how to put together an outline, see the directions for making a formal outline on page **341**.) After you have made the outline, you can number your cards according to the place they have in the outline.

An outline for a research paper will be longer than the outline for an essay. It should be made up of the thesis statement and three or four main headings or main points. Some main headings will be divided into subheadings, and some of these subheadings will have supporting points or details. Use Roman numerals (I, II, III) for main headings, capital letters (A, B, C) for subheadings, and numbers for supporting points. (See **26c** for outline form.)

The student who wrote "The Growth and Development of 'Doonesbury' " made the following outline:

Outline

Title: The Growth and Development of "Doonesbury"

Thesis Statement: Since its introduction in 1968 under the name "Bull Tales," the comic strip "Doonesbury" has developed into one of the most popular and significant comic strips of its time due, in part, to Trudeau's method of expanding the strip.

Introduction: "Doonesbury's" satire and expansion allowed the strip to grow from a university newspaper cartoon to a winner of the Pulitzer Prize.

I.   The original strip
   A.   Focus
   B.   Characters

II.   Rise to syndication
   A.   Discovery
   B.   Format changes
      1.   Changing the name
      2.   Reworking old situations
      3.   Broadening the scope
   C.   New characters
      1.   Phred the Terrorist
      2.   Mr. Slackmeyer
      3.   Joanie Caucus

III.   Problems due to satirical content
   A.   Censorship
   B.   Switch to editorial page

IV.   Success of the strip
   A.   Popularity
   B.   Coverage of issues

Conclusion: Garry Trudeau's ability to deal effectively with a wide range of topics can be seen in the expanded scope of the comic strip. His humor never loses its freshness nor his satire its brilliance.

When you finish your outline, look it over to check the following things:

1. Make certain that your subheadings are really parts of the headings under which they appear.
2. Make certain that each heading is different from the others. There should be no overlapping.
3. Make certain that each heading that you have divided has at least two subheadings. If you have a I, you need a II; if you have an A, you need a B; if you have a 1, you need a 2.

If you have problems writing logical headings and subheadings, review **26c**. Then test your understanding of outline form by doing the following exercise.

EXERCISE 5

This is an outline for the paper "Who Will Make the Squad?" (page 331). What mistakes has the author of the outline made? Rewrite the outline, correcting the errors.

Who Will Make the Squad?

Thesis statement: While playing basketball in high school, I found out that high expectations and hours of difficult practice did not help me make the squad.

   I. Because I was a sophomore I thought I had a good chance of making the squad.
  II. I practiced basketball every night.
     A. I wanted the coach to see how hard I was playing.
 III. I survived the first cut.
     A. I was one of the thirty left after the first cut.

B. We practiced hard to see who the five starters would be.
IV. The final list did not contain my name.
   A. I was not one of the five starters.
   B. I was bitterly disappointed.

27d
Prepare a list of works cited and notes.

Because you are using information gathered from different sources to write your library paper, you must give credit to these sources for providing the information you need. The information is not your own, and if you do not credit the author, you are guilty of literary theft, or plagiarism.

   To credit your sources, you must use a list of works cited and notes in parentheses in the body of your paper. A list of works cited is a list of all the books, magazines, and other sources you quote or paraphrase (rewrite in your own words) in your library paper. Each entry gives the exact page in a particular book, magazine, or other source from which you took some specific information.

27d(1)
Prepare a list of works cited.

Each entry in the list of works cited has three basic parts:

1. Author (Write last name first; begin at left margin.)
2. Title (Underline and capitalize correctly; give subtitle.)
3. Publication information (Give place of publication, name of publisher, and latest copyright date.) For journals, give first and last pages of article. Use the page numbers only; p. and pp. are not used in this style of documentation. Months with long names may be abbreviated (e.g. Nov.).

Entries are listed in alphabetical order according to the author's last name. If a book or article does not have an author given, use the title of the book or article to place it in the list alphabetically.

Sample Entries for the List of Works Cited

A book by a single author:

> Adams, Samuel Hopkins. Incredible Era. Boston:
> Houghton Mifflin, 1939.

A book with a subtitle, written by two or three authors:

> McQuade, Donald, and Robert Atwan. Popular
> Writing in America: The Interaction of Style
> and Audience. New York: Oxford Univ. Press,
> 1977.

A book by more than three authors:

> Grohmann, Will, et al. Art Since 1945. New York:
> Harry N. Abrams, 1958.

An edited book in its second edition:

> Hammel, William, ed. The Popular Arts in America.
> 2nd ed. New York: Harcourt Brace Jovanovich,
> 1977.

A translated work:

> Breton, Andre. Nadja. Trans. Richard Howard. New
> York: Grove Press, 1960.

An edited multi-volume work (no author):

> Kepes, Gyorgy, ed. Vision and Value. 6 vols. New
> York: George Braziller, 1965–66.

An article in a popular magazine:

> Jordan, Hamilton. "Crisis: The Last Years of the
> Carter Presidency." New Republic, 6 Dec. 1982,
> 28–30.

An article in a scholarly journal:

> Hamill, Pete. "Robert Grossman." Graphis:
> International Journal of Graphic Art and
> Applied Art 32, no. 186 (1976/77), 342–47.

An article from an edited collection:

> Kauffman, Stanley. "The Film Generation:
> Celebration and Concern." In The Popular Arts
> in America. Ed. William Hammel. 2nd ed. New
> York: Harcourt Brace Jovanovich, 1977, 72.

A newspaper article:

> Baker, Russell. "No More Mr. Clean Guy." New York
> Times, 2 March 1983, A27, cols. 5–6.

An encyclopedia article:

> Lash, Joseph P. "Roosevelt, Eleanor."

```
Encyclopedia Americana. 1982 ed.
```

An unsigned article:

```
"Dada at M.O.M.A." Newsweek, 8 April 1968, 132-
33.
```

A recording:

```
Niles, John Jacob. An Evening with John Jacob
Niles. Tradition Records, TLP 1036, 1959.
```

A television (or radio) program:

```
Firing Line. Writ. and prod. William F. Buckley.
PBS, 25 July 1982.
```

A book review (unsigned):

```
"The Beloved Agitator." Rev. of Eleanor
Roosevelt: A Friend's Memoir, by Joseph P.
Lash. Newsweek, 23 Nov. 1964, 121A.
```

A motion picture:

```
Spielberg, Steven, dir. E. T. The Extra-
Terrestrial. With Dee Wallace and Henry Thomas.
.Universal, 1982.
```

An interview:

```
Ireland, Richard. Personal interview. 15 April
1983.
```

A public document:

> Public Papers of the Presidents of the United
>
> States. Washington, D.C.: GPO, 1966.

EXERCISE 6

The following is some information that a student gathered for a paper on modern art. Arrange the information in correct form so that the entries are listed as they actually would be in a list of works cited for a paper. Be sure to punctuate and abbreviate correctly. Omit any unnecessary information.

Charlotte Willard; 1971; *Famous Modern Artists: From Cezanne to Pop Art*; Platt and Munk; New York; pages 16–21.

New York Times Magazine; "Remember Dada: Man Ray at Eighty"; DeGramont, S.; pages 6–7; September 6, 1970.

Pages 55–57; *Saturday Review*; Katharine Kuh; Volume 4; "Preservation of the Avant-Garde"; October 30, 1976.

June 20, 1966; "Love and Hiccups"; *Newsweek*; page 67; vol. 66.

Baldwin, James; *The Popular Arts in America*; New York; edited by William Hammel; 2nd ed.; 1977; "Mass Culture and the Creative Artist"; p. 30; Harcourt Brace Jovanovich.

J. Canaday; pp. 28–31; March 24, 1968; *New York Times Magazine*; "Dada and Its Offspring; Exhibition at Museum of Modern Art"

Holt, Rinehart and Winston; *Purposes of Art*; Pages 38–42; Elsen, Albert; 1967; New York.

27d(2)
Prepare parenthetical notes.

When you quote or paraphrase a particular source, show where the information comes from by putting a note in parentheses after the material quoted or paraphrased. This note shows the reader exactly where to look to find the passage in the book or article that you used. A parenthetical note should be brief. In fact, since detailed information about all your sources appears in the list of works cited at the end of the paper, all you need in most parenthetical notes are the author's last name and the page numbers of the material you used. The following reference is a quotation from page 50 of a book by Roland Penrose that was part of a student's list of works cited.

> Man Ray was criticized for "destroying art by painting by mechanical means" (Penrose, 50).

If the author of a source is mentioned in the text of the paper itself, that name need not be repeated in the note. In that case, only the page number is necessary.

> Marcel Jean pointed out that in the early twentieth century people were used to the idea of a nude as a subject for a painting, but the idea of a nude descending a staircase seemed incredible to viewers (34).

If more than one work by the same author appears in the list of works cited, a short version of the title of the work referred to should be used. The following reference is to Thomas Hardy's *The Return of the Native*. The student has also referred to Hardy's *Tess of the D'Urbervilles* in his paper.

> Egdon Heath is presented to us as a "vast tract of uncleared wild" (Hardy, *Return*, 3).

27d(3)
Prepare content notes, if necessary.

A list of notes is not necessary if you use the style of documentation given here in **27d**. You may find, however, that you wish to comment on some of the sources you have used or to tell your reader something that is not part of the main discussion in your paper. If you do, you may want to use content notes; they contain content, other than documentation, that could be of interest to the reader. For example, in a paper on Thomas Hardy's use of nature, you might give this note about a tavern you mentioned in your discussion:

[1]Hardy himself often visited this tavern which figures prominently in his Wessex novels.

27e
Write the paper.

Using your outline and note cards, first write a rough draft of your library paper. To write your paper, you must organize in a unified way all the information you have gathered and chosen from various sources. Since you have probably eliminated some unnecessary information in writing your outline, you, of course, should not include this information in your paper. That means you cannot simply copy your note cards in the order your outline calls for. Instead, you must make sure that the information you have gathered is put together smoothly and logically with sentences and paragraphs that join ideas for your reader.

This quoted information is used without anything to join ideas:

Contradiction existed even among the Dadaists themselves. Kurt Schwitters was "absolutely, unreservedly, twenty-four hours-a-day, PRO art." "The whole swindle that men call war was finished. . . . I felt myself freed and had to shout my jubilation out to the world."

This quoted information is used with words and sentences to join ideas:

Contradiction existed even among the Dadaists themselves. For example, one of the members of the movement, Kurt Schwitters, was not anti-art. He was, according to Hans Richter, "absolutely, unreservedly, twenty-four hours-a-day, PRO art." He believed that everything was art. Though most of the Dadaists joined the movement because of their feelings of despair about the war, Schwitters became a Dadaist for just the opposite reasons: "The whole swindle that men call war was finished. . . . I felt myself freed and had to shout my jubilation out to the world."

Just as you do for any paper you write, you must proofread the rough draft of your library paper carefully to eliminate errors and to make sure that what you have written is clear. Then, using the principles in Chapter **28** of this text or any specific directions your instructor has given you, type the paper in final form.

Your final library paper should include:

1. Title page
2. Outline page
3. Paper itself
4. Notes page (if needed)
5. Works cited page

You may also be asked to submit, with your final paper, your note cards, original outline, and rough draft.

The following is the library paper, "The Growth and Development of 'Doonesbury,' " written by a student who started out with the general topic of cartoons.

The Growth and Development of "Doonesbury"

by

Joseph Witte

April 29, 1982

Outline

Title: The Growth and Development of "Doonesbury"

Thesis
Statement: Since its introduction in 1968
                under the name "Bull Tales," the
                comic strip "Doonesbury" has
                developed into one of the most
                popular and significant comic
                strips of its time due, in part, to
                Trudeau's method of expanding the
                strip.

Introduction: "Doonesbury's" satire and expansion
                have allowed the strip to grow from
                a university newspaper cartoon to a
                winner of the Pulitzer Prize.

I.   The original strip
    A.   Focus
    B.   Characters
II. Rise to syndication
    A.   Discovery
    B.   Format changes

---

1. Changing the name

2. Reworking old situations

3. Broadening the scope

  C. New characters

1. Phred the Terrorist

2. Mr. Slackmeyer

3. Joanie Caucus

III. Problems due to satirical content

  A. Censorship

  B. Switch to editorial page

IV. Success of the strip

  A. Popularity

  B. Coverage of issues

Conclusion: Garry Trudeau's ability to deal effectively with a wide range of topics can be seen in the expanded scope of the comic strip. His humor never loses its freshness nor his satire its brilliance.

The Growth and Development of "Doonesbury"

In 1968 an undergraduate at Yale University named Garry B. Trudeau introduced a comic strip in the Yale Record. Only seven years later this comic strip, under the title "Doonesbury," earned him the first Pulitzer Prize for cartooning ever awarded to a comic-strip artist (World Encyclopedia, 219). "Doonesbury's" phenomenal rise in popularity and critical acclaim was largely due to Trudeau's sometimes bitter but always funny satirical style. However, the way Trudeau originally expanded the strip played an important role in its rise to national renown.

The comic strip created by Trudeau was first called "Bull Tales" (World Encyclopedia, 219). In "Bull Tales" Trudeau spoofed the life and the people on Yale's campus. In fact, Trudeau based two of his original characters on real-life Yale figures: Yale's president, Kingman Brewster; and Yale's star quarterback, Brian Dowling, alias B. D. (Wills, 1). The other significant members of the original cast were derived from characteristics that were common among the

students of the 1960s. These characters included
Mike Doonesbury, "B.D.'s klutzy roommate;"
"Megaphone Mark" Slackmeyer, a campus radical; and
Zonker Harris, a "flowery freak out" (Wills, 2).

In 1970 Trudeau's work came to the attention
of scouts from Universal Press Syndicate, who were
searching for promising new comic strips
(Biography, 420). They were impressed with "Bull
Tales" and urged Trudeau to allow UPS to syndicate
the column (Biography, 420). One of the scouts,
Jim Andrews, stated: "It was clear he (Trudeau)
was a comic genius" (Current Biography, 420).

Trudeau decided to syndicate the strip, and
to appeal to a wider audience, he changed some of
the college-based humor of his original strips
(Wills, 2). As Gary Wills put it: "The 'Y' got
scrubbed off of B. D.'s helmet, naked girls put
their clothes back on, and the swear words
disappeared" (2). The name of the strip was
changed to "Doonesbury" because "Bull Tales," it
was felt, might be offensive to some readers
(Current Biography, 420).

The increased circulation brought about a
more important change in the comic strip. It

allowed Trudeau to expand the scope of the strip. Now he could comment not only on college life but also on national social and political issues (Wills, 2). Trudeau considered Doonesbury "his vehicle to inveigh against social and political wrongdoing, and to cuff wrongdoers" (Parachini, 4).

In order to cover these broad new subject areas, Trudeau needed to expand the cast and setting of the strip. He accomplished this by allowing his characters to move away from the campus and into the world. B. D., for example, joined the army and was sent to Vietnam. While in Vietnam, B. D. was captured by Phred the Terrorist. The pair got lost and almost starved before they were saved by finding a hidden cache of Schlitz beer. This sequence was revolutionary in that it allowed the readers to laugh at the Vietnam war even though the war itself did not seem a suitable subject for laughter. Meanwhile, in New Jersey, Mark Slackmeyer left school to visit his family for Christmas vacation. Trudeau, in this sequence, introduced Mark's father, Mr. Slackmeyer, an upper-middle-class business executive with right-wing political tendencies.

Mark, a left-wing radical and a perfect example of
a rebellious youth, considered his father a
fascist. Readers of "Doonesbury" will notice that
Trudeau directed his satire at both political
extremes. As William F. Buckley, Jr., stated:
"Trudeau, who sprang from the loins of the Vietnam
antinomianism, quickly achieved perspective" (4).

Another new character became one of Trudeau's
most successful creations. Her name was Joanie
Caucus, a runaway homemaker turned women's libber,
who left her family to free herself from what she
felt was the stifling role of homemaker and to
define herself by her own accomplishments.
Trudeau's poignant satire of the American family
culminated when Joanie's husband asked her to come
back, not because he missed her, but because he
missed her cheeseburgers. Nora Ephron calls Joanie
"so downtrodden and yet so plucky, so saggy and
yet so upright, so droopy-eyed and yet wide awake,
so pessimistic and yet deep down slyly sure that
she's on the right track" (94-95).

Trudeau quickly became one of the most highly
regarded cartoonists of the time.[1] However, his
potent satire caused some papers to stop running

the strip. Howard Simons explained that the Washington Post decided to drop "Doonesbury" in 1973 because of the cartoon's treatment of the Watergate issue, commenting that "it is profoundly dangerous for comic-strip artists to ignore the fundamental right of defendants to be presumed innocent" (Maynard, A18). An objection occurred even earlier, in May 1972, when Zonker Harris put the blame on John Mitchell, the Attorney General, for causing the Kent State deaths. Because of that installment the managing editor of Akron, Ohio's Beacon Journal stopped running "Doonesbury." The Journal's subscribers protested the censorship so vehemently, however, that the strip was returned to the paper, and the editor "sent an emissary to New Haven to take Trudeau to dinner" (Current Biography, 420). Other newspapers started running the strip across from the editorial page, where its contents seemed more suitable (Current Biography, 420).

In the years since its introduction, "Doonesbury" has become a fixture in the realm of political satire. The strip has dealt with almost every important issue of its era: Watergate, civil rights, fuel shortages, and labor movements, just to name a few. As Art Buchwald, one of the most popular political columnists, wrote: "It is not only the best comic strip, but the best satire that's come along in a long time" (Cover). Trudeau has consistently appealed to young readers and has a wonderful ear for dialogue (Parachini, 7). Garry Trudeau's ability to deal effectively with a wide range of topics can be seen in the expanded scope of the comic strip.[2] His humor never loses its freshness nor his satire its brilliance.

Notes

[1] His cartoons have been collected in several volumes. I have used The Doonesbury Chronicles, Doonesbury's Greatest Hits, and Joanie extensively in preparing this paper.

[2] Trudeau is currently taking a sabbatical to reevaluate his satirical aims and to write a play based on his cartoons.

Works Cited

Buchwald, Art. Cover. The Doonesbury Chronicles.
    By Garry P. Trudeau. New York: Holt, Rinehart
    and Winston, 1975.

Buckley, William F., Jr. "Overture." Doonesbury's
    Greatest Hits. By Garry P. Trudeau. New York:
    Holt, Rinehart and Winston, 1978.

Ephron, Nora. "Afterword." Joanie. By Garry P.
    Trudeau. New York: Sheed and Ward, 1974.

"Garry Trudeau." Current Biography Yearbook, 1975.

Maynard, Robert C. "The Comic Strip Isn't a
    Court." The Washington Post, 31 May 1973, A18.

Parachini, Allan. "Social Protest Hits the Comic
    Pages." Columbia Journalism Review, Nov.–Dec.
    1974, 4–7.

Trudeau, Garry P. The Doonesbury Chronicles. New
    York: Holt, Rinehart and Winston, 1975.

———. Doonesbury's Greatest Hits. New York:
    Holt, Rinehart and Winston, 1978.

———. Joanie. New York: Sheed and Ward, 1974.

Wills, Garry. "Introduction." The Doonesbury
    Chronicles. By Garry P. Trudeau. New York:
    Holt, Rinehart and Winston, 1975.

The World Encyclopedia of Comics. Ed. Maurice
    Horn. New York: Chelsea House, 1976.

27f
Use a bibliography and endnotes, or footnotes, if this alternate style is recommended.

Section **27d** shows you how to prepare a list of works cited and to give notes in parentheses in the body of your paper. You may find, however, that your instructor prefers that you use a bibliography (a list of all the works you consulted) and notes given at the end of your paper or footnotes at the bottom of each page of your paper. This section should help you do so.

27f(1)
Prepare a bibliography.

A bibliography looks just like a list of works cited except that a bibliography includes *all* the works you looked at—not just the ones you refer to in your paper. Each entry includes author, title, and publication information.

Works Cited	Bibliography
Buchwald, Art. _____	Buchwald, Art. _____

See section **27d(1)** for help in preparing a bibliography and for sample bibliographical entries. For a sample bibliography, see the one for the "Doonesbury" paper on p. **412**.

27f(2)
Prepare notes.

You may use footnotes or endnotes to credit your sources. They are like parenthetical notes (described in **27d(2)**) since they tell the particular page or pages you used from a book or other source, but they contain more information. *Footnotes* are placed at the foot, or bottom, of each page of the paper. *Notes* are placed on a separate page after the final page of the paper.

FOOTNOTES

¹Hamilton Jordan, "Crisis: The Last Years of the Carter Presidency," *The New Republic,* 6 Dec., 1982, p. 28.
    ²Jordan, p. 30.

ENDNOTES

Notes

¹Hamilton Jordan, "Crisis: The Last Years of the Carter Presidency," *The New Republic,* 6 Dec. 1982, p. 28.
    ²Jordan, p. 30.

The numbers on the notes page correspond to numbers you write in the text of your paper. When you use information from a particular source, place a number in your text immediately after the information and a half-space above the line you are writing on. The first time you do this, the number you write will be *one*(¹). The next time, the number will be *two*(²); the third time, *three*(³); and so on. These numbers refer to the notes giving credit to the sources you used to get the information. If you are using endnotes, write the notes themselves on a separate page immediately following the final page of your paper. For a sample page of endnotes, see the one for the "Doonesbury" paper on p. **410.**

The first time you write a note giving credit to a particular source, include this information:

1. Note number (Write the same number here that you wrote in your paper after the information you took from this source).

2. Author (Write first name first).

3. Title (Underline and capitalize correctly; give subtitle.)

4. Publication information (Give place of publication, name of publisher, and latest copyright date.)

5. Page number(s) (Write the page number[s] from which you took the information.)

Sample First-Reference Notes

A book by a single author:

[1] Samuel Hopkins Adams, Incredible Era

(Boston: Houghton Mifflin, 1939), p. 71.

A book with a subtitle, written by two or three authors:

[2] Donald McQuade and Robert Atwan, Popular

Writing in America: The Interaction of Style and

Audience (New York: Oxford Univ. Press, 1977),

p. 56.

A book by more than three authors:

[3] Will Grohmann et al., Art Since 1945 (New

York: Harry N. Abrams, 1958), p. 17.

An edited book in its second edition:

[4] William Hammel, ed., The Popular Arts in

America, 2nd ed. (New York: Harcourt Brace

Jovanovich, 1977), p. 10.

A translated work:

[5] Andre Breton, Nadja, trans. Richard Howard

(New York: Grove Press, 1960), p. 27.

An edited multi-volume work (no author):

> [6] Gyorgy Kepes, ed., Vision and Value (New York: George Braziller, 1965–66), V, 101.

An article in a popular magazine:

> [7] Hamilton Jordan, "Crisis: The Last Years of the Carter Presidency," New Republic, 6 Dec. 1982, p. 29.

An article in a scholarly journal:

> [8] Pete Hamill, "Robert Grossman," Graphis: International Journal of Graphic Art and Applied Art, 32, No. 186 (1976/77), 345.

An article from an edited collection:

> [9] Stanley Kauffmann, "The Film Generation: Celebration and Concern," in The Popular Arts in America, ed. William Hammel, 2nd. ed. (New York: Harcourt Brace Jovanovich, 1977), p. 60.

A newspaper article:

> [10] Russell Baker, "No More Mr. Clean Guy," New York Times, 2 March 1983, Sec. A, p. 27, cols. 5–6.

An encyclopedia article:

> [11] Joseph P. Lash, "Roosevelt, Eleanor," Encyclopedia Americana, 1982 ed.

An unsigned article:

12 "Dada at M.O.M.A.," <u>Newsweek</u>, 8 April 1968, p. 132.

A recording:

13 John Jacob Niles, <u>An Evening with John Jacob Niles</u>, Tradition Records, TLP 1036, 1959.

A television (or radio) program:

14 <u>Firing Line</u>, Writ. and prod. William F. Buckley, PBS, 25 July 1982.

A book review (unsigned):

15 "The Beloved Agitator," rev. of <u>Eleanor Roosevelt: A Friend's Memoir</u>, by Joseph Lash, <u>Newsweek</u>, 23 Nov. 1964, p. 121A.

A motion picture:

16 <u>E. T. The Extra-Terrestrial</u>, directed by Steven Spielberg, with Dee Wallace and Henry Thomas, Universal, 1982.

An interview:

17 Personal interview with Richard Ireland, 15 April 1983.

A public document:

18 <u>Public Papers of the Presidents of the</u>

United States (Washington, D.C.: GPO, 1966),
p. 17.

The second time you write a note giving credit to a particular source, use a shortened form:

1. Author's last name
2. Page number(s) (if different from that given in the first-reference note for this source)

If you use works by two or more authors with the same last name, give the authors' first initials when you write second-reference notes giving them credit.

If you use more than one work by the same author, give both the author's last name and the title of the work you are giving credit to when you write a second-reference note for it.

Sample Second-Reference Notes

5 Goldin, p. 72.

6 McQuade and Atwan, p. 60.

7 Kauffmann, p. 62.

Credit for different information also taken from page 72 of Goldin's article:

8 Goldin.

9 Canaday, p. 105.

If you refer extensively to one particular work, you may choose to omit entirely second-reference notes to that work. Instead, your first reference will indicate that subsequent references will be in the body of your paper:

¹ Katherine Mansfield, "Miss Brill," in
Literature: <u>Structure, Sound, and Sense</u>, ed. Lawrence
Perrine, 3rd ed. (New York: Harcourt Brace Jovanovich,
1978), p. 470. All subsequent references to this work
will be indicated by page number in the text of this
paper.

You will then show second references to that work in the body of
the paper itself, not in the footnotes or endnotes.

Miss Brill "has a kinship with other people in
the park" (p. 472)––a kinship which she feels very
keenly.

This type of reference is particularly appropriate when you are writing a literary analysis and most of your references are to one particular work of literature.

EXERCISE 7

Arrange the information given in Exercise 6 (p. **380**) in correct first-reference note form so that the notes are listed as they
would actually appear on a note page in a library paper. Number
the notes consecutively, beginning with any source you wish. Use
any page numbers you wish.

Write second-reference notes for three of the sources given.
Number these consecutively with the first-reference notes.

The following are the outline, text, endnotes, and bibliography
for the paper "The Growth and Development of 'Doonesbury.' "

The Growth and Development of "Doonesbury"

by

Joseph Witte

April 29, 1982

Outline

Title: The Growth and Development of "Doonesbury"

Thesis: Since its introduction in 1968
Statement: under the name "Bull Tales," the
                oomio strip "Doonesbury" has
                developed into one of the most
                popular and significant comic
                strips of its time due, in part, to
                Trudeau's method of expanding the
                strip.

Introduction: "Doonesbury's" satire and expansion
                have allowed the strip to grow from
                a university newspaper cartoon to a
                winner of the Pulitzer Prize.

  I.   The original strip
       A.   Focus
       B.   Characters
 II.   Rise to syndication
       A.   Discovery
       B.   Format changes
            1. Changing the name
            2. Reworking old situations
            3. Broadening the scope

C. New characters

   1. Phred the Terrorist

   2. Mr. Slackmeyer

   3. Joanie Caucus

III. Problems due to satirical content

A. Censorship

B. Switch to editorial page

IV. Success of the strip

A. Popularity

B. Coverage of issues

Conclusion: Garry Trudeau's ability to deal effectively with a wide range of topics can be seen in the expanded scope of the comic strip. His humor never loses its freshness nor his satire its brilliance.

The Growth and Development of "Doonesbury"

In 1968 an undergraduate at Yale University named Garry B. Trudeau introduced a comic strip in the Yale Record. Only seven years later this comic strip, under the title "Doonesbury," earned him the first Pulitzer Prize for cartooning ever awarded to a comic-strip artist.[1] "Doonesbury's" phenomenal rise in popularity and critical acclaim was largely due to Trudeau's sometimes bitter but always funny satirical style. However, the way Trudeau originally expanded the strip played an important role in its rise to national renown.

The comic strip created by Trudeau was first called "Bull Tales."[2] In "Bull Tales" Trudeau spoofed the life and the people on Yale's campus. In fact, Trudeau based two of his original characters on real-life Yale figures: Yale's president, Kingman Brewster; and Yale's star quarterback, Brian Dowling, alias B.D.[3] The other significant members of the original cast were derived from characteristics that were common among the students of the 1960s. These characters included Mike Doonesbury, "B.D.'s klutzy roommate;" "Megaphone Mark" Slackmeyer, a campus radical; and Zonker Harris, a "flowery freak out."[4]

In 1970 Trudeau's work came to the attention of scouts from Universal Press Syndicate, who were searching for promising new comic strips.[5] They were impressed with "Bull Tales" and urged Trudeau to allow UPS to syndicate the column.[6] One of the scouts, Jim Andrews, stated: "It was clear he (Trudeau) was a comic genius."[7]

Trudeau decided to syndicate the strip, and to appeal to a wider audience, he changed some of the college-based humor of his original strips.[8] As Garry Wills put it: "The 'Y' got scrubbed off of B.D.'s helmet, naked girls put their clothes back on, and the swear words disappeared."[9] The name of the strip was changed to "Doonesbury" because "Bull Tales," it was felt, might be offensive to some readers.[10]

The increased circulation brought about a more important change in the comic strip. It allowed Trudeau to expand the scope of the strip. Now he could comment not only on college life but also on national social and political issues.[11] Trudeau considered Doonesbury "his vehicle to inveigh against social and political wrongdoing, and to cuff wrongdoers."[12]

In order to cover these broad new subject

areas, Trudeau needed to expand the cast and setting of the strip. He accomplished this by allowing his characters to move away from the campus and into the world. B.D., for example, joined the army and was sent to Vietnam. While in Vietnam, B.D. was captured by Phred the Terrorist. The pair got lost and almost starved before they were saved by finding a hidden cache of Schlitz beer. This sequence was revolutionary in that it allowed the readers to laugh at the Vietnam war even though the war itself did not seem a suitable subject for laughter. Meanwhile, in New Jersey, Mark Slackmeyer left school to visit his family for Christmas vacation. Trudeau, in this sequence, introduced Mark's father, Mr. Slackmeyer, an upper-middle-class business executive with right-wing political tendencies. Mark, a left-wing radical and a perfect example of a rebellious youth, considered his father a fascist. Readers of "Doonesbury" will notice that Trudeau directed his satire at both political extremes. As William F. Buckley, Jr., stated: "Trudeau, who sprang from the loins of the Vietnam antinomianism, quickly achieved perspective."[13]

Another new character became one of Trudeau's

most successful creations. Her name was Joanie Caucus, a runaway homemaker turned women's libber, who left her family to free herself from what she felt was the stifling role of homemaker and to define herself by her own accomplishments. Trudeau's poignant satire of the American family culminated when Joanie's husband asked her to come back, not because he missed her, but because he missed her cheeseburgers. Nora Ephron calls Joanie "so downtrodden and yet so plucky, so saggy and yet so upright, so droopy-eyed and yet wide awake, so pessimistic and yet deep down slyly sure that she's on the right track."[14]

Trudeau quickly became one of the most highly regarded cartoonists of the time. However, his potent satire caused some papers to stop running the strip. Howard Simons explained that the Washington Post decided to drop "Doonesbury" in 1973 because of the cartoon's treatment of the Watergate issue, commenting that "it is profoundly dangerous for comic-strip artists to ignore the fundamental right of defendants to be presumed innocent."[15] An objection occurred even earlier, in May 1972, when Zonker Harris put the blame on John Mitchell, the Attorney General, for causing the Kent State deaths. Because of that installment the managing editor of Akron, Ohio's Beacon Journal stopped running "Doonesbury." The Journal's subscribers protested the censorship so vehemently, however, that the strip was returned to the paper, and the editor "sent an emissary to New Haven to take Trudeau to dinner."[16] Other newspapers started running the strip across from the editorial page, where its contents seemed more suitable.[17]

In the years since its introduction, "Doonesbury" has become a fixture in the realm of political satire. The strip has dealt with almost every important issue of its era: Watergate, civil rights, fuel shortages, and labor movements, just to name a few. As Art Buchwald, one of the most popular political columnists, wrote: "It is not only the best comic strip, but the best satire that's come along in a long time."[18] Trudeau has consistently appealed to young readers and has a wonderful ear for dialogue.[19] Garry Trudeau's ability to deal effectively with a wide range of topics can be seen in the expanded scope of the comic strip. His humor never loses its freshness nor his satire its brilliance.

Notes

[1] "Doonesbury," World Encyclopedia of Comics,
ed. Maurice Horn (New York: Chelsea House, 1976),
p. 219.

[2] "Doonesbury."

[3] Garry Wills, "Introduction," The Doonesbury
Chronicles, by Garry P. Trudeau (New York: Holt,
Rinehart and Winston, 1975), p. i.

[4] Wills, p. ii.

[5] "Trudeau, Garry," Current Biography
Yearbook, 1975, p. 420.

[6] "Trudeau, Garry."

[7] "Trudeau, Garry."

[8] Wills, p. ii.

[9] Wills, p. ii.

[10] "Trudeau, Garry."

[11] Wills, p. ii.

[12] Allan Parachini, "Social Protest Hits the
Comic Pages," Columbia Journalism Review,
November–December 1974, p. 4.

[13] William F. Buckley, Jr., "Overture,"
Doonesbury's Greatest Hits, by Garry P. Trudeau
(New York: Holt, Rinehart and Winston, 1978), p.
iv.

[14] Nora Ephron, "Afterword," _Joanie_, by Garry P. Trudeau (New York: Sheed and Ward, 1974), pp. 94–95.

[15] Robert C. Maynard quotes Simons in "The Comic Strip Isn't a Court," _The Washington Post_, 31 May 1973, p. A18.

[16] "Trudeau, Garry."

[17] "Trudeau, Garry."

[18] Art Buchwald, Cover, _The Doonesbury Chronicles_, by Garry P. Trudeau (New York: Holt, Rinehart and Winston, 1975).

[19] Parachini, p. 7.

Bibliography

Berger, Arthur Asa. The Comic-Stripped American.
New York: Walker, 1973.

Buchwald, Art. Cover. The Doonesbury Chronicles.
By Garry P. Trudeau. New York: Holt, Rinehart
and Winston, 1975.

Buckley, William F., Jr. "Overture." Doonesbury's
Greatest Hits. By Garry P. Trudeau. New York:
Holt, Rinehart and Winston, 1978.

Ephron, Nora. "Afterword." Joanie. By Garry P.
Trudeau. New York: Sheed and Ward, 1974.

"Garry Trudeau." Current Biography Yearbook, 1975.

Maynard, Robert C. "The Comic Strip Isn't a
Court." The Washington Post, 31 May 1973,
p. A18.

Parachini, Allan. "Social Protest Hits the Comic
Pages." Columbia Journalism Review, Nov.-Dec.
1974, pp. 4-7.

A Subtreasury of American Humor. Ed. E. B. White
and Katherine S. White. New York: Coward-
McCann, 1941.

Trudeau, Garry P. The Doonesbury Chronicles. New
York: Holt, Rinehart and Winston, 1975.

———. Doonesbury's Greatest Hits. New York:
    Holt, Rinehart and Winston, 1978.

———. Joanie. New York: Sheed and Ward, 1974.

Wills, Garry. "Introduction." The Doonesbury
    Chronicles. By Garry P. Trudeau. New York:
    Holt, Rinehart and Winston, 1975.

The World Encyclopedia of Comics. Ed. Maurice
    Horn. New York: Chelsea House, 1976.

CHAPTER TWENTY-EIGHT

Putting the Paper in Final Form

> **Be sure that your paper is in good form when you give it to your instructor.**

28a

Use the correct materials.

Unless your instructor gives you special directions, use these materials when you *write* formal papers:

1. Standard-size, white, wide-lined paper, not torn from a spiral notebook
2. Blue or black ink

and these materials when you *type* formal papers:

1. Standard-size, white, unlined paper
2. Black ribbon

28b

Write or type so that your paper is easy to read.

1. When typing, leave one-inch margins at the top, the bottom, and on each side of the page. When writing, leave one-inch margins at the

right and bottom of each page and use the printed lines for top and left margins.

2. Write or type your name and the date at the top of the first page or on a title page.

3. Center the title at the top of the first page. Do not underline or put quotation marks around the title. Capitalize the first, last, and all important words. Skip a line, or double space, after the title.

4. Indent the first word of each paragraph about one inch, or five spaces, from the left margin.

5. Double-space when typing. Write on every other line when writing.

6. Number the pages with Arabic numbers (1, 2, 3, . . .), beginning with page 2. Place the number at the top center or top right-hand corner of each page.

7. If you have to divide a word at the end of a line, look it up in your dictionary to find out where you can divide it. (See Chapter **20** if you need help in dividing words.)

8. Write each letter clearly. Be sure that your capital letters are different from your lower-case letters. Be sure that you cross your *t*'s and dot your *i*'s. Use solid dots, not circles, for periods.

9. When typing, avoid erasures and strike-overs. Use correction fluid to make corrections neatly.

28c
Proofread your paper carefully.

Correct any mistakes you find before you give your paper to your instructor.

1. When writing papers in class, always reserve at least five minutes to proofread your paper carefully and make corrections.

2. When writing papers out of class, write your paper once, leave it for a while, and then proofread it carefully and make corrections. Recopy or retype any page that has more than one or two corrections.

3. After you have written two or three papers, you will begin to see the mistakes you make most often. Proofread your papers, looking especially

for each of these mistakes. It is easy to find a mistake when you are looking for a particular one.

The following paragraph shows the changes the student writer made after proofreading.

The ~~Worse~~ Worst Day in My Life

It all started on October 26, 1972, the day I was inducted into the United States Army. On the twenty-sixth, I was ordered to report to the Greyhound Bus Station in Norfolk, and from there proceed to Richmond for a complete physical and mental examination. I have never stood in line for such a ~~great length of~~ long time. It was like nothing I had ever experienced before. After I completed my testing, I was released for lunch. After lunch I had to report to the Train Station in Richmond, where I was told to board a train and stay on until the conductor said, "Fort Jackson, South Carolina," my home for six weeks of basic training. October 26, 1972, was the worst day of my life, but it was also the first of many bad days I spent in the Army.

EXERCISE 1

Proofread the following paragraph carefully and make any necessary changes.

The Discotheque

The discotheque is where day ends and night life begins. On the outside of the discotheque there are neon lights flashing and blinking. People standing around laughing and talking listning to the loud music that echoes from the inside as they wait to get in. On the inside of the discotheque their are large number of people at the bar drinking beer some at tables and some anywhere they can find enough room. The discotheque is famous for it's loud music and draft beer. It has a small stage where go go dancers preform and men sit around drinking beer and watching the dancers. People talking loud to be heard over the music but saying nothing of very much importance. Despite the noise and the crowd, the discotheque is still favorite amoung many people it is a exciting way to spend a night after a dull work day.

28d

When your instructor returns your paper, be sure to make any corrections suggested.

1. Find the correct section in this handbook.
2. Study the section that explains the change you need to make.
3. Make the necessary change on your paper.
4. If you need to make major changes in sentences and paragraphs, rewrite your paper.

If you follow this procedure, it will help you to understand why you need to make the changes your instructor suggests. It will also help you avoid repeating the same mistakes.

Here is a paragraph marked by an instructor using the section numbers found in this book.

The Old Telephone Building

Yesterday I made an appointment to see the old telephone build-

ing, which is for sale. The building was in fair condition on the

outside, except the windows was boarded. As I enter the building

2 2a   *6a (3)*   *22*   *7a (1)*   *9b*

6a(3)   7b(1)

there was papers scatter in the halls and rooms. Going upstairs was

    3d   6a(3)   2/c

hazardous the steps was weak. The second floor was an disgrace, with

    12a   22a

paint pilling off the walls piles of trash on the floor. The building

    2/c

was a total lost.

Here is the same paragraph as it was corrected by the student who
wrote it.

The Old Telephone Building

Yesterday I made an appointment to see the old telephone build-

ing, which is for sale. The building was in fair condition on the

  22a   *that*   6a(3)   22 ,   7a(1)

                were   *entered*

outside, except the windows ~~was~~ boarded. As I ~~enter~~ the building

 9b   6a(3)   7b(1)

I saw that   *were scattered*

~~there was~~ papers ~~scatter~~ in the halls and rooms. Going upstairs was

    3d   6a(3)   2/c

         because *were*

hazardous the steps ~~was~~ weak. The second floor was ~~an~~ *a* disgrace, with

12a   22a

 peeling   *and*

paint ~~pilling~~ off the walls piles of trash on the floor. The building

       loss 2/c

was a total ~~lost~~.

EXERCISE 2

Make the necessary changes in this paragraph, using the sections
in this book to help you.

The Corner Grocery Store

                  3c

I approached the store on the corner I could see it was a poor

              6a(3)

store because of the rubbish outside. There was boxes, papers, and

cans filled with trash on the street in front of the store. I opened the
12 a (6)   *12 a*
door, and it slammed shut behind me as if some one else were closing
                                    6a (3)   *22*
it in anger. The store were filled with most of everyday needs, but it
7a (1)   *7b (1)*   *22b 13a*   *22b*
look overstock. The shelves filled and cases of canned goods sitting
                        12a   *22a*   *7a (1)*
on the floor in the isles. The clutter of the inside of store explain
                6a (3)   *1d (2)*
why the trash were piled outside in such large amount.

EXERCISE 3

Practice proofreading. Edit the following paragraphs by inserting changes where necessary.

1. There is many disadvantage of the pass–fail grading system in college. For one thing it require only a little effort from the student. Instead of learning. A student is concern with only passing a subject and just go through the motions of education. Another disadvantage is the the pass–fail system discourage a student progress, a student who would ordinarily try to do well in their courses are trying only to pass them these students become underachievers and they learn less than their ability will allow. Competition is reduce to the lowest level—between those who past and those who do not. It is also argue that the pass–fail system reduce the prestige of a college education. And that the college degree become less valuable, the better argument seem to be that this

system has no motivation. A good student is not recognize, but he seen as one of many passing student, there is no motivation to excell. The importance of motivation in college reflect a person need to grow and change. Under the pass–fail grading system. A student don't have this moitvation and will suffer as a result.

2. Ray Bradburys *August 2026*, a short story considered by many to be a warning of the nuclear holocaust envisioned by the narrator is a protest against the automation of our lifes. Bradbury creates a moving story without the use of a single human character. He used what Americans relate to more readily than there fellowman; time. The entire house runs on a precise schedule, automaticaly preparing meals, cleaning and even entertaining, at exact intervals. In spite of the absence of people, the house continues with it's work, we get the impression that the persons living their were almost as automated and isolated as the mechanical mice, who clean the house. Bradbury seemed to be criticizing our emphasis on time as well as our feelings of importence by virtue of being human. He shows that not only will the world continue, but our creations will live on after we are gone from the earth.

CHAPTER TWENTY-NINE
Writing Business Letters

Learn how to write a correct and effective business letter.

There are many occasions when you need to write a business letter. You may be applying for a job, ordering some merchandise, inquiring about some matter, or perhaps requesting an adjustment in something you purchased. Since you probably do not know the people to whom you are writing and since you wish to make a favorable impression so that they will understand your needs and assist you, it is important to express yourself clearly, directly, simply, and correctly. The following suggestions should help you to do this.

29a
Observe certain guidelines when writing business letters.

Here are some principles to remember when writing a business letter:

1. Make the purpose of your letter clear immediately—in the first paragraph of your letter.

2. Express yourself clearly. Use simple language, and avoid jargon or wordiness.

3. Use correct grammar, spelling, and punctuation. Proofread your letter carefully.

4. Be polite, even when you are dissatisfied with an order you received or with some other matter. You do not want to anger your reader.

5. Make your letter short. You want to say only as much as necessary to make your point clearly. You do not want to lose the attention of readers or distract them from the purpose of your letter.

6. Use acceptable letter form **(see 27b)**.

7. Be sure your letter is neat. It is best to type your letter and to use standard 8½ × 11 paper.

29b
Use a standard letter form.

There are many acceptable forms for a business letter. Two common ones illustrated in this chapter are the modified block (Letter 1, page **426**) and the full block (Letter 2, page **427**). In the modified block form, everything except the heading, the complimentary close, and the signature are even with the left margin. In the full block form, everything is even with the left margin. The basic parts of the business letter are labeled in Letter 2.

The Heading

The heading is the complete address of the writer and the date. Notice that the address generally contains no abbreviations. There are no periods at the ends of any of the lines in the heading. There is no comma between the state and the zip code. In modified block form, the heading begins to the right of center and ends at the right margin.

The Inside Address

The inside address appears several spaces below the heading and even with the left margin. It contains the name of the person who is receiving the letter, a title, if there is one, and the person's address.

The Salutation

The salutation greets the person receiving the letter. It is followed by a colon and appears two spaces below the inside address.

> Dear Mr. Jones:
> Dear Ms. Andrews:
> Dear Dr. Samuels:

If you are writing to a married woman, you may write *Mrs.* or *Ms.*; if the woman is unmarried you may write *Miss* or *Ms.* Sometimes you do not know the name of the person who will be receiving the letter (as in Letter 2). In that case the salutation may read

> Dear Sir or Madam:

The Body

The body of the business letter is generally one to five paragraphs long. You should state your purpose in writing the letter near the beginning. Keep the letter as brief and precise as possible. The body appears two spaces below the salutation and even with the left margin. In the full block and modified block letters, the first lines of the paragraphs are not indented.

The Complimentary Close

The complimentary close is a way of ending the letter courteously. In modified block form it appears two spaces below the body of the letter and is lined up with the heading. The most common expressions used in the complimentary close are *Sincerely, Sincerely Yours,* and *Yours truly.* Capitalize only the first word of the complimentary close.

The Signature

There is always a handwritten signature. If you are typing the letter, type your name as well four spaces below the complimentary close, and sign your name in the space in between. You may include your title if you are writing as an official representative of an organization.

Sincerely,   Yours truly,

Jane Edwards   *Samuel Johnson*

Jane Edwards   Samuel Johnson
                                         Editor

The following may also be included in some business letters:

The Attention Line

If you wish to direct your letter to a particular department or one of its representatives, but do not know the name of a specific individual in the organization, use an attention line. The attention line is usually placed two spaces below the inside address. (See Letter 2.)

The Subject Line

Sometimes you will want to identify the subject of your letter so that someone can act on the matter concerning you quickly and efficiently. Do this by using a subject line. The subject line usually appears two spaces under the inside heading, even with the left margin. If you have an attention line as well, place the subject line two spaces below the attention line.

Subject: Order #7814, rubber gloves

Enclosures, Carbon Copies, and Reference Initials

Sometimes you will want to indicate at the end of a letter that you are enclosing something or that you are sending another person a copy of your letter. Occasionally you may want to show that you have prepared a letter that another person has written. Notations like these are shown even with the left margin and a couple of spaces below the signature. (See Letter 2.)

Enc. personal data sheet (*enclosure*)
cc: District Manager (*copy sent to another*)
LL/cf (*letter typed by another person*)

29c
Prepare the envelope and fold the letter correctly.

When you use a standard business envelope (4 × 10), fold your letter horizontally into thirds. If you are using a small business envelope (3½ × 6½), fold your letter once horizontally and twice vertically A sample envelope is shown below.

SAMPLE ENVELOPE

```
David C. Foster
1214 Windfall Avenue
Portsmouth, Virginia 23320




            Mr. John Clark
            Parts Manager
            Shopsmith, Inc.
            750 Center Drive
            Vandalia, Ohio 45377
```

LETTER 1

1214 Windfall Avenue
Portsmouth, Virginia   23320
August 9, 1983

Mr. John Clark, Parts Manager
Shopsmith, Inc.
750 Center Drive
Vandalia, Ohio   45377

Dear Mr. Clark:

Thank you for the prompt delivery of the two drum
sanders I ordered on August 2, 1983. I have your
Invoice #387295, dated August 7, 1983. My original
order also included a request for two 5/8 inch arbors,
Catalog Number 505506, listed at a price of $18.50
each, and my check included $37.00 to cover the cost
of these arbors. Since your invoice did not show a
back order, I believe there may have been an error in
filling my order.

Because I am having to delay using my Shopsmith Mark
IV until I receive the arbors, please ship them by
United Parcel Service as soon as possible. I would
appreciate your prompt attention to this matter.

Yours truly,

David C. Foster

David C. Foster

LETTER 2

3340 Brandywine Drive Chesapeake, Virginia 23321 August 16, 1983	} HEADING
ABC Electronics Patton Drive Portsmouth, Virginia 23705	} INSIDE ADDRESS
Attention: Personnel Department	} ATTENTION LINE
Dear Sir or Madam:	} SALUTATION

I believe that my experience and training in
electronics qualify me for the position of
technician that you advertised in the
Virginian Pilot of August 15, 1983.

For the last twelve years I have been
employed by a major manufacturer of home
entertainment equipment, the last four years
in development of new circuits, including
the design and construction of printed
circuit boards. I have taken courses in
microprocessors and digital electronics as   } BODY
well as courses in programming in BASIC and
FORTRAN. I hold a diploma in radio and
television repair from Pitt Technical
Institute in Greenville, North Carolina, and
I am currently enrolled in the Associate in
Applied Science in Engineering Technology
program at Tidewater Community College.

May I schedule an interview at your
convenience? I can be reached at the above
address or by phone at (804) 484-8788 after
5 p.m. weekdays.

Sincerely yours,   } COMPLIMENTARY CLOSE

Thomas A. Slate, Jr.

Thomas A. Slate, Jr.   } SIGNATURE

Enc. personal data sheet   } NOTATION

29d
Send a résumé along with a letter of application.

Most letters of application are short. (See Letter 2.) Along with a
letter of application, you will probably be sending a résumé or personal data sheet giving information a prospective employer would
like to have about you. The résumé generally includes your name,
your address, the job you are applying for, your education, your
experience, honors, awards or special training, and references. Here
are some tips for writing the résumé.

1. Be specific about the job you want. Do not say you will take anything.

2. When you describe your education, start with your current or most
   recent education and work back. It is usually not necessary to list
   anything before high school.

3. When you describe your experience, start with your current or most
   recent position and work back. Try not to leave any long gaps of time.
   Be as specific as possible about the kind of work you did at each job.

4. Check with all people you use as references before listing them on your
   résumé. Give them written permission to answer questions about you.
   Try to use at least one former employer (preferably recent) as a reference. If you have references on file at your school, you do not need to
   list them individually.

```
RÉSUMÉ
Thomas Alexander Slate, Jr.
3340 Brandywine Drive
Chesapeake, Virginia 23321
Telephone: (804) 484-8788

Employment Objective

To associate with a progressive electronics company
and work with state-of-the-art products and
developments

Employment Experience

February 1969        General Electric Company,
to present           Portsmouth, Virginia 23705;
                     worked as circuit analyst, quality
                     control  auditor,  product  analyst
                     and engineering assistant
```

| September 1967 to August 1968 | WOOW Broadcasting, Inc., Greenville, North Carolina 27834; worked as part-time announcer and studio maintenance technician |
| September 1965 to March 1967 | WWDR Broadcasting, Inc., Murfreesboro, North Carolina 27855; worked as part-time announcer and assistant to engineer |

Education

1980 to present	Associate in Applied Science in Engineering Technology, Tidewater Community College, Portsmouth, Virginia 23508; expected graduation: June 1983
August 1968	Diploma, Radio and T.V. Repair Pitt Technical Institute, Greenville, North Carolina 27834
June 1966	Diploma, Murfreesboro High School, Murfreesboro, North Carolina 27855

Special Training

BASIC and FORTRAN programming courses and color television design course at General Electric Company, Portsmouth, Virginia 23705.

Digital electronics, microprocessor and electric motor continuing education courses at Old Dominion University, Norfolk, Virginia 23508

Photography and small engine repair courses at Tidewater Community College, Portsmouth, Virginia 23705

Interests

Mechanics, photography, electronics, woodworking

References

Placement Office, Student Services
Tidewater Community College
Portsmouth, Virginia   (804) 484-2121

EXERCISE 1

Mark any errors that you see in the following letter.

```
                              Apt. 3d.
                              709 Cherokee Road.
                              Portsmouth, Va., 23701.

August 2, 1983

Mr. James Wilson
Advertising Mgr.
Hadley Gifts

New York, N. Y., 10021

Gentlemen,

        It has come to my attention that your illustrious
firm stocks Reek-No-More cologne in 2-ounce bottles. I
have long admired this scent and would like to order
some for my cousin. Please send it by return mail and
bill it to me at my present address. I would also like
to know if you can identify the scent on the piece of
cloth that I am enclosing.
        Your prompt attention to this matter will
certainly not go unappreciated.
                              Most Respectfully, I
                              remain

                              Janet Dawson
                              encl--one piece of
                              perfumed cloth
```

EXERCISE 2

Choose one of the following:

1. Find a want ad in the help wanted section of your local newspaper. Then write a letter of application and a personal data sheet that you might send in response to the listing.

2. Write a letter ordering something that you saw advertised in a newspaper or magazine.

3. Write a letter to accompany an item you are returning to the seller because it is unsatisfactory for some reason.

4. Write a letter to an insurance company, asking for a review of a claim that was denied.

5. Write a letter to the placement office of your college requesting that your file be sent to a prospective employer.

Index

Division of words, **28b:** 409
Double negatives, **1c(2):** 17–18

E

each
    agreement with pronoun, **6b(3):** 82
    agreement with verb, **6a(1):** 72
-ed words
    as adjectives, **4a(1):** 48–50
    as verbs, **7a(1):** 88–89; **7b(1):** 98–99
Editing. *See* Proofreading, **28c:** 415–17
effect, affect, **21d:** 282
Ellipsis marks, **17a(4):** 233; **27b(3):** 369–71
Enclosure, in business letters, **29b:** 424–25
everyone, everything
    agreement with pronoun, **6b(3):** 82
    agreement with verb, **6a(1):** 72
except, accept, **21d:** 282
Exclamation point, **17c:** 234–35
Expletive. *See* Subject, **1b(3):** 11–12

F

fewer, less, **21d:** 284
foot, feet, **21d:** 284
Footnotes. *See* Notes and footnotes
Fragment. *See* Sentence fragments.
from, off, **21d:** 284
Full-length paper, **26:** 330–60
    avoiding incomplete paragraphs in, **26d:** 354–57
    conclusion of, **26f:** 358–59
    defined, **26:** 330
    introduction of, **26e:** 357–58
    outlining for
        formal outline, **26c:** 338–51
        rough outline, **26b(2):** 334–35
        sample outlines for, **26c(5):** 344–48
        sentence outline, **26c(1):** 339–40

topic outline, **26c(2):** 341–42
    paragraph development in, **26d:** 351–56
    thesis statement in, **26b(3):** 335–47
    topic selection for, **26a:** 332–33
Fused sentence. *See* Run-together sentences, **3:** 35–44
Future, **7g:** 127. *See also will, would,* **7g:** 130–33
Future perfect, **7g:** 128

G

Gerund. *See -ing* words, **7h(1):** 135–36
good, well, **4e:** 57–58
Guiding readers
    about person (point of view), **11b:** 170–72
    about time, **7g(1):** 128–30; **11a:** 168–70
    about writing style, **11c:** 172–73
    making clear references, **6b:** 80–84; **11d:** 173–77

H

Heading, for business letters, **29b:** 422
Helping verb
    defined, **7:** 85–86
    fixed form helpers (*will, would, can, could,* etc.), **7e:** 116–18
    forms of *be* (*is, are,* etc.), **7d:** 111–16
    with past participle, **7b:** 97–98
    with present participle, **7c:** 109–10
hold, hole, whole, **21d:** 286
Hyphen
    in compound numbers, **12b(2):** 190
    in fractions, **12b(3):** 190
    to divide words, **12b(5):** 190–91
    with compound adjectives, **12b(1):** 189–90
    with prefixes *self-, all-, ex-,* **12b(4):** 190

I

Imperative Sentence. *See* Command.
in, into, **21d:** 284
Incomplete comparison. *See* Words, omission of part of comparison, **22c:** 293
Independent clause. *See* Main clause, **1a(4):** 8; **1b(5):** 13–14
Indexes to magazines, **27a(2):** 364–65
Indirect question, end punctuation of, **17a(2):** 231–32
Infinitive
   defined, **1a(4):** 9
   fragment, **2e:** 32–34
   spelling of, **7h(2):** 136–38
-ing words
   as adjectives, **4a(1):** 48–50
   that look like verbs, **7h(1):** 135
   with helping verbs, **7c:** 109–11
Inside address, for business letters, **29b:** 423
Interruptors. *See* Comma with nonessential expression, **13h:** 199–202
Introduction, of full-length paper, **26e:** 357–58
Italics. *See* Underlining
its, it's, **21d:** 284; **15d(2):** 221

J

Jargon, **21c(4):** 281

L

lay, lie, **7f(1):** 119–21
learn, teach, **21d:** 284
leave, let, **21d:** 285
lend, borrow, **21d:** 283
less, fewer, **21d:** 284
let, leave, **21d:** 285
Letters, *See* Business letters.
Library, use of
   card catalog, **27a(1):** 362–64
   indexes, **27a(2):** 364–65
Library paper, **27:** 361–413

bibliography cards for, **27b(2):** 367–68
outline for, **27c:** 372–76
sample, **27e:** 384–94
sources for, **27b(1):** 366
styles of documentation
   new MLA style
      list of works cited, **27d:** 376–81
      notes, content notes, **27d(3):** 381–82
      parenthetical notes, **27d(2):** 380–81
   traditional MLA style
      bibliography, **27f(1):** 394
      notes or footnotes, **27f(2):** 396–401
lie, lay, **7f(1):** 119–21
like, as, **21d:** 283
Limiting of topic. *See* Topic selection
Linking verbs, with adjectives, **4c:** 53–54
List of works cited, **27d:** 376–80
Logic. *See* Nonsense sentence, **8c:** 152–53
loose, lose, **21d:** 285

M

Main clause. *See* Sentences, **1a(4):** 8; **1b(5):** 13–14
Manuscript form, **28:** 414–20
   arrangement on page, **28b:** 414–15
   correct materials, **28a:** 414
   division of words, **28b:** 414–15
   indentation, **28b:** 414–15
   legibility, **28b:** 414–15
   margins, **28b:** 414–15
   numbering of pages, **28b:** 414–15
   proofreading, **28c:** 415–17
   revision, **28d:** 417–20
   title, **28b:** 414–15
mind, mine, **21d:** 285
Misplaced parts, **9a:** 157–58
Mixed constructions. *See* Mixed-up sentences, **8a:** 139–49

Mixed-up sentences
  in which, for which error, **8a(1):**
    139–40
  is when, is where (definition),
    8a(4): 145–46
  mixed sentence and question,
    8a(3): 143–45
  two mixed thoughts, **8a(6):**
    147–48
  using *who, which* or *that* for *and,*
    8a(2): 141–43
  with no subject, **8a(5):** 146–47
Modal auxiliaries. *See* Helping verb,
  Fixed form helpers, **7e:**
  116–18
Modifier
  dangling. *See* Dangling parts, **9b:**
    158–60
  myself, yourself, himself, **5c:** 68–70

N

Negative statements
  contractions of, **1c(1):** 16–17
  double negatives, **1c(2):** 17–19
Note cards for library paper, **27b(3):**
  368–71
Note-taking, for library paper, **27b:**
  366–72
Notes and footnotes, **27f(2):**
  396–401
  first reference, **27f(2):** 396–400
  second reference, **27f(2):** 400–401
  See also Parenthetical and content
    notes, **27d(2)** and **27d(3):**
    380–82
Nouns
  defined, **1a(2):** 5
  possessive forms, **5b(4):** 66
  singular and plural, **1d:** 19–21
    no plural forms, **1d(4):** 21
    special plural forms, **1d(3):** 21
    with plural markers (*six, many,*
      etc.), **1d(2):** 20
    with singular markers (*a, one,*
      each, etc.), **1d(1):** 19–20
Numbers, **19c:** 259–60
  expressed in one or two words,

  19c: 259
  for addresses, **19c(2):** 259
  for dates, **19c(6):** 260
  for decimals, **19c(3):** 259
  for figures in series, **19c(1):** 259
  for identification, **19c(5):** 260
  for money, **19c(3):** 259
  for pages and divisions of books,
    19c(4): 259
  for percentages, **19c(3):** 259
  for telephone numbers or TV
    stations, **19c(5):** 260
  for times of day, **19c(6):** 260
  for ZIP code, **19c(2):** 259

O

Object
  with *lay* and *set,* **7f:** 119–23
Objects (pronouns), **5:** 59–61; **5a:**
  61–64
off, from, **21d:** 284
Omission
  of words in sentence, **22:** 291–94
  shown by ellipsis marks, **17a(4):**
    233
one
  agreement with pronoun, **6b(3):**
    82
  agreement with verb, **6a(1):** 72
Outline
  for full-length paper. *See* Full-
    length paper, Formal outline
    for, **26c:** 338–51
  for library paper, **27c:** 372–75
  working (rough) outline, **26b(2):**
    334–35

P

Paragraph
  adequate development of, **25e:**
    323–24
  conclusion of, **25g:** 326–27
  defined, **25:** 315
  length of, **25:** 315
  methods of development of, **25d:**
    319–23

Q

R

S

CORRECTION SYMBOLS ALPHABETICALLY ARRANGED

ab	19	abbreviations
ad	4	adjectives and adverbs
agr	6	agreement
apos	15	the apostrophe
bus	29	business letters
cap	18	capitals
comp	26	the full-length paper
cs	3	comma splices
dang	9	dangling parts
dict	20	dictionary
edit	28	editing
emp	10	emphasis
ex	21	exact words
frag	2	fragments
lib	27	library paper
log	8	logic
mis	9	misplaced parts
mixed	8	mixed-up sentences
n	19	numbers
org	26	organization of composition
ref	11	reference of pronouns
rep	23	repetition
rts	3	run-together sentences
shift	11	shifts
spo	5	subjects, possessives, objects
s/p	1	singulars and plurals
sp	12	spelling
ss	1	sentence sense
sub	24	subordination
und	19	underlining
var	24	variety of sentences
vb	7	verb forms
vt	7	verb tenses
w	23	wordiness
¶	25	paragraphs
∧	22	omission of words
//	10	parallel sentences
, /	13	commas
; /	14	semicolons
" "	16	quotation marks
./?/:/—/()/[ ]	17	periods and other marks

B 5
C 6
D 7
E 8
F 9
G 0
H 1
I 2
J 3

4